The Mutiny Within

The Mutiny Within

*The Heresies of
Percy Bysshe Shelley*

by

James Rieger

GEORGE BRAZILLER
NEW YORK

Copyright © 1967 by James Rieger
All rights reserved.
For information address the publisher:
George Braziller, Inc.
One Park Avenue
New York 10016
Library of Congress Catalog Card Number: 67-12475
First printing
Printed in the United States of America
Designed by Jennie R. Bush

For My Parents,

Henry George
and
Grace Virgo Rieger

Acknowledgments

The second sections of Chapters One and Three, Chapter Four, parts of Chapter Five, and the Appendix are based upon my Harvard doctoral thesis, directed by Walter Jackson Bate and Douglas Bush.

Chapter Four and the Appendix were first published, in slightly different form, in *Studies in Romanticism*, IV (1965), 169–184, and *Studies in English Literature*, III (1963), 461–472.

The bulk of my research was undertaken at the Harvard College Library, the Bodleian Library and the British Museum. A Dexter Travelling Fellowship enabled me to work in England in the summer of 1961. I wish also to thank John D. Gordan, Curator of the Berg Collection in the New York Public Library, and David Bruce Cratsley of the Philip H. and A. S. W. Rosenbach Foundation, Philadelphia.

James Richard Scarlett, Lord Abinger, has graciously permitted me to quote from the Godwin MSS. in his possession.

The Marianne Hunt bust of Shelley, reproduced on the dustjacket by the courtesy of H. K. Prescot, the Librarian of Eton College, is thought by many to be the most nearly authentic likeness. The photograph is by Cecil Greville, Ltd.

Fred Leventhal transcribed the Roberts letters for me in the British Museum. William Abrahams, Howard Felperin, David Kalstone, David Perkins, Edgar Rosenberg, Preston Smith and Alex Zwerdling read my manuscript at various stages. Each knows what I owe him. *Plurimum in amicitia amicorum bene suadentium valeat auctoritas, eaque et adhibeatur ad monendum non modo aperte, sed etiam acriter, si res postulabit.*

J. R.

Contents

Introduction   13

I Disinheritance   23
Field Place
Superstition and Jacobinism;
   Godwin's *Caleb Williams*

II The Rosy Cross and the Wandering Jew   49
Hogg as an Allegorist
Ahasuerus and the Elixir; Science and the New Eden
The Freemasonic Synthesis: "Rose Croix"
   and the Abbé Barruel
Transformations of the Jew

III Mont Blanc and the Magus Zoroaster   79
Whiteness
Frankenstein; or, The Modern Prometheus (1818)
Dualisms and Doublegangers

IV The Paterin Beatrice   111
Introduction
The Cenci
Valperga
Beatrice and Prometheus

V The Ophite Demogorgon   129
Vulture and Serpent
The Ophite Genesis
The Demiurgic Imagination
Nous and Logos

Ophis and Uroboros
Natural Gnosticism: Godwin and
   the Shelleys Once More

VI *Orpheus and the West Wind* 163

VII *Actaeon, the Phrasemaker* 183
Marriages and Metaphors
Quod enim scelus error habebat?

VIII *Motes of a Sick Eye* 207
Naïve, Sentimental, Gnostic and
   Polysemous Poetry
"... the sea is flooding the house & it
   is all coming down"

Appendix 237

Notes 249

Index 273

The Mutiny Within

Introduction

My title comes from *The Triumph of Life:*

> "*their lore*
> *Taught them not this—to know themselves; their might*
> *Could not repress the mutiny within,*
> *And for the morn of truth they feigned, deep night*
> *Caught them ere evening.*"

Shelley's final, fragmentary epic exposes the myopia of statesmen, the wishful thinking of metaphysicians, the brittleness of art, the grotesqueness of sex, the folly, in short, of every human hope. There are no morns of truth; there are only false dawns. The night goes on.

At last, and at his best, Shelley played grimly with Socrates' awareness that he knew only that he knew nothing. More typically, and unlike Socrates, he coveted the martyr's crown. When in Keats's fate he "wept his own," his melancholy was tinged with self-congratulation. His revolutionism notwithstanding, Shelley wished to be imperfectly understood by a public he could not love. His Evangel was autobiographical, intended far less to save the gentiles than to help the Man of Sorrows know himself. He wrote, by his own admission, coterie verse. My purpose is to show how and why he set about doing so and to suggest that the present unpopularity of his work would not have displeased him. His intellectual and artistic heresies mirror an inward mutiny which never was put down and which is the subject of this essay.

Shelley derived many of his major symbols from the magic, hagiology, and obscene creation myths of the Gnostic and dualist Christian heresies. Our chronological survey of his writings through 1819 will show him selecting progressively more refined *topoi* from these heterodox materials as he moves backwards historically among them. This, his basic heresy, is perhaps the least important of the three we shall discuss.

Amos Wilder has thought of Shelley "on the analogy of the great heretics of the second century. His hatred of the God of the Old Testament, his antinomianism combined with heroic devotion to love and freedom, his oracular view of the poet, his sense of the reality of evil and tragedy, his mythological reading of existence—all suggest the operation of the Christian faith in him, but in an errorist form."[1] Shelley's piety, errorist or otherwise, is questionable. But he did lard his first published works with the bourgeois occultism of eighteenth-century Freemasonry; then he experimented with the theodicy and emblems of Zoroastrian and Manichean dualism. In 1814 he picked up a working knowledge of the more economical, or more nearly monistic, heresies of the early Church. Four years later he fused a personage from Platonic myth with its Gnostic descendant to establish in the nethermost deep of *Prometheus Unbound* his most recondite symbol of the "imageless" Imagination. In the autumn of 1819 he assumed the persona of Orpheus; the "numbers" of "Ode to the West Wind" are literally magical.

The second or "critical" component of Shelley's heresy unfolds and partially justifies the first. It may be expressed by a question. Does God transcend the world, or does He reside in and breathe through it? Does He do neither? The problem is as central to romantic aesthetics as it is to theology. It doubts the possibility of metaphor. Poets like to think they prophesy, but are their utterances ontologically trustworthy? Can the Word be made flesh? Is the tenor really present in the vehicle? The rhapsode must know the answer to these questions, for if he has been wrong, if his frenzies are self-suggested and his songs are froth, then he cheats, corrupts, and even risks annihilating the souls of his listeners. For Coleridge a negative answer to these questions meant pathetic fallacy and "dejection." Shelley, who in the end did not worry seriously about personal survival after death, was at least out to save minds in this world. In his major poetry through *Prometheus Unbound* he debated the question of the validity of metaphor by an analogy from symbol to the Incarnation. The later long poems argue it mainly in terms of metaphor itself. This problem and others arising from it are the topics of the final chapters.

It can be argued that the mythological framework of Christian orthodoxy is at once too rigid and too protean to serve a poet fretting over metaphor. The problem of immanence against transcendence exists and does not exist in Thomistic Christianity, which destroys the alternatives by comprehending both. God is in the mystic's heaven, and He is in the communicant's wafer too. The Gnostics preferred to chop logic with a difference; their inelegant versions of the Fall and the Redemption belabor and complicate Incarnation to the virtual neglect of all other topics. The free-swinging libel of Origen and Saint Irenaeus, as they blast heretical crankiness and illiteracy in page after rancorous page, is equally single-minded. These orthodox refutations contain the only source materials on the Gnostics available in the early nineteenth century. They provided too the most precise symbols, passionately read in two conflicting ways, for Shelley's more sophisticated purpose. But was clarity an ancillary aim? When we read that "Prometheus was never intended for more than 5 or 6 persons" and that *Epipsychidion* "is to be published simply for the esoteric few," we wonder.[2]

Obscurantism enters the main tradition of English verse with Shelley. It is the third of his heresies, and it embraces the other two. Shall a poet's obscurantism be condemned as crankiness, a mental tic, a fraudulent impulse that can only yield fake art? When Blake notes that he "must Create a System or be enslav'd by another Man's," we think he is sincere. When Yeats rummages through one hermetic rag-and-bone shop after another in search of shiny talismans, we are not sure. Yet the product is in either case great as well as darkly learned. Obscurity, the accomplished fact, must be dealt with pragmatically; the critic has no standard of appraisal but the successful dissolution of privateness, genuine or affected, into the poem itself. He does not permit himself to ask whether such success has been honestly or dishonestly inspired. Should he refrain from doing so, or should he not?

The question of obscurantism, like that of sincerity,[3] is one of intention and regards dead men, not living poems. We have been too well bred to address it. Yet it must be addressed, for it gapes wide and is itself obscure in the history of poetic practice. To pretend that it is not there, or worse, to post signs warning of an open fallacy, is surely the giddiness of dogma. Willful mystification was at least a partial motive for some symbolists, and many lovely and baffling poems survive to prove that it was not the dissembler of confusion or incompetence. Obscurantism is a legitimate object of historical inquiry because poets are also, and so is the ethics of their craft. The use of words is at all events a moral enterprise. Should we or should we not have something braver to say about it than that nothing succeeds like success? Let us see.

When Yeats placed *Prometheus Unbound* "among the sacred books of the world," he did not mean that it belongs to Talmudists.[4] Yet textual scholia and critical glosses upon this single poem (not to mention the rest of the corpus) have already achieved patrologian dimensions. Because he loaded every rift with arcane learning, Shelley like Scripture has been cited to nearly every purpose, many of them distinctly ill-advised. He invites critical synecdoche. "We have found in him," Bennett Weaver writes, "that for which we sought, and Shelley scholarship has tended to become a record of overemphases."[5] We should not blame ourselves too harshly for this. The critic's job of illumination is particularly vexed when the poet has set out to puzzle him. Essays in the explication of Shelley will often seem lopsided, pedantic, even obsessed, because Shelley was himself rather a pedant.

To say, for example, that *Prometheus Unbound* is not on one level a maddeningly recondite allegory of the operations of the human mind is so much whistling in the dark and runs counter to

Shelley's explicit statement to that effect in his Preface. Yet critics have never agreed on the significance of Demogorgon, the central figure of the allegory. I hope to show in a later chapter that Demogorgon is the product of Platonic and Gnostic syncretism and by virtue of that ancestry an exact emblem of the Shelleyan Imagination. This identification may even appear obvious when it is read back into the poem itself. Helpful though it may be to know this, a far touchier and more elementary question arises from it. What are we to make of poetry which cannot be enjoyed in an intelligent way without a detailed knowledge of its sources?

Once we have tracked down and comprehended a difficult allusion, it may or may not turn out to enrich the poem on whose behalf we ran to the library in the first place. Demogorgon passes this test satisfactorily, if not brilliantly. But it also becomes clear fairly quickly that for all his missionary zeal, and although he does indeed create "beautiful idealisms of moral excellence" in his lyrical drama, Shelley is showing off. So Yeats after him showed off Rosicrucian symbolism and secondhand folklore, and so Pound strewed the later *Cantos* with private references and polyglot tags. Shelley was the first poet in English who kept one eye on the learned journals. The anachronistic suggestion is not made facetiously. Shelley out-Heroded the dons he despised and envied and who had not helped matters by expelling him. Like Yeats he frequently displays the pedantry of the haphazardly self-educated.

"Allusion," I. A. Richards has written, "is a trap for the writer ... It invites insincerity. It may encourage and disguise laziness. When it becomes a habit it is a disease."[6] In the following chapters we shall see Shelley stooping time and time again to cuteness, to allusions which are at best supererogatory and whose frivolousness, at worst, will raise questions regarding his metaphoric honesty.

The foible is a form of overcompensation. It has always seduced autodidacts and provincials—Irishmen, for example, or Americans. In the late eighteenth century cultural exile was function of class, which included sect. The Dissenting artisan who went on to embrace Freemasonry, Swedenborgianism, or any other eccentric system had already been barred from the universities, the one route to intellectual catholicity. Genealogically and (if he was a "Jacobin") politically, he descended from the Levelling peasant who had cursed the Norman Yoke and whose accents still reverberate in Blake's suspicion of the Latin heritage. Although he detested Mystery for its own sake, Blake occasionally fulfilled the law according to which the shopkeeper-turned-prophet speaks in tongues which he alone can understand and enjoy. Shelley, as an aristocrat, is a sport in this setting.

The man on the fringe—the American or Irishman who is neither English nor a "foreigner," the London clerk who is neither learned nor unlettered—may choose to fly towards the center. The history of literary expatriation in this century reminds one of Leonard Bast's bedsitter, cluttered with *The Stones of Venice*, and suggests that the center is not simply a coterie, but a background as well. Alternatively, the outsider may run still further afield, into a truculent and shrill disestablishmentarianism or, if he is a symbolist, into the occult. So the bards Blake admired took refuge in the mountain fastnesses of Wales.

But the writer *born* in the center, and as alien to it as Shelley was, is certain to seek the periphery. When any of these men puts on his donnish singing robes, he will sound cranky some of the time, for he will ignore Saint Paul's warning that "whatsoever things were written aforetime were written for our learning, that we through patience and comfort of the Scriptures might have hope" (Romans xv. 4). There is much in this sentence for poets and for textual exegetes. When the Nun's Priest referred the Monk to it, he added a "moralite" of his own: "Taketh the fruyt, and lat the chaf be stille."

Condescension is among the defensive stratagems of the parvenu. The writer anxious to infiltrate circles where, in Yeats's phrase, "all's accustomed, ceremonious" will emulate the manner which he was not born and, if he turns critic, the manner in his will most likely degenerate into that tone which silences discussion by turning intellectual questions into social ones. What student has never been cowed by T. S. Eliot's remarks on Milton and Dryden? "Each of these men performed certain poetic functions *so magnificently well* that the magnitude of the effect concealed the absence of others. The language went on and *in some respects improved.*"[7] The stance is Olympian and the diction patronizing, but the ground of argument does not begin to appear. Here is Eliot on Shelley: "from a poet who tells us, in a note on vegetarianism, that 'the orangoutang perfectly resembles man both in the order and the number of his teeth,' we shall not know what not to expect."[8] One might call the tone pure Bloomsbury or, if a relevant answer were really demanded, that of a very "county" hostess. For the question is actually about the *mannerliness* of romantic humanism, compared by T. E. Hulme to "pouring a pot of treacle over the dinner table." The analogy is invidious, but it must be seen that of all major modern critics the unswervingly centripetal Eliot was least qualified by temperament to sympathize with the man Shelley or to assess his verse.

Eliot once wrote that Shelley "borrowed ideas—which, as I have said, is perfectly legitimate—but he borrowed shabby ones, and when he had got them he muddled them up with his own intuitions." Like Wordsworth, La Rochefoucauld, and D. H. Lawrence, but for different reasons, Shelley belongs "with the numbers of the great heretics of all times."[9] Because one may ask whether the mystic emblems of the *Four Quartets* are any more accessible for being nominally traditional, these animadversions, one-third of a century old and later modified, retain a double historical interest. They are of course answerable. Referential propositions only appear to exist in poetry; their ancestry does not signify, because they have no ancestry. The conceptual content of art may seem traditional or heterodox, but it can actually be neither, for symbolistic language is always private. "Familiarity" is a stratagem—a sop or a seduction—and is not to be trusted as a sign of sincerity or the lack of it. Conversely, a defender of Pound's polyglot could say that Chinese ideographs have an internal logic totally unlike that imposed by analytic Western syntax. Only if we fooled ourselves that poetic language makes "sense" and is susceptible of paraphrase could we quarrel with Robert Lowell's grammatical and metaphorical idiosyncrasies: "Hide,/ Our steel, Jonas Messias, in Thy side." It is that it is, and it thunders.

The objection that people like their commas in the right places and that very few can read Chinese is even more futile. If the size of the audience mattered at all, an illiterate might justly complain of the modern bias towards written as against oral transmission and of the death of normative formulae. Ideas are never borrowed and muddled with intuitions. Lowell has not confused Jonah and Christ with Leviathan; his trope is what Richards has called a pseudo-statement, with "meaning" in the poem and nowhere else. Our catholic culture is something other than the private utterances which daily impinge upon and reform it. There is no such thing as stylistic or emblematic heresy.

From the beginning of the nineteenth century through the first two-thirds of this, poets have addressed an ever narrowing circle of readers. Much contemporary poetry is gnomic and elliptical because the syntactical conventions of prose discourse have long been mistrusted. References to personal experience have grown increasingly oblique, and many writers have reacted against the old, stale figurative conventions by adapting eccentric symbol systems to their private purposes. The search for a unique voice is the search for an honest voice. Paradoxically, when a poet enlists an out-of-the-way tradition—the Christian heresies, say—in aid of sincerity, he becomes at the same time hard to understand.

The original problem remains. What is to be made of the poet who *wants* to limit his audience to a handful of initiates? A contemporary of Coleridge's, impressed by Germanic analogies from God's primal Word to the Imagination and from darkly reflective sacrament to obscure symbol, might regard mystification as a legitimate and pleasing device, mimetic of Mystery. Mystery, the mother of abominations, would be in this view the mother of Muses too.

"You ought to know," Blake chides us, "that What is Grand is necessarily obscure to Weak men. That which can be made Explicit to the Idiot is not worth my care. The wisest of the Ancients consider'd what is not too Explicit as the fittest for Instruction, because it rouzes the faculties to act."[10] Shelley agreed that the poet's function is hieratic, and like Blake he did not always distinguish in practice between oracular music and what might be called the Pythian hum. The desire to be either less or more than lucid is usually perverse; in the very young it may be bumptiousness, fitfully cogent and with less than an even chance of growing into originality.

The business of our first chapter will be to suggest some causes of Shelley's passionate singularity and to fix it in its cultural context. There was more to it than pedantry, though that remains its most salient aspect. We shall be dealing at some length with a schoolboy, no older than an American high school senior, a scribbler with sloppy personal habits, a fondness for chemical stenches and bangs, and no discernible talent. Shelley's extreme youth will be emphasized not to excuse his earliest writings, which are lazy and plagiaristic, but because there is more salt than bromide to the proposition that the ignorant and fractious child is father to the man.

I
Disinheritance

> *In its acuter stages every religion must be a homeless Arab of the desert. The church knows this well enough, with its everlasting inner struggle of the acute religion of the few against the chronic religion of the many, indurated into an obstructiveness worse than that which irreligion opposes to the movings of the Spirit.*
>
> —William James, *The Varieties of Religious Experience*

Field Place

"Now the misfortune of revolutionists," Santayana wrote in *Winds of Doctrine*, "is that they are disinherited, and their folly is that they wish to be disinherited even more than they are. Hence, in the midst of their passionate and even heroic idealisms, there is commonly a strange poverty in their minds, many an ugly turn in their lives, and an ostentatious vileness in their manners." This character does not apply to Shelley, nor was it meant to without qualification. "The mind of Shelley was thoroughly disinherited; but not," Santayana reminds us, "like the minds of most revolutionists, by accident and through the niggardliness of fortune, for few revolutionists would be such if they were heirs to a baronetcy." Shelley's revolutionism and his early deism grew out of and away from his family's Whig connection.[1]

When Shelley was a boy, the Whig cause was one of parliamentary opposition, not popular but formidably "established," reformist but ineffectually so. His deviations towards the left can be explained in part as a protest against his heritage of respectable impotence, as well as against the common Tory enemy. Just so the nominal or "Independent" Whig radicalism of Sir Francis Burdett, who was committed briefly to the Tower for his outspokenness in the same year (1810) that Shelley dedicated *The Wandering Jew* to him, blended nostalgia for what the cause had been under Charles James Fox with impatience for what, at the time of Shelley's death, it seemed likely to become again. But unlike the manner of Santayana's revolutionists, Burdett's throughout was as cavalier as his title. And Byron, a severe judge of such matters, remembered Shelley to have been "as perfect a Gentleman as ever crossed a drawing-room, when he liked, and where he liked."[2]

Students of literature can still be fooled by the ancient canard that the Whigs were what Samuel Johnson variously labeled them: a vile faction, greedy for "innovation," the detractors of "establishment." "Whiggism," he told Bennet Langton, "is a negation of all principle." Macaulay and his nephew, G. M. Trevelyan, falsely traced an unbroken, apostolical line from 1689 to the "peace, retrenchment and reform" of Victorian Liberalism. Recent historical scholarship has shown that Whig zeal knew many backslidings and demoralizations—none worse, perhaps, than during the doldrum years of Napoleon—before Gladstone became its latter-day evangelist.[3] And it had never, at any time, been middle-class, democratic, or otherwise meanly bred. Still, readers of poetry remain more likely than not to reply to the question, "What is Whiggery?" as Yeats did in "The Seven Sages":

A levelling, rancorous, rational sort of mind
That never looked out of the eye of a saint
Or out of drunkard's eye.

The great Whig "connections," or family juntos, socially outranked their Tory opposites, with whom they quarreled over the means by which both could salvage hereditary prerogatives in a rapidly blackening land. Such methods sometimes looked like altruism or puffed themselves as democratic sentiment. At the turn of the nineteenth century, the Whigs were the mighty and venerable landholders. Their names were the names of great mansions and parks, or even whole counties: the Dukes of Norfolk, Bedford, and Devonshire, the Marquess of Lansdowne, the Earls of Derby, Gilford, and Moira, Earl Fitzwilliam, Lord King and Lord Holland.[4] They led the town too with their salons and patronage, relics of the age before. Holland House in Kensington was the center of fashion, and there Byron, Rogers and Moore kept up the literary tone.

The term "party" conveyed nothing so ideologically rigid as its modern meaning; there were no "platforms." Politics worked by blood and marriage, not by principle. Some years before, Chatham had called for "measures, not men," but his cry was politely unheard. The younger Pitt (to add to modern confusion) professed himself a Whig, though he founded what has since grown into the Conservative Party. One of the few issues on which the Whigs were united in 1800 was Catholic Emancipation. Their eagerness to repeal religious disabilities perfectly illustrates the protean nature and complex ironies of party politics under the four Georges. The Test Act of 1673 had been a Whig maneuver and had remained a rock of offense to the Jacobitical Tories throughout decades of opposition, stretching well past the Pretender's defeat at Culloden. But in 1780 the future Duke of Norfolk (a supporter of Fox and later famous for his treasonous toast to "our Sovereign's health—the Majesty of the People") was forced to abjure his Catholic faith in order to enter politics.[5] His bitter and single-minded fight against legalized intolerance spurred the Whig campaign for Emancipation, though it did not create it. And the Duke's interest ensured the religious liberalism of his creature, his silent vote, Mr. Timothy Shelley, M.P. for New Shoreham.

The Shelleys of Fen Place and Field Place were distinctly *arrivistes*. The younger son of a younger son, Bysshe Shelley of

Newark, New Jersey, had profited from insanity and childless death among more immediate heirs to the modest family holdings. He turned his athletic good looks to advantage too, by eloping with two girls of fortune, whom he mistreated and on whom he sired Timothy and a line who were to become the Barons De L'Isle and Dudley. Numerous others were got either lawfully or on the wrong side of the sheets. By 1790 he was as rich as any landholder in Sussex, a condition hardly likely to escape the notice of the borough-mongering Norfolk. The Duke enlisted Bysshe's aid, put his eldest son in Commons, and in 1806, when his grandson, the poet, was fourteen years old, paid him off with a baronetcy. Sir Bysshe, having founded his desiderated dynasty, retired to the squalor of a cottage in Horsham, near the public house where he spent most of the waking hours that remained to him talking atheism with the village Hampdens.

Timothy Shelley, like many a son of a colorful parvenu, wanted only to be quietly "county." Phlegmatic by temperament and a prig by choice, he was of little use to Sir Bysshe except as the target of round, blue oaths. Timothy was pusillanimous, to put it more faintly than the evil old man must have. Young Percy Bysshe claimed to have modeled the curses against his father with which he amused his friends at Oxford upon those that had electrified the drawing-room air at Field Place. Other forms of Shelleyan "blasphemy" seem a throwback to Sir Bysshe; the poet was eventually to sign himself *atheos*, though in a very special and no doubt a different sense from his grandfather's. Sir Bysshe was rather fond of the boy, who at least had some life to him, whose first printing bills he paid, and in whom he lived to see and deplore a return to the republicanism of the land of his own birth.

Three years before he died, Sir Bysshe was in turn damned by the one descendant who in any way resembled him: "He is a bad man. I never had respect for him, I always regarded him as a curse on society.—I shall not grieve at his death."[6] Shelley was angry that his grandfather had refused to answer his letters since his expulsion from Oxford; his father's priggishness was speaking through him too. But the older, wild and sportive seed was still in his blood, detested but ineradicable. The fruit proclaims the disorderly tree. Shelley was never the seraph (or putto) he remains in what has been called the hagiographical tradition of literary biography. He was one of Yeats's saints, however, and we shall presently examine his hostility to a brand of "Whiggery" unknown by the later poet. Shelley saw the world, despite himself, much as his grandfather had seen it: "out of drunkard's eye."

England's dirty weather spawned as a relief the bright days of Chaucer's mid-April, Wordsworth's childhood, and Forster's Italy. This is a critical commonplace. The dullness of English country life, from the stately houses to the rectories, has not been so heavily speculated upon, though it generated many antithetical worlds of wish, fairylands, Gothic demesnes, exotic landscapes haunted by gnomes and what Arnold called "nature magic." Beckford feverishly transformed his father's Fonthill into Vathek's Samarah and the infernal halls of Eblis. Herrick pixilated "this dull Devonshire." Take a rusticated family in which an elder child, a fanciful and manic boy, has only his sisters to play with—take Haworth Parsonage or Field Place—and watch the towers of Angria rise of themselves and the meadows and moors of Sussex and Yorkshire change to the floor of the underworld. As Dante Rossetti told William Allingham, the action of *Wuthering Heights* "is laid in hell,—only it seems places and people have English names there."

Shelley, his sister Elizabeth, and their Grove cousins strolled through the moonlight at St. Irving's Hills, the Duke of Norfolk's estate at Horsham Strode, in the spring of 1810. The Elizabethan manor house became in Shelley's second published novel "le Château de St. Irvyne," shaken by November's blasts, its vaults the scene of agonizing horror and forbidden arts. In the same springtime Shelley and the sixteen-year-old Elizabeth asked Edward Fergus "H + D +" Graham to meet them on Clapham Common:

> . . . mind & keep yourself concealed as my mother brings a blood stained stiletto whic[h] she purposes to make you bathe in the life blood of her enemy. Never mind the Death-demons,

> & skeletons dripping with the putrefaction of the grave, that occasionally may blast your straining eyeball—Persevere even though Hell & destruction should yawn beneath your feet. . . .
> The fiend of the Sussex solitudes shrieked in the wilderness at midnight—he thirsts for thy detestable gore impious Fergus—But the day of retribution will arrive. H + D + means Hell Devil. . . .
> Death + Hell + Destruction if you fail.
> Mind & come for we shall seriously expect your arrival. . . .[7]

Life was dull, very dull, in "the Sussex solitudes." Shelley was a fairly enthusiastic shot, but he preferred Gothicizing the landscape to destroying its game as an antidote for the daily tedium. Hellen, the third of his four sisters, recalled half a century later how he would talk of "the 'Great Tortoise,' that lived in Warnham Pond" and of "an Alchemist, old and grey," who practiced in a sealed-off room in the garret.[8] They planned someday to dig him a cave in the orchard, which would suit him better. Hogg remembered that a "great Old Snake" had crawled through the Field Place gardens for more than three hundred years. And the girls, to please their brother, would dress themselves "in strange costumes, to personate spirits, or fiends."

Shelley would sit up whole nights watching for ghosts. Because these never materialized, he decided to remove his vigils to the "charnel-house" at Warnham Church, but failed to devise a way of sneaking in and staying after dark. He devoured books of magic and witchcraft in his spare hours at Eton, but even the incantations he learned from them did not work. Finally, uncalled for, the "shadow" of Intellectual Beauty fell on him, the first, surprising fruit of the boyhood quest he describes in the 1816 "Hymn" to that spirit:

> While yet a boy I sought for ghosts, and sped
>   Through many a listening chamber, cave and ruin,
>   And starlight wood, with fearful steps pursuing
> Hopes of high talk with the departed dead.
> I called on poisonous names with which our youth is fed;
>   I was not heard—I saw them not.

Shelley read as many books of chemistry as he did horror novels and occultist tracts. He possessed an electrical machine and a galvanic battery at Field Place. "Whenever he came to me," Hellen reported, "with his piece of folded brown packing-paper under his arm, and a bit of wire and a bottle . . . my heart would sink with fear . . . with as many others as he could collect, we were placed hand-in-hand round the nursery table to be electrified."[9] Science was the new magic.

Ginotti, the central character in *St. Irvyne*, reveals that like Godwin's Caleb Williams and like Shelley himself, " 'From my earliest youth, before it was quenched by complete satiation, *curiosity*, and a desire of unveiling the latent mysteries of nature, was the passion by which all the other emotions of my mind were intellectually organized.' " Metaphysics having been mastered and love scorned, " 'Natural philosophy at last became the peculiar science to which I directed my eager inquiries.' "[10] When we speak of Shelley as "a Newton among poets," we must beware of misinterpreting his researches exclusively as an eagerness for understanding his environment. He wanted to control it. New chemistry is but old alchemy writ legibly; both are ciphers for politics.

Faust, the seeker after the philosopher's stone, wishes to know and to wield all things. Harry Levin has pointed out that *libido sciendi* and *libido dominandi*, the lust of the eyes and the pride of life, are virtual synonyms in the theurgist's vocabulary.[11] But the despair and damnation of Marlowe's sorcerer are functions of his spiritual torpor, his *accidie*, and in Goethe's version Faust dies blind, not knowing that he has been betrayed by his lemur workmen; he has commanded them to build the Republic, but they have dug his grave. So too, Godwin's St. Leon finds the elixir a mockery and a cheat when he tries by its means to heal the wounds of Central Europe. He and Godwin's daughter's Frankenstein, both of whom have sold their souls too cheaply, are among the mages of the laboratory and elsewhere who will be dealt with in the next two chapters. It is sufficient to say now that Shelley practiced his necromancy and his science in aid of politics, the more free and ready way of dealing with social outrage, and for religion's sake, which saves us to all time. The *Quarterly Review*'s comments (as reported by Hogg) on Shelley's experiments with gunpowder and a magnifying glass are very much to the point: "The Quarterly Reviewer, telling a story, partly true and partly false, of his destroying some old trees at Eton with a burning-glass, remarks, that you might foresee the future opponent of superstition and tyranny in the author of this exploit."[12]

Timothy Shelley was a parliamentary nonentity in a do-nothing party. The Whigs had withdrawn from the House (though retaining their seats) for three years following their defeat in the reform debates of 1797 and the passage of the Treasonable Practices and Seditious Meetings Bills. For years afterwards they dozed on their benches. Even by these degraded standards Timothy lacked moral initiative, though he remained a pliable tool. He sat in Commons through the abolition of the slave trade and sporadic revivals of the 1797 issues without opening his mouth. *Hansard* records only one short speech, a report of good order at a meeting of reforming mechanics and apprentices in a Horsham tavern.[13] His was the silent complacency and dull provincialism typical of "Whiggery" during its leanest years. It was against this degeneration of Foxian vitality that the young Shelley revolted. His quixotic trip to Dublin in 1812 can be viewed as a reactionary gesture, an adventure both radical and restorative of the older Whig ideal.

The influence of the anarchist Godwin, his ghostly father and future father-in-law, was also in the ascendant. Shelley was claiming his reforming and republican birthright by direct action, rather than by keeping his fine feelings to himself on a back bench, as his father had done. Irish rights and Catholic Emancipation were supported in Parliament by Grattan, the Duke of Norfolk, and other "left" Whigs and Irish members, but seventeen more pussyfooting years were to elapse before the latter cause would be won. Shelley rejected Timothy's and the Duke's urgings that he enter regular politics because the thought of temporizing with social evil sickened him. At the end of his life Shelley saw that the cancer was moral and in the bone. But only a disabused revolutionist can have sarcastic visions of the triumph of "life." Timothy never did. "If I die tomorrow," Shelley said the day before he drowned, "I have lived to be older than my father, I am ninety years of age."[14]

"But he *is* nothing," Shelley said of his father—"no *est* professes no *ism* but superbism & irrationalism."[15] Timothy made his servants attend divine worship and sometimes went to church himself; otherwise, as when he subscribed pseudonymously for the Unitarian sermons of the Reverend Mr. Sadler, he styled himself "a friend of religious liberty." He boasted while drunk that he had anticipated the deistical arguments from design of William Paley's *Evidences of Christianity* (1794) and *Natural Theology* (1802). These works, together with the same author's utilitarian reading of Christian ethics in *Principles of Moral and Political Philosophy* (1785), seem childish to modern theologians; Shelley thought them pernicious. His mother's liberalism and toleration were more to his taste: "she says, 'I think *prayer* & thanksgiving is of no use. If a man is a good man, atheist or Xtian he will do very well in whatever future state awaits us.' This I call liberality."[16]

Having failed to promote a love affair between his sister and his best friend, Shelley reported in disgust to Hogg that Elizabeth "is no more a Xtian than I am, but she regards as a sacred criterion the opinion of the world."[17] No euphemism will do; the Shelleys of Field Place were hypocrites. They supported outwardly a Church whose dogma they disbelieved, but whose institutional and eschatological sanctions would, they hoped, effectively cow whichever of their tenants and between-stairs maids dreamed of dancing the *carmagnole* in their blood. Timothy tried to have it both ways. Shelley reports continual frustration in argument with the "friend of religious liberty." He would get his father to assent to certain common, antimiraculous premises: "But when I came to *apply* the truths on which we agreed so harmoniously, he ... silenced me with an equine argument—in effect these words 'I believe because I do believe.' "[18] And his otherwise free-thinking mother "fancies me in the High road to Pandemonium, she fancies I want to make a deistical coterie of all my little sisters."[19]

The Shelleys' middle-class instincts appear most clearly in their dread of adverse gossip. As with all phlegmatic people, their moral cowardice exceeded their sense of physical and financial peril; they were intimidated more by the thought of what Lady Grundy might say than by the nightmare of what the servants might do. Timothy's anger over his son's expulsion from Oxford was directed less at the arguments contained in *The Necessity of Atheism* than at the publicity Shelley courted for them. He knew that the work was a joint production, though Shelley was probably too proud to tell his father that he had contributed only the third point (that religious belief or disbelief is involuntary) and that he had shielded Hogg by refusing to claim or disclaim sole authorship when the Fellows of University College had put the question to him.[20] The Hogg-Shelley correspondence of December 1810–January 1811 shows that the poet was an anticlerical deist at the time the pamphlet was conceived and written; in these letters, many of whose arguments derive directly from Paley, Shelley tries to counter his friend's atheism. He explained to Godwin a year later that when he had subscribed himself, in the Advertisement to the pamphlet, "*Thro' deficiency of proof*, AN ATHEIST," he had meant atheism only "in the popular sense of the word 'God.'"[21]

Timothy worried about public scandal, not about the reasonings of Locke, Hume, or his own favorite "Palley" (as he mispronounced it), whose arguments from design had simply been inverted by Hogg. The two boys recognized the actual cause of concern when, in an attempt to deprecate paternal wrath, they proposed that "They will not obtrude Atheistical opinions upon any one whatever, they will refrain from publishing Atheistical Doctrines or even speculations."[22] Hogg later garbled the printed texts of his dead friend's letters in order to disguise Shelley's anticlericalism and his own youthful atheism. But when he substituted "Intolerance" for "Christianity" as the name of the poet's archenemy, he did not so much distort as reveal the essence of the category. By following Timothy's reasoning further than Timothy had had the wit or nerve to do, Shelley had entered into a tragicomedy of disinheritance. That act of disinheritance both impoverished and strengthened every future gesture and utterance.

It is natural for an adolescent boy to despise his father, and frequently it is commendable. We have seen that Timothy Shelley was the emblem of a dull, smug, provincial world, intellectually timid, petty-bourgeois in morals, half-hearted in politics, and hypocritical in religion. "Shelley's mind," Santayana continues, "disinherited itself out of allegiance to itself, because it was too sensitive and too highly endowed for the world into which it had descended. It rejected ordinary education, because it was incapable of assimilating it." By "ordinary education" Santayana did not mean just that of Oxford, which was, as it had always been, Aristotelian. "Must I care about Aristotle?" Shelley had asked his tutor; "what if I do not mind Aristotle? I then left him, for he seemed to be in great perplexity."[23] Santayana meant that Shelley, one of the "spokesmen of the *a priori*," sprang fully formed from the womb "like a bee or a butterfly"—or, one might add, like Minerva or Milton's Sin from the brow of unfathomable power.

This graceful, even stimulating reading of the facts is not of much help to the literary historian. Shelley substituted flaming affectation for his father's respectability, delusions of persecution for his smugness, cosmopolitan exile for provincialism, intellectual bravado for cautious inconsistency, theoretic syndicalism for wishy-washy reformism, and heresy for the Church of England. He rejected ordinary education because it *was* ordinary—because, for the heart that craved instruction, there was nothing to be learned.

If we dismiss Shelley's revolt—his thirst for visionary experience, his pacifism, his campaign for Irish rights, and above all his sense of the holiness and the fragility of the body's affections—as no more than the antibourgeois barbarism of middle-class youth, we are guilty of the genetic fallacy. But James's logical category has no converse; it is no longer a fallacy when urged against an audience. Pragmatically, the genesis and the fruit of a critical response will be identical. Pope's dictum still holds true: the reader's jaundice *is* the yellow he sees. Eliot admitted this when he remembered "an enthusiasm for Shelley" as "an affair of adolescence ... for how many does Shelley remain the companion of age?"[24] When we reflect how few good things survive even into middle age—audacity, flexibility, and candor, for instance, are rarely among them—the question answers itself.

Superstition and Jacobinism; Godwin's *Caleb Williams*

Jesuit educators are popularly supposed not to care who teaches a boy after the age of twelve, so long as they have had charge of him until that time. The history of London politics in the 1790's suggests that such a boast, whether or not any Jesuit ever made it, would not be unjustified in a Protestant context. Joseph Priestley and Burke's detested Dr. Price were among the founders of English "Jacobinism," and both were Nonconformist ministers. The three anti-ecclesiastical Pantisocrats, Southey, Coleridge and Wordsworth, all ended their days as strong Church of England men. Those revolutionary essayists and novelists who, like Godwin, built their republicanism and anarchism upon axiomatic atheism could not rid their rhetoric of Biblical and Miltonic phrases and draped their political parables upon structural metaphors borrowed from Protestant theology. Twenty years later Byron marked the incestuous and fratricidal heroes of his tales and dramas with the brand of a Calvinist Cain; their ravings of predestined anguish and of the helplessness of the corrupted will are legacies from the Aberdeen childhood of their creator, the limping Mulciber with the studied, Radcliffean mien.

Many French Catholics in the post-Jansenist lull of the eighteenth century inherited with gently-born Anglicans a lackadaisical, "class" attitude towards their instituted religion. Theirs was that "chronic" conformism which William James contrasts with the "acute" religious feverishness symptomatic of all new, enthusiastic, and dissenting sects. Yet when these Frenchmen made the apparently easy leap into rationalism and materialism, they found it a far simpler matter to exorcise the specter of deductive logic than to get quit of hell. As we shall see in the next chapter, the philosophical fraternities of Paris infused a dash of illuminism into their ritual and borrowed signs and incantations from alchemy, Christian heresy, and Persian magic.

There we shall see too that Shelley, *because* he had imbibed only the most watery of religious gruel at home, was never and could never have been an atheist in the now current sense of the term. If we can believe Hogg, Shelley at Oxford "adopted the scheme of the sceptics"[25] as a weapon of "defensive warfare"[26] in aid of Platonistic idealism. "One thing at least is certain, the denial of the existence of gods, and devils, and spirits, if it was to be found in him at all, was only to be found in his words and arguments; practically, his turn of mind was towards superstition, by no means towards irreligion and materialism."[27] When a mind disposed to awe has found orthodoxy shrunken to the shadow of a once vital and insistent norm, its instincts will spin outwards to embrace the eccentric and the occult. Insofar as that mind is also scholarly and critical, it will fly after the heresies and other unexploded errors and will winnow them carefully, for whatever peripheral anathema may in fact be truth.

Both these traditions—that of the acute religionist, lapsed into uneasy infidelism, and that of the chronic conformer who passes through rationalism into superstition and heresy—coalesce in William Godwin. "Jacobinism loves a rabbi," Matthew Arnold observed, and Godwin's *Enquiry concerning Political Justice* (1793) was at the time of Pitt's State Trials the closest thing to a Jacobin Bible in English. Arnold's metaphor seems especially apt when we remember that some years before Godwin became the spokesman for English utopian materialists, he had been a dissenting preacher. But it is not generally known that the sect Godwin had been reared in was an heretical offshoot of Calvinism, and that *Political Justice* attacks all positive institutions in the name of this heresy.

Political Justice was of course the greatest single determinant of Shelley's own radicalism. But Godwin's novels and those of his daughter had an even stronger influence upon Shelley's psychological metaphors and the characters of his dramatic and narrative poems. These connections will be drawn in the next three chapters. Let us now consider William Godwin and the upstart servant, Caleb Williams, a knowledge of each of whom qualifies one's understanding of the other. The literally heretical bent of the most nearly catholic revolutionary gospel of the age will illuminate several major Shelleyan themes. The most important of these is the redemptive power of the imagination.

Caleb Williams; or, Things As They Are (1794) is, in brief, the "mangled tale" of an orphaned and *déclassé* secretary who cannot resist opening a forbidden trunk in which his master, Mr. Falkland, has secreted some compromising documents. Godwin compared Caleb to Bluebeard's wife, and Hazlitt called him "the very demon of curiosity personified."[28] The trunk contains evidence that Falkland is a coward and a murderer. To the point of this discovery the story has been a political allegory, culminating in the exposure of the secret that cashiers governors: the secret that the British constitution is a fraudulent and violent imposition, so rotten at the core and propped up by such timid hypocrites that an enlightened understanding can bring both crashing to the earth.

But Caleb does not denounce his employer. Rather he allows himself to be falsely imprisoned on a capital charge and, following his jailbreak, to be harried like a beast of prey throughout the English countryside, now *locus inamoenus*. Godwin develops a chilling metaphor of enchained Albion as herself the most insensate and least corruptible of jailors. Caleb at last turns upon and exposes his tormentor, who falls into his arms and dies. He then sees that he has loved Falkland as a god, and that if the master is a murderer, the servant is a deicide. *Caleb Williams* is a puzzling sequel to *Political Justice* until it is recognized that Godwin has developed in the novel doubts latent in and crippling his tract.

The reader senses a mythic dimension in *Caleb Williams* because the narrative persona, Caleb himself, orders his world within the framework of a secularized Calvinism. The pathos of external, fallen reality is a projection of the sickly consciousness through which we meet nature and society in this story. Caleb's character is rotted away by a conviction of merited and universal persecution; he may be crudely labeled Prometheus-as-Protestant. Similarly, the source of Godwin's rude power as a novelist and polemicist was not the speciously rigorous logic admired by his contemporaries, but rather the hangover of religious paranoia from which he still suffered when he wrote his two most famous books. Thomas De Quincey made some appropriate phrases for it: "In . . . his *Political Justice*, Mr. Godwin advanced against thrones and dominations, powers and principalities, with the air of some Titan slinger or monomachist from Thebes and Troy, saying—'Come hither, ye wretches, that I may give your flesh to the fowls of the air.' "[29]

There is an organic bond between Jacobinism and Dissent. It has been described and analyzed many times, but never adequately with regard to Godwin. Godwin had been one of the brighter young men at the Hoxton Academy. Hazlitt, who had been trained at a similar institution and later arrived at political opinions as radical as Godwin's, remarked that, "In private, the author of *Political Justice* at one time reminded those who knew him of the metaphysician engrafted on the Dissenting Minister."[30] Godwin's doctrine of social and psychological Necessity is a materialistic restatement of Predestination. His anarchist's emphasis upon the political priesthood of every citizen and his assaults upon the Procrustean cruelty of Law derive, perhaps less obviously, from the old antinomianism.

Between the years of his education and the spring of 1794, when he both published *Caleb Williams* and launched his pamphlet attack upon "the Moloch of Legitimacy"[31] in the State Trials, Godwin was a Nonconformist minister at Ware, Stowmarket, and Beaconsfield, and a teacher at Epsom. He also wrote a *Life of Chatham*, three novellas (two of which remain lost),[32] and a volume of sermons, upon which Lamb later twitted him with relish. These last are models of orthodox Calvinism, except for the occasional startling sentence, prophetic of the later Godwin: "God himself has not a right to be a tyrant";[33] "Impotence and blindness are the parents of vice."[34]

When such a man came to write a murder mystery, it is not surprising that he should take as his models, besides the *Newgate Calendar* and *Lives of the Pirates*, a book concerning the persecution and flight of a female French Huguenot and "a tremendous compilation entitled 'God's Revenge against Murder,' where the beam of the eye of Omniscience was represented as perpetually pursuing the guilty, and laying open the most hidden retreats to the light of day."[35] Just so Caleb thought himself "allied to the army of martyrs and confessors"[36] and compared his persecution by Falkland to "what has been described of the eye of omniscience pursuing the guilty sinner, and darting a ray that awakens him to new sensibility at the very moment that, otherwise, exhausted nature would lull him into a temporary oblivion of the reproaches of his conscience. Sleep fled from my eyes. No walls could hide me from the discernment of this hated foe."[37]

Here the inquisitive eye, Caleb's chief weapon, has been turned against him. Curiosity is the active function of the understanding, which Godwin made passively dependent upon the senses. Throughout the earlier chapters of the novel's second volume, the "eye" of "penetration" is perpetually upon Falkland: "I will watch him without remission. I will trace all the mazes of his thought."[38] Later the mechanical facility which is the fruit of Caleb's boyhood curiosity enables him literally to penetrate the walls of his prison, where, again literally and also Miltonically, "all was a sightless blank."[39] But now his senses have been deranged by terror; reason is useless, and there is no way "to escape from the lynx-eyed jealousy of Mr. Falkland."[40] Caleb is at the mercy not only of the "suspicious eye" and the "penetration" of every amateur thief-taker, but also, by a kind of *lex talionis*, of "the gaze of indiscriminate curiosity."[41]

Falkland recognizes his godlike position and warns Caleb of it: " 'Why do you trifle with me? You little suspect the extent of my powers. At this moment you are enclosed with the snares of my vengeance unseen by you. . . . You might as well think of escaping from the power of the omnipresent God, as from mine! If you could touch so much as my finger, you should expiate it in hours and months and years of torment.' "[42]

The persecution of Caleb originates in paranoia. Falkland, like Blake's Nobodaddy, is deified at the start by a mind predisposed to worship. "I have reverenced him," says Caleb near the end of the book, "he was worthy of reverence: I have loved him; he was endowed with qualities that partook of the divine."[43] In other words, Caleb asks for trouble. This is the downfall of empirical *superbia*, gibbering its superstitious terrors in diction that mocks Scripture and Marlowe's Faustus:

> Did his power reach through all space, and his eye penetrate every concealment? Was he like that mysterious being, to protect us from whose fierce revenge mountains and hills, we are told, might fall on us in vain? No idea is more heartsickening and tremendous than this. But, in my case, it was not a subject of reasoning or of faith; I could derive no comfort, either directly from the unbelief which, upon religious subjects, some men avow to their own minds; or secretly from the remoteness and incomprehensibility of the conception: it was an affair of sense; I felt the fangs of the tiger striking deep into my heart.[44]

Neither faith nor what Caleb had substituted for it, "reasoning," helps him now. The context shows that he even misuses the term "sense." What he means by it is not sensation or even emotion, but something that transcends the faculties and, if its supremacy is denied, strikes into the heart as terror. This is the imagination, a power excluded, significantly, from the psychological system of *Political Justice*. Its most important appearance in the novel under its true name is at the end of a passage in which Caleb fruitlessly attempts exorcism through the understanding:

> In vain I said, "Mr. Falkland . . . acts by human, not by supernatural means. . . . he cannot produce a great and notori-

ous effect without some visible agency, however difficult it may be to trace that agency to its absolute author. He cannot, like those invisible personages who are supposed from time to time to interfere in human affairs, ride in the whirlwind, shroud himself in clouds and impenetrable darkness, and scatter destruction upon the earth from his secret habitation." Thus it was that I bribed my imagination.[45]

Shelley's Imagination is a double faculty of intuition and synthesis, making images from the sensible analogues of Ideas it alone is equipped to perceive.[46] It roughly combines Coleridge's Reason with his Secondary Imagination, and will be understood throughout this study as the higher principle against which the "atheistic" and, later, the Promethean understanding rebels, to its own confusion. The few times Godwin uses the term in his work, he does so in a sense closer to Shelley's than to that of other poets after, or associationist critics before, his time. The imagination desires to see God and may in fact do so, because it loves Him first. It is the artist's strength, not the mechanic's.

Caleb is frightened because he is unimaginative. He can barely see the Idea behind the sensuous appearance and cannot make a coherent picture from the few glimpses he has. Immediately before the catastrophic final interview with his tormentor, he still expostulates and protests too much: "It is true Mr. Falkland was mortal."[47]

Even if Jehovah seems a devil, deicide is not easily accomplished. Caleb's curiosity represents one of many ways of setting about it. He seeks to destroy his God by *knowing* him and does in fact escape temporal, bodily torment by exposing Falkland to the common light as a painted idol. This is salvation through the understanding, and a very peculiar brand of Calvinism it is. We do not have to search far for its name, yet its significance has to date been overlooked by Godwin's commentators. His untitled memorandum of 10 March 1800 gives a precise definition of the variety of Protestant hangover from which he suffered:

Disinheritance

> The Enquiry concerning Political Justice I apprehend to be blemished principally by three errors. 1. Stoicism, or an inattention to the principle, that pleasure and pain are the only bases upon which morality can rest. 2. *Sandemanianism, or an inattention to the principle, that feeling, and not judgment, is the source of human actions.* 3. The unqualified condemnation of the private affections.
>
> It will easily be seen how strongly these errors are connected with the Calvinistical system, which had been so deeply wrought into my mind in early life, as to enable these errors long to survive the general system of religious opinions of which they formed a part.[48]

Godwin goes on to note that the second and third of these errors "owe their destruction to a perusal of Hume's Treatise of Human Nature" in 1795. This means that he still was, however uneasily, beneath their yoke when he wrote *Caleb Williams*. The novel takes on the quality of myth insofar as it purges by demonstrating the errors of Sandeman's insolent understanding. Mythopoetic art characteristically develops tendencies of which the myth-maker had not been aware before he expressed them.

Godwin's fragmentary "Memoirs" unlock the meaning of *Caleb Williams*. Their account of his three years (from the age of eleven to fourteen) as the sole pupil of Samuel Newton of Norwich diagnoses the infection of which he cured himself by forcing it to crisis in his character of the snooping secretary. Since very little of this manuscript has been published before (and that the part least relevant to Godwin as a novelist), it is worth quotation at length:

> His [Newton's] religious creed was happily adapted to the peculiar bias of his disposition. I had hitherto been sufficiently accustomed to the warning cry of hell & damnation. But the damnatory doctrines of Doddridge, or even of Calvin, could not satisfy the harsh and exclusive character of my preceptor. His doctrines were drawn from the writings of

Sandeman, a celebrated North country apostle, who, after
Calvin had damned ninety-nine in a hundred of mankind, had
contrived a scheme for damning ninety-nine in a hundred of
the followers of Calvin. Calvin has sufficiently guarded against
the merit of good-works, but Sandeman undertakes to show a
flaw in his passport for the elect, & demonstrates that, after we
have dispossessed the devil of the battery of good-works, he
gains possession of the citadel by imposing upon us the merit of
faith. In a word, he incontestibly shows that many repented
orthodox divines have represented faith as an act of the will or
a disposition of the heart, *whereas God works to save or damn
a man but according to the right or wrong judgment of his
understanding.* Hence he infers, that these repented orthodox
divines in addition to the acknowledged corps of heretics,
pagans, & infidels, shall without doubt perish everlastingly.

This scheme for damning those good, simple souls, who
never suspected a word of the matter, but thought themselves
cock-sure of everlasting life, was the favourite topic of
Newton's discourses. These persons he dignified with the
name of Pharisees; & the leading trait of the character of the
Almighty, according to this system, consisted in a scurvy sort
of a joke; the language of the day of judgment being in effect,
"Whither away, my friends? You are out in your reckoning;
your goal lies that way. You mistook the meaning of a material
word in my declaration. You thought & perhaps your neighbors thought too, that you were pious, humble Christians. But
I am of a different opinion, & it is my pleasure that you be
burned with fire & brimstone to all eternity.[49]

Here and throughout the "Memoirs" the schoolmaster takes on
the qualities of the God he worships. The narrative continues
directly with this self-portrait of the student:

It was scarcely possible for any preceptor to have a pupil
more penetrated with curiosity & a thirst after knowledge,
than I was when I came under the roof of this man. All my
amusements were sedentary; I had scarcely any pleasure but in

reading. . . . added to this was a trembling sensibility & an insatiable ambition; a sentiment that panted with indescribable anxiety for the stimulus of approbation.

The boy's eagerness received no encouragement or understanding from Newton. Young Godwin, as he describes himself in this last passage, had qualities which would be developed both in Caleb and in the honor-obsessed Falkland. Those of the former predominated as Godwin continued to fight the Sandemanian rabbi-Jehovah at his own game and with his own weapon, knowledge:

> The pleasantest hours I spent at Norwich were, when my lessons were finished, & my instructor abroad, in stealing down to his library. I was uncertain whether my conduct in this respect would meet with his disapprobation. . . . I seated myself on these occasions in a chair close to the shelf to which the book belonged, that I might restore it to its place in a moment.
> Why did I do this? Why did I not ask for the loan of the book, which would probably not have been refused? This was an essential part of my character. It might have been refused; & what then? What should I have done then? Besides, I never asked for a thing then, when there was a chance of being refused. I was under the control of a despot; & I resolved he should not be a despot to me, where I could avoid it. Never mortal felt more energetically the sentiment, "My mind, my mind shall be the master of me!"[50]

The parallel between the library and the prohibited trunk is too obvious to bear much comment. Whoever belongs to the class of the perpetually uninvited must storm the chambers of forbidden knowledge.

Godwin's harshest words for his preceptor are these: "It would be a curious speculation, to draw a comparison between this sort of man, & one of the early Roman emperors, Caligula or

Nero."⁵¹ A startlingly apposite passage occurs near the end of *Caleb Williams:*

> When Nero and Caligula swayed the Roman scepter, it was a fearful thing to offend these bloody rulers. . . . Falkland! art thou the offspring in whom the lineaments of these tyrants are faithfully preserved? Was the world, with all its climates, made in vain for thy helpless, unoffending victim?
>
> Tremble!⁵²

Very few literal correspondencies can be drawn between Newton and Falkland; the analogy lies entirely in the character of the protagonist, Caleb-William, and in the situation. The young Godwin's behavior at Norwich is a classic example of what Anna Freud calls "identification with the aggressor." Long after leaving school Godwin continued to seek the "stimulus of approbation" for his old tutor. He was surprised and hurt by Newton's objections to *Political Justice:* "When I knew you, you were an ardent champion for political liberty. I cannot easily suppose that you have changed your sentiments on that head. . . . We are both of us I conceive enemies to that servility under which the species have so long laboured."⁵³

The use of Newton's own values as an instrument of rebellion created a guilt-situation which, already "an epoch in the mind" of Godwin himself, was then essentially transferred to the fiction. Hazlitt, who knew both well, was the first to observe that "The work (so to speak) and the author are one."⁵⁴ In that work Caleb seems willfully to intensify his guilt by repeated insistence upon the godlike attributes of his persecutor.

Years later De Quincey was to recall of *Political Justice* and of its author's liaison with Mary Wollstonecraft, "Such was the awe inspired at that time by these shocks to public opinion, that most people felt of Mr. Godwin with the same alienation and horror as of a ghoul, or a bloodless vampyre, or the monster created by Frankenstein."⁵⁵ The last simile says more than De Quincey perhaps intended. The same monstrosity of cold intellect is punished in Mary Shelley's scientist and in the scapegoat alter ego, Caleb Williams. Godwin's novel does much to explain his gradual but total decampment from his position of intransigent radicalism after the years of immediate political crisis (he ended his career in a sinecure, as Yeoman Usher of the Exchequer). If the writing of *Political Justice* is represented by the opening of the trunk (significantly, only the half-opening), then the public exposure of the trunk's owner as a false god simultaneously reveals the sin of the snooping servant and the even greater untruth of his own deity, the "demon of curiosity." This latter exposure is the writing of *Caleb Williams*.

Recalling in 1832 the inception of his novel, Godwin remembered saying to himself "a thousand times, 'I will write a tale, that shall constitute an epoch in the mind of the reader, that no one, after he has read it, shall ever be exactly the same man that he was before.' "[56] One wonders if he knew, as he set out to rip the mask from "the existing constitution of society" and from "the modes of domestic and unrecorded despotism, by which man becomes the destroyer of man,"[57] precisely which idols would weather worst in sunlight and fresh air. Caleb, at all events, cannot see the pit he is digging under himself as he resolves at last to effect the damnation of Falkland: "I will unfold a tale—! I will show thee to the world for what thou art; and all the men that live shall confess my truth! . . . Didst thou believe me impotent, imbecile and idiot-like, *with no understanding* to contrive thy ruin and no energy to perpetrate it? I will tell a tale—!"[58]

Twenty pages earlier Caleb had experienced a momentary doubt of his faith in empirical reason. If properly reflected upon, that moment might have saved his sanity, as grace saves souls alive: "My original conceptions of the genius and perseverance of Mr. Falkland had been such that I could with difficulty think anything impossible to him. I knew not how to set up my own opinions of material causes and the powers of the human mind, as the limits of existence. Mr. Falkland had always been to my imagination an object of wonder, and that which excites our wonder we scarcely suppose ourselves competent to analyse."[59] Caleb should have asked himself what he meant, precisely, by "imagination." This is the faculty that saves Shelley's Gnostic Prometheus; its denial by the reason ruins his Beatrice. Her Paterinism is, as we shall see in Chapter Four, a literary variant and an historical precursor of Samuel Newton's Sandemanianism.

The disordered brain of Caleb Williams reflects his creator's growing mistrust of the materialism and sensationalism upon which *Political Justice*, the final critique of the impure understanding, had shut the library door forever. If the novel proves anything whatever, it is that the feast of reason and the flow of soul are not necessarily synonymous.

Although Shelley admired *Caleb Williams* so much that he read it in whole or in part at least four times, there is no evidence that he did so before his expulsion from Oxford. By this time he had already twice treated the legend of the Wandering Jew in prose and verse narrative. His lifelong fascination with this figure is the subject of the next chapter, where the resemblances between Ahasuerus, the proto-Prometheus, and Godwin's Caleb and St. Leon will emerge more clearly than they can be made to do here.

The boy Godwin and the boy Shelley resented the petty tyranny of a teacher and a father's paradoxical lack of authority, a moral and intellectual debility which in either case seemed by extension to enervate the total ambiance. Both rebelled "curiously," even pedantically, sharpening the understanding as a sword. Empirical reasoning led both from religion into radical politics, but the structure of Godwin's thought remained Sandemanian, and Shelley, superstitious all his life, returned for a time to a god beyond the God of Canterbury. Shelley forsook the intolerant narrowness of induction once he saw, as Godwin saw late in life and as Caleb and Frankenstein saw too late, that he had dethroned any number of imperious bogeys only to set up a more fearful abstraction, the understanding's naked self, stalking at noonday. But whereas Godwin and Caleb continued to adore their fancied or real persecutors, Newton or Falkland, Shelley never ceased to mistrust whatever logically elegant code was offered him by authority as sufficient truth. He continued to curse whatever banal fact of nature stood to him *in loco parentis* and veiled the divinity he would love if he could see it.

Caleb Williams and *Prometheus Unbound* are epistemological exercises. The moral development of the central character of each is couched in terms of perception. Godwin implies more than unhappy social fact in his subtitle, *Things As They Are*. But if we are not to err in our quest for the *Ding an sich*—which, according to Arnold, is the goal of criticism too—we must know how many cognitive faculties the mind has and which of them to trust. For his own day Godwin established that the sense-fed understanding is one of many locks on each man's prison of flesh. The proposition has a corollary: the heart of another is to each of us a sealed chamber, a strongbox, and our only key to it is the imagination. This is also the one medium of religious revelation. The intuitive imagination regards a light clearer than any shattered in Newton's prism or dreamt of in Hartley's optics. Caleb learns, when such knowledge can no longer help him, the truth shown in Godwin's evaluation of his own marriage to Mary Wollstonecraft:

> I have been stimulated, as long as I can remember, by an ambition for intellectual distinction; but . . . I have been discouraged, when I have endeavoured to cast the sum of my intellectual value, by finding that I did not possess, in the degree of some other men, *an intuitive perception of intellectual beauty*. I have perhaps a strong and lively sense of the pleasures of the imagination; but I have seldom been right in assigning to them their proportionate value, but by dint of persevering examination, and the change and correction of my first opinions.
>
> What I wanted in this respect, Mary possessed, in a degree superior to any other person I ever knew. The strength of her mind lay in intuition. . . .
>
> This light was lent to me for a very short period, and is now extinguished for ever![60]

Prometheus awakens simultaneously to love and to imagination, which were for Shelley "the great secret of morals" and "the great instrument of moral good."[61] When he *sees* the beneficent principle above all understandable powers of earth and air, and above Jupiter, who is the perverse father and torturer of this world, he loves or at the least pities and forgives all created things. His chains fall off of themselves. A hymeneal chorus celebrates the cancellation of cycles and of that divorce which had crucified the Titan: "The wise want love; and those who love want wisdom."

But the Wandering Jew must always blaspheme; every smile seems a mocking grimace, because he laughed once in ignorance. Caleb's touch kills. Both are self-betrayed. Before Shelley perceived that science is not a synonym for wisdom, that the only practical political program is the reformation of the human heart, and that the letter murders without the spirit, his learning and his artistic aims were as eccentric as his geographical wanderings were pointless later. Caleb and Ahasuerus circle forever around the unapprehended axis of their desire, the great secret of morals, which is always there in the middle and which, Frost knew, always knows.

II
The Rosy Cross and the Wandering Jew

"You atheist?" [*Evtushenko*] *asked me in English.*
"Well yes, but it's more that I hate him."
—Kingsley Amis[1]

Hogg as an Allegorist

Early in the Michaelmas term of 1810 Jefferson Hogg, entering Shelley's rooms in University College for the first time, stumbled upon a mess suggesting that which was made firmament by the first of all poetic utterances:

Books, boots, papers, shoes, philosophical instruments, clothes, pistols, linen, crockery, ammunition, and phials innumerable, with money, stockings, prints, crucibles, bags, and boxes, were scattered on the floor and in every place; as if the young chemist, in order to analyse the mystery of creation, had endeavoured first to re-construct the primeval chaos. The tables, and especially the carpet, were already stained with large spots of various hues, which frequently proclaimed the agency of fire. An electrical machine, an air-pump, the galvanic trough, a solar microscope, and large glass jars and receivers, were conspicuous amidst the mass of matter. Upon the table by his side were some books lying open, several letters, a bundle of new pens, and a bottle of japan ink, that served as an inkstand. . . . There were bottles of soda water, sugar, pieces of lemon, and the traces of an effervescent beverage. Two piles of books supported the tongs, and these upheld a small glass retort above an argand lamp. I had not been seated many minutes before the liquor in the vessel boiled over, adding fresh stains to the table, and rising in fumes with a most disagreeable odour.[2]

This must be a composite memory, for Shelley could hardly have made such a malodorous chaos of his rooms during his first few days of residence. Nor does Hogg's disagreeable tone—patronizing, facetious, sentimental, and wounded by turns throughout the *Life*—dispose us to trust him.[3] He lacks good will towards both his readers and his subject. Thirty-six years after Shelley's death, the healthiest component of Hogg's infatuation with him is still the envy that leers through it. We know, too, that Hogg deliberately garbled the texts of Shelley's letters, and that he hid such eerie matters as his own urge to sleep with every woman loved by his friend, from Elizabeth Shelley to Jane Williams (whom Hogg eventually married). Still, his pictures of the ungainly, stoop-shouldered boy striding at an oblivious tilt, neck outstretched, along the Oxford High Street with a Greek text held inches from his nose—or of Shelley sailing his clumsy paper boats across a puddle on some bleak upland common in a cutting northeast wind, while Hogg whines—these have a likeness that engages belief. So too Hogg's reproductions of talks with Shelley, which he does not pretend to render verbatim, have the note of authenticity, for all the vulgarity of the reporter's manner.

The archness of Hogg's references to "the primeval chaos" and "the mystery of creation" does not betray an ironic cast of mind, but rather his embarrassment with those quirks of metaphor which now seem the book's one critical strength. Hogg tends on the whole to invest Shelley's every clumsy gesture and personal untidiness with heavier symbolic freight than it should be made to bear. At times, however, his analogies from the tangible ambiance and the visible oddity to the twists of temperament that produced them illuminate his subject more brilliantly than the accuracy of single vision could have done.

Shelley's rooms must have looked to his scout the way a pigpen would if a pig were to turn apothecary. But to his biographer, who continually refers to Shelley as a "wizard" and "alchemist" throughout the Oxford portions of the *Life*, the poet's spirit was about to make the stinking jumble pregnant. Nothing was wanting but light. Magic had become science, "left" Whiggism was about to turn radical, and within two months a mildly anticlerical deism would have yielded in his letters to the accents of Voltaire and Antichrist. This witches' or alchemists' brew found a concrete and noxious correlative in that room where Shelley literally confused poison with nourishment, crucibles with crockery, and once tried to serve Hogg tea in a cup partly filled with aqua regia, the solvent of gold.

The allegorical habit of Shelley's mind surpassed that of his friend's. Hogg saw in a college sitting-room the vehicle of a metaphor actually being lived. Shelley turned to fiction, and adopted as the unifying type of his own occultism, thaumaturgic chemistry, loneliness, and emergent blasphemy that cousin-german of Cain, the Wandering Jew. By November, 1810, he had already used this figure in his second published romance, *St. Irvyne* (1811), and in his first long poem, *The Wandering Jew* (alternatively called "The Victim of the Eternal Avenger").[4] In *Queen Mab* (1813) Ahasuerus becomes a Godwinian revolutionist. Before reappearing for the last time in *Hellas* (1821), he learns forgiveness, and his elixir of unending torment is transmuted into the fire of the Titan.[5]

Ahasuerus and the Elixir; Science and the New Eden

The Wandering Jew was originally not a Jew at all, but Pontius Pilate's janitor, a native Roman named Cartaphilus.[6] As Jesus was led forth to be crucified, Cartaphilus shoved Him from the door, saying, "Vade Jesu citius, vade, quid moraris?" "Ego vado,"

Christ replied, "et tu exspectabis me, donec redeam." Twelve centuries later, when he recounted his history to a certain Armenian archbishop over the dinner table, Cartaphilus was still waiting. He had become devout, and his remorse was tempered only by the hope of forgiveness on Judgment Day. Roger of Wendover picked up this story from his fellow-monks at St. Albans; they had had it from the archbishop himself when he visited England in 1228. From Wendover's *Flores Historiarum* and Matthew Paris' *Chronica Maiora* the legend passed into popular tradition, from which the more or less stationary Cartaphilus re-emerged in a *Volksbuch* of 1602 as the fugitive Ahasuerus. The Armenian archbishop's tale had parodied the most baffling crux in the Gospel According to Saint John. Christ's last words concerning His beloved disciple ("If I will that he tarry till I come, what is that to thee?") had been twisted into the curse on the brutal porter: "I'm going, but *you* shall wait until I return." The *Volksbuch* added to this corrupt echo of Gospel the fatigue and the homesickness of the Diaspora.

The Wandering or Eternal Jew entered German and English Romantic literature by way of *Ahasver* (pub. 1786), a verse "rhapsody" by Christian Friedrich Daniel Schubart (1739–1791). Shelley based parts of *The Wandering Jew* and the Ahasuerus section of *Queen Mab* on a prose translation of this poem. Rather than confess that he had read it in *Bell's Court and Fashionable Magazine*, he claimed that the excerpt quoted in a Note to *Queen Mab* was "part of some German work, whose title I have vainly endeavoured to discover. I picked it up, dirty and torn, some years ago, in Lincoln's-Inn Fields."[7]

As might be expected from a writer of the Storm-and-Stress school, Schubart exaggerated the *Weltschmerz* implicit in the *Volksbuch* version. There, however, and in the later popular treatments inspired by it, the theme of unending flight had been the most transparent of gimmicks, a framing device which justified the writer's inclusion of historically unrelated incidents and a variety of splashy settings. The Jew had, after all, visited every land on earth in the course of better than one and one-half millennia. The "world-sick" posturings of Schubart's Ahasver are as sophisticated an improvement upon the picaresque sensationalism of the *Volksbuch* as the physical disgust of Tennyson's demoralized Tithonus and the ghastly humor of Mary Shelley's "Mortal Immortal" are upon Schubart.

Ahasver is also tinged with what would become open satanism in later characterizations. Although his bent is suicidal rather than revolutionary, he does complain that God's wrath seems vindictive, not condign. He longs for reconciliation mainly as the instrument of release from an immortality that can never consume him utterly. A fugitive and a vagabond in the earth, his punishment like Cain's is greater than he can bear. Shelley's Jew, taking a logical giant step, renounces both it and its Author as more than he *will* bear.

Paulo, the title character of *The Wandering Jew*,[8] has bound his brow with a gray fillet, which appears at times to blaze. He explains this chameleonic property by untying the ribbon and revealing his forehead:

> A burning Cross was there;
> Its colour was like to recent blood,
> Deep marked upon his brow it stood,
> And spread a lambent glare.
>
> (III, 249–252)

The brand is a greater mockery than was Jehovah's "mark upon Cain, lest any finding him should kill him": it proclaims that the body of Ahasuerus cannot be rid of consciousness and pain, no matter how ingeniously he or his enemies contrive to mortify it. Such symbols hold all our horror of live burial: "to lie in cold obstruction and to rot." Like Shakespeare's Claudio, we fear less the simple return of flesh to clay than what we may *feel* as we dissolve, the slime and the ice, the sensible conversion into "a kneaded clod." Even Lucifer is awed by the seal on Paulo's head; if God did not interpose, the "magic spell" of that Cross would be so potent that

> fiends would obey my mandates dread,
> To twilight change the blaze of noon,
> And stain with spots of blood the moon.

(III, 243-245)

The badge of blasphemy is the stigma of martyrdom. It bleeds like that made by a circlet of thorns on the forehead of Our Lord, the Eternal Avenger. It looks forward to the mutilated Prometheus' coronation "over himself."

Shelley derived Paulo's mark of pariahood from the Wandering Jew who rescues Don Raymond in the Bleeding Nun episode of M. G. Lewis' *The Monk* (1796). There also he found the "chilling gaze" that shoots "a lurid gleam of light," a "secret spell" and "mystic . . . fear" through the soul of Rosa, Paulo's beloved (I, 240, 242-244). Lewis' anonymous wanderer is a mesmerist, and versed, like Paulo, in the thaumaturgical arts. He conjures up the ghost of Beatrice, the Nun, by means of a magic circle composed of "sculls, thighbones" and blood, the last traced on the floor with a wooden crucifix. A chalice serves as his paint-pot. Paulo is clearly his disciple:

> "On Death resolved—intent,
> I marked a circle round my form;
> About me sacred reliques spread,
> The reliques of magicians dead,
> And potent incantations read—
> I waited their event."

(III, 317-322)

Lewis' Raymond reports that many thought the Jew "Doctor Faustus, whom the devil had sent back to Germany." This not unreasonable hunch further complicates the strongly agglomerative myth of Ahasuerus. Unlike the bully who kept Pilate's gate and unlike Cain, Faustus premeditates the murder of his own soul. Cartaphilus did not know that he was blaspheming, and the first fratricide was condemned for murder ex post facto; but presumption is by definition deliberate. The necromancer does not stumble upon his occult learning; he steals it. The posture of Ahasuerus-Faustus is henceforth openly defiant. He flings his arts, as Vanni Fucci flung his obscene "figs," square in the face of God.

The charmed circle exorcises a revenant, but cannot bring repose to the magician himself. In *St. Irvyne*,[9] substantially finished at the same time as *The Wandering Jew* (April, 1810), Shelley equates the magical or, more properly, the alchemical overreaching of Ahasuerus, with the blasphemy that perpetuates and blights his life. Ginotti, the central character, has Paulo's hypnotic glance but not his burning scar; he did not mock the convict Christ. His existence is protracted instead by the *elixir vitae*, the philosopher's stone, which a devil once gave him in return for his soul. Whoever possesses this talisman will not die until he gulls another malcontent into hearing the formula from his lips. Shelley did not invent this twist of plot, by which the newer, pseudoscientific bent of Ahasuerus was made to reinforce the cautionary intent of the original legend. He borrowed it from Godwin's second novel, *St. Leon: A Tale of the Sixteenth Century* (1799). The device turns up again in the finest of all Gothic romances, Charles Robert Maturin's *Melmoth the Wanderer* (1820).

Like Caleb Williams and Ginotti, St. Leon has been possessed since his childhood by "curiosity, resistless curiosity" (II, 9),[10] an urge which we have already defined as the willed activity of the discursive understanding. Curiosity betrays St. Leon into accepting from the pseudonymous Zampieri (a Wandering Jew stereotype) "the *great secret*, which can endow a man in a moment with every thing that the human heart can wish" (I, 5). This is of course the elixir, the deceitful gift that ensures its recipient youthful immortality and, because it transmutes metals, limitless wealth. St. Leon continues: "What adept or probationer of the present day would be content to resign the study of God and the profounder secrets of nature, and to bound his ardour to the investigation of his own miserable existence?" The remainder of the narrative answers St. Leon's rhetorical question with an object lesson much like that learned later and expressed as follows by Mary Shelley's "modern Prometheus," the chemist Frankenstein: "If the study to which you apply yourself has a tendency to weaken your affections, and to destroy your taste for those simple pleasures in which no alloy can possibly mix, then that study is certainly unlawful, that is to say, not befitting the human mind" (p. 49).[11]

As Frankenstein directly though "unwillingly" destroys his kindred and friends by the agency of the obscene Adam stitched together in his laboratory, so the elixir decrees that St. Leon shall outlive or devastate the objects of his love. His acts of benevolent patronage in Hungary turn to fire and famine; at the book's end his son simultaneously denounces and fails to "recognize" him in the fullness of the many Godwinian meanings of that verb. More will be said of Frankenstein and the Shelley of "Mont Blanc" in the next chapter. We have only to see now that Godwin and his daughter preach the same homily: the elixir, chemical or alchemical, dooms its owner to moral isolation; an emblem of the sense-fed intellect, it confirms the prison of the body, within which Blake's Newtonian sleeper, the man of "single" or "vegetative" vision, has been sentenced to life upon life upon life of emotional short-circuit. Because he has inverted the faculties, forswearing imaginative insight to follow the false god of induction, he is mocked and paid in kind.

No one sees the man beneath the superficial aspect: the branded brow and glaring eye of the Jew, St. Leon's eerily youthful countenance, the naked hideousness of Frankenstein's prodigy and alter ego. The "enlightened" or "illuminated" adept is blind, mistaken and mistaking through the lust of the eyes, and can never, "as he is," be loved by anyone. "How unhappy the wretch," St. Leon declares, "the monster rather let me say, that is without an equal; that looks through the world, and in the world cannot find a brother; that is . . . cut off for ever from all cordiality and confidence, can never unbend himself, but lives the solitary, joyless tenant of a prison whose materials are rubies and emeralds" (II, 234–235).

When Shelley wrote *St. Irvyne*, more than a decade had still to elapse before he would announce that love was a mystery of morals more potent than that other "great secret" communicated by Zampieri to St. Leon. His trust in science and his delight in its magical and blasphemous connotations were unqualified. Yet the philosopher's stone is poisonous in *St. Irvyne*; its owner cannot wait to get rid of it. Wolfstein, whose position parallels St. Leon's, does not inherit the detested immortality which Zampieri-Ginotti has hoped to pass on to him with the elixir. Although he has been told the formula, Wolfstein dies swiftly, "blackened in terrible convulsions," because he has refused to deny his Creator (199). Ginotti is less lucky. The "frightful prince of terror" appears out of a sulphurous whirlwind to renege the elixir's escape clause: " 'Yes, thou shalt have eternal life, Ginotti.' " The flesh suddenly rots and falls from Ginotti's living skeleton. Shelley leaves him only his leading, mesmeric feature—"two pale and ghastly flames glared in his eyeless sockets"—and concludes the episode with morbid relish: "Yes, endless existence is thine, Ginotti—a dateless and hopeless eternity of horror."

We shall see later that Shelley's disenchantment with the natural sciences, with political amelioration, and with inductive reasoning, which erects abstract notions upon sensory perceptions, coincided with a contempt for the human body that verged at times on physical disgust. The elixir, which deviates so horribly from its conventional effect at the end of *St. Irvyne*, should be an integrative symbol of these two areas of nausea. Yet Shelley had boundlessly sanguine prospects of a technological utopia when he talked away the evenings of his one November at Oxford, while awaiting publication of the romance he had completed seven months earlier. The reasons for this inconsistency will also explain the eminent badness of his earliest works and excuse our having spent so much time on them.

When Hogg and Shelley first found themselves seated next to each other at dinner, they fell into an argument over the comparative merits of Italian and German literature. Shelley soon dismissed the topic as " 'of little importance, for polite letters are but vain trifling; the study of languages ... is merely the study of words and phrases, of the names of things; it matters not how they are called; it is surely far better to investigate things themselves. ... through the physical sciences, and especially through chemistry.' "[12] At this moment only matter was "real" to the future Platonic realist. His philological corollary seems even more ominous: words bear no relation to things "as they are"; names are signs devoid of significance, Idols of the Market-place. Yet the boy who could upset his tutor by doubting whether he would "mind Aristotle" patently wanted to convince himself of his opinions. No harm could come of trying them out in their most extreme form on the first freshman who happened to strike up a conversation at table. Several days later Shelley burst angrily into Hogg's rooms after walking out of a geology lecture early and noisily; the professor had talked about " 'stones!—stones, stones, stones!—nothing but stones!—and so drily. It was wonderfully tiresome—and stones are not interesting things in themselves!' "[13]

The question reduces itself to the timeless one of correspondency. On either hand we have denotation and the thing denoted, the name and the stuff of category, the formal and telic against the material "cause" of an object. These contraries became in time metaphysical noumenon and phenomenon, theological Word and flesh, and the tenor and vehicle of metaphor. Shelley reconciled them briefly when he wrote *Prometheus Unbound*. At Oxford, however, he worried whether stones in fact spoke sermons and had already decided that the artifice of language contained no matter. Were science and deism, as "natural" philosophy and "natural" religion, rational absurdities as well as oxymora? If he could not resolve the question, he could at least transcend it. This he did when he escaped into scientific fantasy, into golden views of a utopia which evaded the contradictions because it was "then," not "now," and neither here nor there. We shall presently find the eternal and homeless Jew native to that place.

Shelley talked of science as if its end were politics. Yet the

Godwinian anarchism which he was about to swallow whole, with its dream of the abolition of class and the revocation of the curse of work, is at bottom nostalgic, not futuristic. It rephrases the myth of the earthly paradise and plans the restoration of that infant equality which precedes the descent of adolescence through shame into the knowledge of good and evil. Shelley's eloquence to Hogg—*if* we may trust Hogg—remembers Eden: " 'Is not the time of by far the larger proportion of the human species . . . wholly consumed in severe labour? And is not this devotion of our race . . . absolutely necessary to procure subsistence; so that men have no leisure for recreation or the high improvement of the mind? Yet this incessant toil is still inadequate to procure an abundant supply of the common necessaries of life.' "[14]

"Cursed," says God, "is the ground for thy sake; in sorrow shalt thou eat of it all the days of thy life. . . . In the sweat of thy face shalt thou eat bread." But Shelley sees a way to profit from the thorns and thistles of exile and to irrigate the scorched wilderness: " 'by chemical agency the philosopher may work a total change, and may transmute an unfruitful region into a land of exuberant plenty.' "[15] We can distill water from the atmosphere; " 'the arid deserts of Africa may then be refreshed by a copious supply, and may be transformed at once into rich meadows, and vast fields of maize and rice.' "

Inductive reasoning is the wand of the beneficent mage: " 'having ascertained the cause, we shall next be able to command it, and to produce at our pleasure the desired effects. . . . there are many mysterious powers, many irresistible agents. . . . What a mighty instrument would electricity be in the hands of him who knew how to wield it, in what manner to direct its omnipotent energies. . . . how many of the secrets of nature would such a stupendous force unlock!' "[16] The accents of the alchemist, countervening Jehovah's cruel will, sound too clearly here to bear comment.

Shelley draws the political connection at last in imagining the effects of "aeronavigation" over Africa: " 'The shadow of the first balloon, which a vertical sun would project precisely underneath it, as it glided silently over that hitherto unhappy country, would virtually emancipate every slave, and would annihilate slavery for ever.' "[17]

While his friend pauses for breath, Hogg slips in an astute question about metaphysics: " 'is that science, too, the study of words only?' "[18]

" 'Ay, metaphysics,' he said, in a solemn tone, and with a mysterious air, 'that is a noble study indeed! If it were possible to make any discoveries there, they would be more valuable than any thing the chemists have done, or could do; they would disclose the analysis of mind, and not of mere matter!' " Shelley rises from his chair and wanders slowly about the room. He begins to speak of souls and pre-existence. The contraries remain unresolved.

In the last eighteen months of his life, Shelley again feared that existence holds no definitive essence at its core. If the facts of experience have a divine tendency, or any meaning whatever, do words represent that meaning? Does the brain actually comprehend the "reality" the mouth utters, or does it worship in its madness what it invents in monstrous vanity? The wry nominalism of *The Triumph of Life* mocks the dogmatic freshman's insistence on "things themselves." The imagery of *Epipsychidion* is tragically and deliberately bathetic. Both poems document their author's suspicion and, finally, plain doubt of the validity of metaphor. He had lapsed from his creed that honest words are literally invested with an explosive Presence and that the Imagination, the integrator, is a kind of sacrament. But the Eton sixth-former who scribbled prose and verse romances was still unbaptized. He had no faith to lose, or be betrayed by.

Zastrozzi, St. Irvyne and *The Wandering Jew* were written in haste and written to astonish. Their borrowings from "Rosa Matilda," Schubart, Godwin and Lewis are almost as felonious as are the open plagiarisms from Lewis in the so-called *Original Poetry* by "Victor" and "Cazire" (1810). Shelley cared so little for *St. Irvyne* that he barely attempted to harmonize its two independent and contradictory plots. In November, 1810, when he wrote on this point to Stockdale, his puzzled publisher, he was so bored with the story that he forgot that Ginotti does not die at the end.

The Jew's elixir does not point the same frightening moral as the Titan's stolen fire does because Shelley was not yet thinking symbolically. He was not yet pressed by the need to reconcile science, politics, and anticlericalism, the concerns of the here and now, with his magical, romantic, and occultist yearnings towards the unseen and unpredictable. Eton and Oxford insulated him against this need. So long as he raved through the mouth of a fabulous Hebrew and reveled in old-wivish misconstructions of the book of nature, these ruling-class academies were prepared to tolerate his assaults upon the ethos of that class. They had disciplined and subdued many fantastical young men. But it was something else again to read nature through the spectacles of Locke and Hume.

When University College expelled him for *The Necessity of Atheism*, Shelley fell into a world of fact, which, like the beast-woman on the road to Thebes, would eat him alive if he could not unriddle it. Was the world atomic, and therefore measurable, or was it monadic and demanding to be listened to? The question is perhaps one of semantics. The areas of matter and spirit, whether absolute or aspectual, are those which the artist's imagination, Coleridge insisted, "at all events struggles to idealize and to unify." This is *to poiein*, the process of "making" or "esemplasm."

When he wrote *Queen Mab*, the cast-out Shelley needed a narrative emblem of his exile and restlessness. He needed also to connect the magical world with the material or apparent realm of experience. The Wandering Jew, a figure he had used before in aid of nothing more profound than Gothic *frisson*, again answered his purpose. But Ahasuerus arrives at the frontier of modern literature with many superimposed stamps in his passport; the ink has begun to run. No pattern can be detected in this palimpsest, the souvenir of his obscure travels, and the protean

Jew cannot cross over with independent symbolic status until he has been initiated into the first of Shelley's heresies.

The Freemasonic Synthesis: "Rose Croix" and the Abbé Barruel

Paulo, the title character of *The Wandering Jew*, derives his name from a coreligionist, the Apostle who, dazzled by the Christ whose Church he had persecuted, traveled through every civilized nation to spread the good news of his own and the world's enlightenment. Victorio, Paulo's rival for the love of Rosa, triumphs only in removing the girl from both their grasps when he feeds her the poison he mistakes for a love philtre. And what of Rosa herself? Retrospectively, this rescued novice rather resembles Villiers de l'Isle-Adam's Sara, the beloved of Axel, at whose escape from the nunnery the mystic rose bursts into bloom. Shelley may have modeled her upon Lewis' Matilda, who first excites the lust of Ambrosio while she is disguised as the young monk "Rosario." Has her name any deeper significance? The surviving texts of the poem are too corrupt to warrant more than a query. What symbolic union, if any, is shadowed forth by this spiritual marriage of a girl called after the rose with a man known everywhere by the badge of his infamy, the cross that burns on his forehead?

We are on safer ground with *St. Irvyne: or the Rosicrucian*. Stockdale evidently did not understand the subtitle, for Shelley wrote to him on 19 November 1810: "What I mean as 'Rosicrucian' is the elixir of eternal life which Ginotti had obtained. Mr. Godwin's Romance of St. Leon, turns upon that superstition." The acknowledgment is misleading; Godwin does not mention Rosicrucianism, nor is "that superstition" named anywhere in Shelley's story but on the title-page. Shelley most likely learned whatever he knew of the alchemical brotherhood after he had finished *St. Irvyne* in April and before he sent Stockdale his final revisions sometime in the fall. An examination of his source reveals a precedent for the political radicalism mouthed by the Ahasuerus of *Queen Mab*, but of which both Paulo and Ginotti are innocent. The stone of the philosophers of the Rosy Cross is also slung at the forehead of God Himself. The Jew who in 1810 whined of his estrangement from the Avenger becomes a theomachist.

After his expulsion from Oxford, Shelley left behind him at Field Place the first volume of his copy of a book which Hogg says was enormously popular among undergraduates that year. This was Robert Clifford's translation of the Abbé Barruel's *Memoirs, Illustrating the History of Jacobinism* (1797–1798).[19] Augustin Barruel was an aged Jesuit who, driven from his home by the French Revolution, sat down at a desk in England to expose the antimonarchical and anti-ecclesiastical "conspiracy" of recent years as the reawakening of the dragon of "Manicheism." Writing without fear of decapitation or contradiction, Barruel displayed all the vices of scribbling expatriates: garrulousness, ill-temper, and inaccuracy. He blamed the upheaval on three groups, acting in collusion: the antireligious *philosophes*, led by Voltaire and d'Alembert; the republican Freemasons; and Adam ("Spartacus") Weishaupt's Bavarian Illuminists, a band of skeptics who infiltrated and corrupted the originally innocent Masonic lodges. All three elements were combined in the Parisian Lodge of the Nine Sisters, whose members included Condorcet, Camille Desmoulins, and Danton. Lafayette, Montesquieu, and Dr. Guillotin belonged to its sister Lodge of Candor.

According to Barruel, Weishaupt derived the name of his sect from that "which Manes and his disciples first affected, *gloriantur Manichaei se de coelo illuminatos*" (III, v). The object of the Illuminists was of course "enlightenment," and their political code was anarchistic. The abolition of positive institution would, they hoped, yield equality under natural law. They practiced or at least tolerated "mysteries" in their ritual to disguise their blatant atheism. They admired Jesus Christ—to a point—for his communism. Weishaupt's secret purpose, however, was "to *tie hands, to subjugate, fire on, and vandalize* the whole universe" (III, 250).

Barruel divides Freemasonry into three sects. First are the

Hermetic Masons of the "Scotch" degrees. These chemists, pantheists and "Spinosists" follow Hermes Trismegistus in proclaiming that everything in nature is part of a great whole, identical with Jehovah. Then there is the Cabalistic Masonry of the Prussian and French Rosicrucian lodges. More will be said presently of Cabalism, which, Barruel asserts, is merely Martinism under another name. Finally, the deistical, anticlerical, and democratic Eclectic Masons combine the errors of all sects; their clubhouse is the supremely powerful Grand Orient Lodge at Paris.

The Freemasons themselves give two accounts of their origins. One faction claims descent from the priests of Memphis and Eleusis, the Platonic and Eclectic philosophers, Druids, Persian Magi, Mosaic Jews and later Roman sages. Their tradition has been kept underground by an intolerant Church. Because of their diverse ancestry, some modern Masons proclaim the eternity of matter, some are dualists, and still others are Platonic trinitarians. All insist, however, on the hypostatic unity of Jehovah.

The other group traces its origins to the Knights Templar, an order founded by Hugo de Paganis and confirmed by Eugenius III. Hospitalers at first, they degenerated during the Crusades through correspondence with the Saracens and became sodomitic, iconoclastic, and infanticidal. Their Grand Master, Jacques de Molay, was burnt and the order dispersed early in the fourteenth century. The Templars at that time swore vengeance upon their suppressors, Philip the Fair and Clement V; their descendants are dedicated, by extension, to the liquidation of all monarchs and prelates. Mirabeau and Count Volney are the leaders of this party.

Barruel, however, second-guesses both traditions. Having noticed that Condorcet in the *Esquisse* praises a "horde of sectaries known by the names of *Albigeois, Cathares, Patarins, Bulgares*," and so forth, he outlines these medieval heresies in detail and finds in them the source of all Jacobinical Freemasonry (II, 221). Behind them is the ultimate source, "the slave *Curbicus*, more generally known under the name of *Manes*" (II, 224). His dualism survives in the Rosicrucians, who begin their ceremonies by sitting mournfully on the ground and holding reeds, the instrument of the heresiarch's flaying. The meaning of their motto, *Mac Benac* ("the flesh parts from the bone") is thus perfectly clear, although the obscurantist Masons refer it to their legendary founder, Hiram or Adoniram, the martyred Master Mason who built Solomon's Temple. The medieval Templars simply substituted Molay's name for that of Manes.

Third-degree Freemasons are told that Adoniram was murdered by several subordinate workers who wished to discover the secret password of Masters. The word was lost with him, and "Mac Benac," the exclamation of one of Solomon's policemen when he tried to lift the badly decomposed body, is now used in its place. Fourth-degree or Elect Masons are sworn to vengeance against Adoniram's chief assassin, who is not yet named. Next come the three Scotch degrees of High Priest, Pontiff of Jehovah, and Knight of St. Andrew. Here one learns that the Templars discovered the lost word carved on a stone in the ruins of Jerusalem and that they brought the stone back to Scotland with them. The word is "Jehovah," and it stands for deism, the natural religion of which the world has been cheated. The next step, that of *Rosae Crucis* (or *Rose Croix*), reveals that Christ Himself stole and hid the rock of the word. He is our enemy, second only to Adoniram's actual assassin in perniciousness. The final degree, *Kadosch*, exposes the king (Philip the Fair and all his successors) as that murderer; when he is killed the Grand Master Molay and the order of Templars and Masons will be avenged. Christianity too must be destroyed in order to recover "Deism" and "Liberty and Equality," which, we are told at last, constitute the lost word in its fullest significance.

Our immediate concern, of course, is with the ritual of *Rose Croix*. Barruel relates that the initiate is led into a nearly dark room where mourners sit before a painting of three crosses on a hill. This twilight represents the hour when the word "Jehovah" was lost, the veil of the Temple was rent, the implements of Masonry were broken, the light was darkened, and the "flaming star" disappeared (II, 168). This is the dawn of Trinitarianism, the moment in which the Godhead was fragmented by the immolation of a demagogue who pretended to be His rebellious son. A placard on the middle cross contains four letters that denounce this fraud: "I*ew* of N*azareth* led by R*aphael* into I*udea*" to be executed as an impostor (II, 169).

There is a lot of nonsense, misinformation, and outright distortion in Barruel's book: "it is half filled," Shelley wrote Miss Hitchener, "with the vilest and most unsupported falsehoods," though it is "a book worth reading."[20] Most of it is mere melodrama for obvious polemical purposes. English Freemasonry, founded as we know it in 1717, was deistic and materialistic but not revolutionary. Even the French lodges, which added the higher degrees and their ritual, were never opposed to the Church. The "movement" as a whole was characterized by an intense admiration for the sciences and saw itself as a bridge between mystery and rationalistic enlightenment.[21] Even the motto of *Rose Croix*, "I.N.R.I.," is less blasphemous (though heretical) than Barruel would have us believe. It is the perfect alchemical slogan: *Igne Natura Renovatur Integra;* "the whole creation is renewed by fire."[22]

Freemasonry simply incorporated an older, loosely organized brotherhood founded by "Christian Rosenkreuz" ("Father Rosy Cross"), who is sometimes identified with Paracelsus, but was more probably Johann Valentin Andrea, a professor at Tübingen in the early seventeenth century. The handbook *Fama Fraternitatis* (1615) called for a reformation in alchemy along the lines of that then proceeding in religion. The movement's emblem may, in fact, be no more than a modification of Luther's monogram, a cross-crowned heart rising from the center of an open rose.[23] Perhaps roses have nothing to do with it; the name may derive instead from the Latin *ros*, or "dew" (the alchemist's distillations), which, joined to *crux*, signifies the marriage between science and Protestantism. In any case Rosicrucianism was early associated with the forerunners of modern Freemasonry. One H. Adamson connected the two in a work called *The Muses' Threnodie*, published in Perth in 1638:

> For what we do presage is riot in grosse,
> For we are brethren of the Rosie Crosse;
> We have the Mason Word and second sight,
> Things for to come we can fortell aright.

Returning to Shelley, we find that the appeal of *Rose Croix* lies precisely in the area of Barruel's error. By muddling the *philosophes,* the Freemasons, and the quasi-nihilistic Illuminists into one lump of ruination, with hermetic science implied as the catalyst, the *Memoirs* restores the elixir's age-old symbolic potency. There are two prospects from the Rosicrucian Golgotha. The alchemist looks forward intellectually to Voltaire, Hume, Holbach, experimental physics, and empirical philosophy generally. A desert of heresy, blasphemy, and abominable magic opens behind him. Shelley took from this perverse *Charfreitags Zauber* much more than the authority he needed for a final synthesis of his scientific and "Gothic" interests. The ritual is anti-monarchical, anti-paternal, and, in a sense shortly to be developed, atheistic. The Wandering Jew has attained his political majority.

Paulo mocked Christ as He stumbled along the Via Dolorosa. The Ahasuerus of *Queen Mab* follows Barruel's stage directions by jesting at the Crucifixion itself. The fallen world of Shelley's early maturity, like that of Swinburne's poems, has grown gray with the breath of the Galilean, whose institutional triumph has chained man's erotic energy, divorced his Promethean intellect from his emotions, and palsied his will. Shelley's religious iconoclasm is auxiliary to the warfare of the One with the many; it is part of his struggle to mend the fragmented consciousness of the race through the imagination. The antitrinitarianism of the Rosicrucians and their lament for the shattered Word foreshadow this struggle. But insofar as the "Nazarene Jew" of *Rose Croix* rises up specifically against the Father, he is also available as a type of the prophetic poet's revulsion from Jehovah, or of the battle of titanic but impaled human wisdom against "Jupiter." Shelley can and does have it both ways. In the most complicated phase of his syncretistic mythopoeia, Shelley and Ahasuerus merge into Jesus.

It is characteristic of heretical systems that they contradict themselves in the act of inverting orthodoxy. Their symbologies fold ambivalences within enigmas and appeal to the footloose ironist for the same reason that they repel a poet of more "central" loyalties and normative intentions. Their eccentricity is finally a metaphor of their murderousness. Barruel thought that the old regime had lost a war fought on two fronts against a cabal of rationalists and obscene magicians. So Shelley's heretical images and impulses seek resolution in the unbeheld but living truth on which they impinge. All the poet *can* see for the moment, there in the middle, is a cancerous orthodoxy. Centripetal error will crush this infamy as its orbit implodes to a usurped peace.

Transformations of the Jew

Canto VII of *Queen Mab* encloses a factitious narrative within the "real" fiction of Ianthe's vision. Mab introduces Ahasuerus as " 'a wondrous phantom, from the dreams/ Of human error's dense and purblind faith,' " and when she dismisses him at the end, the reader is reminded that he has seen a "phantasmal portraiture/ Of wandering human thought" (64–65, 274–275). The theomachic Jew serves a double purpose here. First, the popular history of his suffering and the main article of his creed—that " 'an almighty God' " exists, " 'And vengeful as almighty!' "—are respectively a superstition and a lie; they point up the actual martyrdom of the atheist whom Ianthe had, as an infant, seen burnt, and they establish the truth of Mab's proclamation, " 'There is no God!' " (84–85, 13). In the second place, Ahasuerus mouths sentiments (*not* opinions) which Shelley had once strewn throughout his private letters and now publicly recants.

The Jew's narrative and its context fuse Schubartian and Freemasonic details with hints of the Gnosticism which Shelley will name in 1814 as the conceptual framework of "The Assassins." As

The Rosy Cross and the Wandering Jew

in the ritual of *Rose Croix*, the fatal dialogue takes place not at the foot of the Via Dolorosa but during the Crucifixion itself. And Christ, who merely fakes His agony, is cursed by a nationalist, not mocked by an idle porter: " 'Indignantly I summed/ The massacres and miseries which His name/ Had sanctioned in my country' " (176–178). The predestinarian Jehovah who stages this puppet-show of Atonement gloats that ignorant and apostate millions will burn forever and howl " ' "the justice of their doom" ' " (152). God's perverse sense of humor and His confession that He planted the " ' "tree of evil" ' " for the sake of death and to sate His malice reflect Gnostic theodicy (110). So does the opposition of *pistis* and *gnosis* in Mab's claim that the divine principle which exists independently of Nobodaddy can be apprehended by the eye of reason only. The jittery self-idolatry euphemistically called "faith" is blindness. The devout project into the darkness a monstrous amalgam of their own most vicious instincts; they are themselves the goblin adored in the churches, " 'the creature of His worshippers' " (28).

The Jew then recounts the holy warfare of Christian upon Christian. The details of his single specific allusion can only fit the "crusade" which Innocent III mounted against the neo-Gnostic Cathari and which triumphed in the bonfire at Montsegur:

> "the red cross, in mockery of peace,
> Pointed to victory! When the fray was done,
> No remnant of the exterminated faith
> Survived to tell its ruin, but the flesh,
> With putrid smoke poisoning the atmosphere,
> That rotted on the half-extinguished pile."
>
> (219–224)

Most Gnostic sects regarded Jesus as a rebel against Jehovah, as one who came not to fulfill but to destroy the Law. Shelley's Prometheus thinks of him this way, and pities his unsuccess. Ahasuerus, however, confounds the Son in the Father, which is another reason why the Jew and his legend must be repudiated.

When the Grove family had broken up the attachment between their daughter and the heterodox Shelley in the Christmas vacation of 1810, he had turned his anger against the source of their prejudice. "Oh!" he had burst out to Hogg, "I burn with impatience for the moment of Xtianity's dissolution, it has injured me; I swear on the altar of perjured love to revenge myself on the hated cause of the effect which *even now* I can scarcely help deploring. . . . I will stab the wretch in secret. . . . Ecrasez l'infame ecrasez l'impie."[24] Barruel had been obsessed by Voltaire's motto, which sounds like a refrain on page after page of the first volume of the *Memoirs*. A fortnight later, Shelley hurled it at Hogg once more: "Oh how I wish I *were* the Antichrist, that it were *mine* to crush the Demon. . . . Oh! Christianity when I pardon this last this severest of thy persecutions may God (if there be a God), blast me! Has vengeance in its armoury of wrath a punishment more dreadful!"[25] Shelley had lifted the last sentence verbatim from the translation of *Ahasver* quoted in the Notes to *Queen Mab*. By the late winter of 1813, when those Notes were composed, he wished to distinguish the historical Jesus—"a man of pure life, who desired to rescue his countrymen from the tyranny of their barbarous and degrading superstitions" —from the fabulous, institutionalized Saviour. The latter "is a hypocritical Daemon . . . the other stands in the foremost list of those true heroes who have died in the glorious martyrdom of liberty."[26] But even then Shelley was not sure. "Since writing this note," he added in a footnote, "I have some reason to suspect that Jesus was an ambitious man, who aspired to the throne of Judea."

The Jew's narrative, Mab's comments upon it, and Shelley's Notes operate dialectically: if the Jew exists—if Mab has raised a legitimate ghost—then Christ is a charlatan and God a sadist. But because Ahasuerus is in fact an optical illusion, Jehovah emerges from the canto's structural syllogism as a priestly hoax, as does any "Christ" imposed upon the historical Jesus. Shelley employs the nightmarish Jew as a two-handed engine, exposing to believers the moral malignancy and to infidels the ontological absurdity of the larger superstition from which this bogey sprang. His paradoxical method has a unified aim—to purge the mind of idols and cant—but it may produce contradictory or even duplicitous feelings within the reader. *Paradise Lost*, Shelley tells us, accidently elicits a mixed response, and we shall see later that he intends the history of Beatrice Cenci to breed a synthetic clarity from affective confusion. It is worth pointing out now what may already be obvious—that although Shelley does not espouse the occult systems which from this point forward yield him major symbols, the tropes themselves are psychologically and morally real. They are the djinns which the human mind enthrones over itself.

Shelley's theological development, or muddlement, from his Oxford days to the publication of *Queen Mab* is mainly of extraliterary interest, but our present critical purpose requires a brief, paraphrastic summary of his position at the end of this period. At the time of his expulsion from University College, Shelley had been an atheist only in the popular sense of the word "God" and through deficiency of proof. His letters to Hogg and Elizabeth Hitchener continued to expound the necessitarian point that because faith or the lack thereof is involuntary, positive religious institution must maintain its hegemony through philosophically irrelevant sanctions in the social sphere. He tempered his agnosticism with a hunch that the soul (though not certainly the personality) will survive the body[27] and with a "Deism" which he sporadically embraced and rejected and fuzzily equated with a rational hatred of Christianity. In 1812, a year after Shelley had repudiated "natural" with revealed religion, Southey proved to him that he was a "pantheist," meaning a panpsychist, and so, for the moment, he was. His Oxford anti-theism had affected only the notion of a *creative* Deity; Shelley never doubted that a "vast intellect animates Infinity."[28] The ground of being, or *"Existing power of existence,"* is synonymous in its cognitive, phenomenal, and ethical aspects with truth, electricity and morality; it "analogises with the *universe*, as the soul of man to his body, as the vegetative power to vegetables, the stony power to stones," and gravitation to a clock.[29] In the speech that introduces Ahasuerus, Queen Mab pulls down the creator who veils from mortal sight what the Notes call "a pervading Spirit co-eternal with the universe":[30]

> "let every seed that falls
> In silent eloquence unfold its store
> Of argument; infinity within,
> Infinity without, belie creation;
> The exterminable spirit it contains
> Is nature's only God; but human pride
> Is skilful to invent most serious names
> To hide its ignorance."
>
> (VII, 19–26)

The vagueness of this hypothesis covers up its implicit dualism and some embarrassing questions arising from it. Necessity may account for the kinetics of a universe divided into spirit and matter, but barring the mediation of daemons, "animal spirits," or some other cumbersome transformation-mechanism, it is not easy to see how one essence can impinge upon, much less affect, the other. What is "perception," and should the epistemologist trust it? Can one believe with Descartes that sensation is a tool of certain knowledge insofar as its reports conform to such clear and simple noumenal structures as, say, the theorems of Euclid? Shelley does not yet face these questions squarely.

If the Deity is non-creative, so is the human mind—as Shelley admits. By 1821 he will have adopted the formula in which Tasso supposedly anticipated Schelling's and Coleridge's analogy from the divine Maker to the poet. His 1813 metaphysics cannot logically include this proposition. Yet no symbolistic aesthetics can do without it. The artistic Idea need not shape the concrete world in any crude sense, as Orpheus set stones dancing. But if words do not precisely correspond to things, as Shelley complained to Hogg at Oxford—if, moreover, spirit or "meaning" is not consubstantial with the matter of the universe—then metaphoric language, which must credit such immanence if it is to enforce similar inherences or identities, is fraudulent, even dangerous. The aesthetic question reduces itself to the phenomenological dilemma. Is the elementary particle an atom, or is it a monad? In order to see it as both, one must, as I have said, accept a sacramental mystery not unlike the doctrine of the Real Presence in the mass. Shelley does so in "Mont Blanc," and in 1818 he literally brings the Logos, the creative and itself incarnate Word, onstage. Having thus resolved his earlier dualism (and Shelley, let it be said again, had never been a simple materialist), he simply discards matter; he climbs to that quasi-Berkeleian height of idealism from which philosophers view matter as an effluence of thought at the risk of tumbling into solipsism. Ahasuerus then reenters one last time, stripped of his legendary, Schubartian and Rosicrucian feathers. The Prospero of *Hellas*, he personifies the conquest, here and now, of space and time, and the poet's repudiation of the concrete realm which those dimensions measure:

> this Whole
> Of suns, and worlds, and men, and beasts, and flowers,
> With all the silent or tempestuous workings
> By which they have been, are, or cease to be,
> Is but a vision;—all that it inherits
> Are motes of a sick eye, bubbles and dreams;
> Thought is its cradle and its grave, nor less
> The Future and the Past are idle shadows
> Of thought's eternal flight . . .
>   What has thought
> To do with time, or place, or circumstance?
>   (776–784, 801–802)

The seer of *Hellas* retains from German, English, and Shelley's own juvenile Gothicism little but his name. His cultural alienation from the Muslim despot provides lateral perspective, and his timelessness erects a cyclic overview; from these two vantage points of better information he can predict the evaporation of all creeds with the temples that house them and the rocks on which they are built. His dissipation of the ephemera of single vision attenuates and sophisticates the theomachy of the classic Ahasuerus. Otherwise, the Jew who fled from Ianthe's sight at a wave of Mab's wand never reappears in Shelley's mythopoeia, though the ruined angel of "The Assassins," written the next year, bears marks of weakness and woe common to both the Jew and Prometheus. The figure of the Wanderer persists, however, and emerges from certain curious transformations as a persona of Shelley himself. The metamorphoses even more curiously epitomize Byronic and later German developments of the legend.

In *Alastor, Epipsychidion* and *Adonais* the Wanderer becomes a poet, and he puts to sea. The differences between him and Coleridge's Mariner far outweigh the resemblances. Rather he looks forward to Heine's Flying Dutchman, "the Wandering Jew of the Ocean" sketched in the *Memoirs of Herr von Schnabelwopski* (1834). The Hollander is doomed to sail till the Day of Judgment, not for having mocked Christ but because he once swore by the Devil. A woman's fidelity can release his body and save his soul, but marriage means the death of both partners. As the Dutchman's bride consummates their love by drowning herself, the enchanted ship goes to the bottom.

The symbolic coincidence of orgasm and death is familiar to us from Donne and Crashaw, among others; Shelley complicates the texture of this metaphor, which dominates much of his later verse, by prescribing with Heine that extinction shall be by water. In the last chapters of this study we shall look more closely at the nympholeptic picaro who steers his boat towards a fused Pole and Evening Star, simultaneously the "lodestone" of his "one desire" and sacred to her in her Aphrodisiac aspect. Urania and her son Adonais will beacon the suicidal sailor towards the burning fountain they inhabit, and the last words before the *tornata* of *Epipsychidion*—"I expire"—will climax a honeymoon voyage with Emily, the most recent mortal form of the One who has ever "lured me towards sweet Death." The eroticism of this poem is incestuous, though disembodied, and Shelley specifically opposes it to the final catastrophe of his first marriage: life had imitated art, and Harriet had been, with gruesome literalism, "quenched."

High-minded incest counterpoises mundane murder in *Epipsychidion*, as it does in *Manfred:* "I loved her, and destroy'd her!" Byron's hero recalls of Astarte, his sister. Incest's libidinal converse is fratricide, the narcissist's rage against his doubleganger. The mark on the forehead of the "fabled Hebrew wanderer" in Canto II of *Childe Harold's Pilgrimage* is therefore interchangeable with that of "curst Cain's unresting doom"— with the sign set on Ahasuerus' legendary stepfather, lest he be killed, by the Father of the Son whose agony will one day be mocked. Cain rises up against his brother, and Ahasuerus in effect spurns himself. The mirror-identity of Jesus and the Jew partially explains the stigma "like Cain's or Christ's—oh! that it should be so!"—which blazes from the "ensanguined brow" of *Adonais'* "phantom" poet as he flees "astray/ With feeble steps o'er the world's wilderness."

Richard Wagner, born in Leipzig the same week that Hookham printed *Queen Mab*, derived *Der Fliegende Holländer* from Heine's tale. *Parsifal*, his last opera, sets up a more traditional Jew-figure in Kundry, the temptress who, having once jested at Christ, must live and laugh always, no matter whether she feels shame, lust, or repentance:

> Da lach' ich—lache—,
> kann nicht weinen:
> nur schreien, wüthen,
> toben, rasen
> in stets erneu'ten Wahnsinn's Nacht.

Water is the sign of her atonement and the agent of her release, as it was for the Dutchman and his bride. Parsifal baptizes Kundry from a holy spring, and the tears she now can shed thaw the frozen earth like sacred rain. Winter's enchantment cracks under the more potent spell of Good Friday, and all the meadow is suddenly spread with flowers.

The whore who anoints Parsifal's feet and dries them with her hair clearly plays Mary Magdalene to the knight's "something else thereby," in Donne's phrase. But Wagner has subtler reasons for making his Ahasuerus a woman. Kundry reproduces the guileless fool, Parsifal himself, who first enters the opera carrying the bow with which, like Coleridge's proto-Dutchman, he has shot a swan, the bird of *gutes Zeichen*. Parsifal and his predecessors—Amfortas and the other Knights of the Grail—are "errant" in a double sense. Like the Jew, they wander in search of salvation, but their self-regard may trap them in a fey mirror-realm, the Garden of the Antichrist, the antitype of the Paradise they seek. Kundry, the Acrasia or mock-Urania of Klingsor's bower, plays a double symbolic role: she is simultaneously the Wanderer and the false goal of his quest.

This ambivalence retrospectively lights up much in Shelley's later practice. After 1817 he radically qualifies the crude epistemological and moral dualisms we have already glanced at and whose symbols are the subject of the next chapter. The world one beholds and that which lies beneath the grave draw ever closer together. *Kakodaimona* mask as good genii, and in June, 1822, the murderous doubleganger shows itself at last to the bodily eye and lures Shelley towards the sea. The sexes grow progressively more alike too. Laon and Cythna are brother and sister, but Emily's soul, the "sister" of the poet's "orphan one," actually blends with his amid the hermaphroditic imagery of an island lovenest, half cave, half tower. It is usually said that the Shelleyan Ahasuerus turns into Prometheus. He becomes as well a cheated Grail-Knight: the poet-errant associates the saving truth he quests after with women, mortal types of the Uranian Aphrodite, each of whom turns out to be an inadequate vehicle, a traitress, or, in Emily's case, a loathly "cloud." And the Wanderer becomes Kundry in the sense that his goal, for good or ill, is his own feminine daemon. He is his own psychopomp into an underworld of personal becoming. The evening star of Aphrodite leads Hermes' soul downward and inward, and their union, depending on how one looks at it, is a mystery or a monstrosity.

Tannhäuser too has taken a symbolic night-journey to the interior of *mons Veneris* (Venusberg). But Wagner's epic or degenerated-epic heroes (Siegfried, the Arthurian Tristan, the quasi-Arthurian Parsifal or Perceval, and his son Lohengrin) are hardly

nympholepts. And the Dutchman's practical need for a wife—
any wife—is matched, to say the least, by Senta's enthusiasm.
This invalidates Nietzsche's very funny comments on "the case
of Wagner." They are pertinent, however, to Shelley. Wagner's
erotic world-view, because it is tragic, makes room for and forgives the woe that is in marriage: nosiness, leaping to conclu-
sions, stupidity and (on the many levels of *Tristan und Isolde*)
bad timing. Shelley's does not. Within a year of his death he
learned too late and confessed to Mary that "love far more than
hatred—has been to me, except as you have been it's object, the
source of all sort[s] of mischief."[31] When in Chapter Seven we
witness the collapse of the romantic wanderer's quest for an
Antigone into bathos and self-justification, Nietzsche's strictures
will seem most germane:

> The Flying Dutchman preaches the sublime doctrine that
> Woman settles even the most restless man or, in Wagnerian
> language, "redeems" him. Here we permit ourselves a ques-
> tion: granting this to be true, would it therefore be desirable?
> What becomes of the "Wandering Jew" whom a wife adores
> and *settles?* He simply ceases to be eternal; he gets married
> and concerns us no longer. Translated into reality, the danger
> of artists, of geniuses—for these are the "Wandering Jews"—
> lies in women: *adoring* women are their corruption.[32]

III

Mont Blanc and the Magus Zoroaster

> *... only bones abide*
> *There, in the nowhere, where their boats were tossed*
> *Sky-high, where mariners had fabled news*
> *Of IS, the whited monster.*
>
> —Robert Lowell

Whiteness

The virgin's wedding dress, the judge's ermine, and the priest's alb are no whiter than the duck jacket, the badge of a crippling and specious innocence, which nearly became Herman Melville's shroud when he fell from the yardarm into the sea. He reminds us in *Moby-Dick* that for all its holy associations, white is the color of the polar bear, the tropical shark, and the albatross; of the revenant and the pale horse of the Apocalypse; of cowardice and the most dread, because invisible, of ocean squalls; of the albino and the leper. Is it for such reasons, he asks, "that there is such a dumb blankness, full of meaning, in a wide landscape of snows—a colorless, all-color of atheism from which we shrink?"

The sky-god of *Prometheus Unbound* perches on a glacier, from which his curses, "Like snow on herbless peaks, fall flake by flake"; under his "wrath's night" humanity "climbs the crags of life, step after step,/ Which wound it, as ice wounds unsandalled feet" (III, i, 12–15). He fails to see that his throne will become a toboggan to perdition as man's mind begins to discharge its collected lightning and Promethean defiance melts into love. "Hark!" Asia cries,

> the rushing snow!
> The sun-awakened avalanche! whose mass,
> Thrice sifted by the storm, had gathered there
> Flake after flake, in heaven-defying minds
> As thought by thought is piled, till some great truth
> Is loosened, and the nations echo round,
> Shaken to their roots, as do the mountains now.
>
> (II, iii, 36–42)

Jupiter's chthonic counterpart in "Mont Blanc" is "the old Earthquake-daemon," who may have "taught her young/ Ruin" among these "frozen floods" (72–73, 64). Her realm snowblinds the bodily eye, one may say, and allows the poet to imagine the Power beyond her, the "secret Strength of things" which "inhabits" the world of mere appearance and cancels its significance (139, 141). The whiteness reflected by Mont Blanc's congealed coldness opposes that which radiates from *Adonais'* living waters, from the "burning fountain" of Eternity.

The Shelleys visited the Chamouni area from the twenty-first to the twenty-seventh of July, 1816. At noon on the twenty-fifth they reached the top of Montanvert: "We ... behold *le Mer de Glace*. This is the most desolate place in the world; iced mountains surround it."[1] Taking the wife first, let us try to illuminate the practice of each by comparing the metaphoric uses to which the Shelleys put the Sea of Ice. For both it symbolizes those spiritual "desert places" whose "blanker whiteness of benighted snow" scared Robert Frost—who knew too that however one might prefer holocaust,

> for destruction ice
> Is also great
> And would suffice.

Frankenstein; or, the Modern Prometheus (1818)

"Mr. Godwin," Hazlitt wrote of *Political Justice* in 1825, "has rendered an essential service to moral science, by attempting (in vain) to pass the Arctic Circle and Frozen Regions, where the understanding is no longer warmed by the affections, nor fanned by the breeze of fancy!"[2] Whether or not Hazlitt nods here towards his old friend's daughter's novel makes little difference.[3] The metaphor is just, as the narrative frame of Robert Walton's voyage to discover the secret of the magnet is the absolutely right emblem of Victor Frankenstein's researches into the *elixir vitae*:

"I try in vain," Walton writes to his sister in England,

> to be persuaded that the pole is the seat of frost and desolation; it ever presents itself to my imagination as the region of beauty and delight. There, Margaret, the sun is for ever visible; its broad disk just skirting the horizon, and diffusing a perpetual splendour. . . . there snow and frost are banished; and, sailing over a calm sea, we may be wafted to a land surpassing in wonders and in beauty every region hitherto discovered on the habitable globe. . . . What may not be expected in a country of eternal light? I may there discover the wondrous power which attracts the needle.[4]

But from that sun no heat. The connection between brilliant light and freezing cold reverses Milton's dark flames and signifies a direct ratio of increase between the knowledge and the loneliness of all northward discoverers. The metaphor is second in importance only to that of the sea-voyage itself. "I desire," says Walton, "the company of a man who could sympathise with me; whose eyes would reply to mine. You may deem me romantic, my dear sister, but I bitterly feel the want of a friend" (p. 16). This cordial lack is felt too by Frankenstein, whom Walton is quick to clasp, shortly after their meeting, as "the brother of my heart" (p. 23). But Frankenstein sees this sympathy for what it really is: "'Unhappy man! Do you share my madness?'" (p. 24).

The absurdity of Walton's belief in eternal light at the pole is an obvious but necessary feature of Mary Shelley's metaphoric irony. The expedition sets sail from Archangel shortly after the vernal equinox and is given up in September, when the ship is locked fast in ice, and night begins again to assert her ancient prerogative. The allegorical meaning is plain: absolute isolation is reached before absolute enlightenment. The arctic frost of the soul is revealed as the only ignorance, and when the novel ends, seasonal darkness is about to bury all.

Mrs. Shelley's use of the sea-voyage to signify the self-destructive pride of an adventurous soul clearly reflects her husband's influence. Even Henry Clerval's removal to the university at Ingolstadt is described as "'a voyage of discovery to the land of knowledge'" (p. 53). The image is also Coleridgean. "I am going," Walton announces, "to unexplored regions, to 'the land of mist and snow'; but I shall kill no albatross" (p. 18). The major application of the metaphor is reserved for Frankenstein; as Walton puts it, "Strange and harrowing must be his story; frightful the storm which embraced the gallant vessel on its course, and wrecked it—thus!" (p. 27). The scientist's moment of greatest moral confusion is that preceding his nervous breakdown, when he has reneged on his bargain to create a mate for the monster. Having fallen asleep in the skiff he has taken out to drown the remains of his experiment, he wakes to find himself compassless on the ocean, with "the sun . . . of little benefit to me" (p. 153). Where is either the true or the magnetic North? With prophetic irony—for a harsher doom is reserved—"I looked upon the sea, it was to be my grave."

The crime of the "modern Prometheus" is partly the conventional overreacher's wish to "explore unknown powers, and unfold to the world the deepest mysteries of creation" (p. 42). "The words of fate, enounced to destroy me," are contained in Professor Waldman's introductory lecture on the modern chemists, who "'penetrate into the recesses of nature. . . . ascend into the heavens. . . . command the thunders of heaven, mimic the earthquake, and even mock the invisible world with its own shadows.'" Equally important is Frankenstein's lifelong exaltation of the technological understanding (Godwin's and Shelley's "reason") at the expense of sensibility and imagination. Unlike Clerval, who reminds one of Godwin's Falkland as he forms his childhood values out of "books of chivalry and romance," Frankenstein's leading passion is a "thirst for knowledge.... The world was to me a secret which I desired to divine. Curiosity, earnest research to learn the hidden laws of nature . . . are among the earliest sensations I can remember" (p. 32). Is his curiosity any less damnable than Caleb Williams' old-womanish nosiness because its object is not human? The answer depends on whether the source of life is material or divine. Mary Shelley seems content to wonder. But Frankenstein himself has little doubt regarding "the metaphysical, or, in its highest sense, the physical secrets of the world" (p. 33).

Muriel Spark asks the reader of the later chapters of *Frankenstein* to "visualise this pattern of pursuit as a sort of figure-of-eight *macabaresque*, executed by two partners moving with the virtuosity of skilled ice-skaters."[5] The compass-directions followed are significant at all times. As Walton voyages towards the pole, Frankenstein goes north to study at Ingolstadt and later removes from Geneva to the Orkneys to set up the laboratory in which he has promised to create a female monster. So long as he considers himself primarily an intellectual, he is the slave of the magnet and of his artifact, although the monster does not address him as such—"'You are my creator, but I am your master'"— until, having fruitlessly tracked him to his northern workshop, it has no further use for him (p. 149).

Frankenstein then reverses his moral and geographical direction, flying southward to restore his frozen heart. He marries Elizabeth Lavenza in Geneva, and they plan to honeymoon even further south at Como. Their destination lies precisely east southeast, but the great *massif* of the Alps bars their way. The new husband decides "to commence our journey by water, sleeping that night at Evian"; he makes the characteristic and fatal error of trying to reach the south by setting out in a northerly direction (p. 172). They sail towards Elizabeth's strangulation, for the mateless monster has resolved to execute the *lex talionis*. Forgetfully (as we shall see), Frankenstein thinks of Mont Blanc as "beautiful," and with even greater irony Elizabeth finds the play of clouds above it " 'interesting' " (p. 173). At other times, "coasting the opposite banks, we saw the mighty Jura"—the antithesis of overreaching, an emblem of domestic humanity—"opposing its dark side to the ambition that would quit its native country" (p. 172).

When Frankenstein's love was frustrated by death, "I awakened to reason, at the same time awakened to revenge" (p. 177). *Eros*, thwarted, yields *thanatos*. The destructive urge becomes " 'the devouring and only passion of my soul' " as scientific curiosity had been earlier (p. 179). Reason and revenge are sides of a coin. Fire and ice, Promethean desire and polar hate, are both opposed to love, and both drive fanatics north. Between these intemperate extremes lies the warmth by which men live.

Invoking " 'thee, O Night, and the spirits that preside over thee' " to his aid, Frankenstein begins the chase to the sunlit, frozen Arctic, where the monster will be in his own element, the reverse of Lucifer's dark flames (p. 181). " 'I seek,' " he tells his maker, " 'the everlasting ices of the north, where you will feel the misery of cold and frost to which I am impassive' " (p. 183). This is the kingdom of uncircumscribed intellect, where the moral needle vacillates ever more wildly as the voyager nears his goal. As in *Caleb Williams*, what appears to be a one-sided bloodhunt is actually a campaign of mutual harassment, a game of catch-me-if-you-can. Neither antagonist is free to break out of the charmed figure-eight danced upon the frozen sea, an antipastoral setting as jail-like as Caleb's England. For the monster, like the rationalist, is " 'filled . . . with an insatiable thirst for vengeance' " and is " 'the slave, not the master, of an impulse which I detested, yet could not disobey' " (p. 197).

The monster had earlier seized the Arve glacier for his domain, as Milton's Devil embraced his horrors and profoundest hell:

"'the caves of ice, which I only do not fear, are a dwelling to me. ... These bleak skies I hail'" (p. 89). Mont Blanc is the southern prototype of the frozen ocean. Frankenstein's first conversation with his creature takes place here, amid summits which Mrs. Shelley described in her *Journal* as "higher one would think than the safety of God would permit, since it is well known that the Tower of Babel did not nearly equal them in immensity."[6] The glacier fills Frankenstein "with a sublime ecstasy that gave wings to the soul, and allowed it to soar from the obscure world to light and joy" (p. 86). The three aesthetic categories of Burke and Uvedale Price are used several times and with precision in this scene. Mary Shelley meant the mountain to be literally terrible in its beauty, just as Babel's sublime tower, the proudest artifact of the overweening, geometrical understanding, was awful in its temerity.[7]

The twofold metaphor of ice and sunlight, emblematic of the unlawful quest, recurs here from Walton's opening reverie and anticipates the climactic encounter at the pole: "The sea, or rather the vast river of ice, wound among its dependent mountains, whose aerial summits hung over its recesses. Their icy and glittering peaks shone in the sunlight over the clouds" (p. 87). When Frankenstein first approaches Mont Blanc through the Arve ravine, it seems to him that the precipices speak of "a power mighty as Omnipotence" (p. 84). The "white and shining pyramids and domes" appear, in the chill sunlight, "as belonging to another earth, the habitations of another race of beings." The summits are "the faces of those mighty friends" (p. 86). But when he stands on the *Mer de Glace* and invokes their help ("'Wandering spirits, if indeed ye wander, and do not rest in your narrow beds'"), he conjures up only the monster, who comes bounding towards him over the crevasses "with superhuman speed" (pp. 87–88).

A higher power does govern man in the material universe, but Frankenstein is cruelly deluded every time he thinks of it as benevolent. The diction and sentiments of what he rejects as superstition are closer to actuality: "the evil influence, the Angel of Destruction . . . asserted omnipotent sway over me from the moment I turned my reluctant steps from my father's door" (p. 40). He cannot make up his mind. At the end of the book, when he knows he must die unsatisfied, he persists in thinking that "the ministers of vengeance" are on his side and will conduct the monster into Walton's hands (p. 187).

Mary Shelley's irony is too obvious when Frankenstein, pursuing the blood-trail northward, insists that "a spirit of good followed and directed my steps; and, when I most murmured, would suddenly extricate me from seemingly insurmountable difficulties. Sometimes, when nature, overcome by hunger, sunk under exhaustion, a repast was prepared for me in the desert that restored and inspirited me" (p. 182). On the next page more manna—this time a dead hare—is left for him by the monster with a note explaining that the scientist must be kept alive until they wrestle to the death at the pole. Even in these last hours of his madness, Frankenstein has half-glimpses of the source of his vindictive efficiency: "I pursued my path towards the destruction of the daemon more as a task enjoined by heaven, as the mechanical impulse of some power of which I was unconscious, than as the ardent desire of my soul" (p. 183).

The world does in fact wag on its poles by a mechanical impulse. Godwin's materialistic Necessity is felt through his daughter's whole creation as magnetism, animal and mineral. It draws the desiring needle, shudders through the scientist's "soul" as the fixed idea, and awakens the constituent clay of his laboratory Adam. Frankenstein never realizes that his self-destructive vengeance is predicated on his murderous curiosity. The perfect incarnation of this power, its Logos and *filius dilectus*, is the prosy monster. Its court of judgment is the arctic ice-cap, and its thrones the pole and Mont Blanc. Mary Shelley keeps the Fates who drive her antagonists morally neutral. The magnetic chemist has not so much defied them as he has interloped in a game which only they know how to play and win. They permit him, in accordance with the rules, to get himself into trouble, but as croupiers everywhere with any amateur, they refuse to get him out again. Shelley's "Strength . . . Which governs thought" is neither malevolent nor insane in his wife's book. It is mindless.

Frost and fire join once more in the suicide that ends the novel. " 'I shall quit your vessel,' " the monster tells Walton, " 'on the ice-raft which brought me thither, and shall seek the most northern extremity of the globe; I shall collect my funeral pile and consume to ashes this miserable frame, that its remains may afford no light to any curious and unhallowed wretch who would create such another as I have been' " (p. 199). The monster is more than a sentimental *Urmensch*, corrupted from original benevolence into a principle of daemonic, insouciant, self-propelled violence by the frustration of love, which should have been his birthright. He is a botched and dangerous experiment which, in destroying itself, discredits the scientific understanding in whose name and image it was made. Hazlitt's words on the final historical import of Godwinian reason may be applied to the monster:

> if it is admitted that Reason alone is not the sole and self-sufficient ground of morals, it is to Mr. Godwin that we are indebted for having settled the point. No one denied or distrusted this principle (before his time) as the absolute judge and interpreter in all questions of difficulty; and if this is no longer the case, it is because he has taken this principle, and followed it into its remotest consequences with more keenness of eye and steadiness of hand than any other expounder of ethics. His grand work is (at least) an *experimentum crucis* to show the weak sides and imperfections of human reason as the sole law of human action.[8]

The flames to which the crucial experiment consigns himself redeem nothing and mean nothing. They are not purgatorial, nor are they pentecostal tongues, like those Eliot thinks of at Little Gidding on a midwinter afternoon, when, "with frost and fire,/ The brief sun flames the ice, on pond and ditches,/ In windless cold that is the heart's heat." Intellectual fire, Yeats says, consumes everything that is not God. But when the creator is a flesh-and-blood intellectualist and his Adam literally the reason's naked self, then the Promethean element, eating up itself, leaves only the obscure night of the Arctic winter and of the atheist's spiritual negation.

What, meanwhile, of the Rationalist himself? As he lies dying on a ship locked in the ice, Frankenstein reproves Walton's mutinous sailors in words that recall yet another voyager:

> "Are you then so easily turned from your design? Did you not call this a glorious expedition? And wherefore was it glorious? Not because the way was smooth and placid as a southern sea, but because it was full of dangers and terror; because at every new incident your fortitude was to be called forth and your courage exhibited; because danger and death surrounded it, and these you were to brave and overcome. For this was it a glorious, for this was it an honourable undertaking. You were hereafter to be hailed as the benefactors of your species. . . . Oh! be men, or be more than men. Be steady to your purposes and firm as a rock. This ice is not made of such stuff as your hearts may be; it is mutable and cannot withstand you if you say that it shall not."
>
> (p. 192)

Or, as it has been better put,

> "Considerate la vostra semenza:
>   Fatti non foste a viver come bruti,
>   Ma per seguir virtute e canoscenza."
>
> (*Inf.*, XXVI, 118–120)

Ulysses, the smooth-tongued, speaks from the flames reserved in the eighth Malebolgia for evil counselors. At one edge of the known world lies Caucasus, with its writhing Titan; in the southern hemisphere, beyond Hercules' pillars, "Acciò che l'uom più oltre non si metta," Purgatory rises from the sea. And at the pole, as Walton's ship swings southward in fright, another beacon, the pyre of the self-immolated monster, blazes out its warning against the proud, the curious, the obsessed and solitary.

It is hard to remember one's origins at the pole, and how one was meant to live. In such utter isolation, one's private moral compass seems the least untrustworthy guide, together with that "private opinion" which, according to Hobbes, sometimes renders the Greek *hairesis*. The accumulated wisdom of men and the claims of the affections are too distant to bear thinking of, even if the cold would permit it.

A generation later, Melville's questing Pierre disregards this lesson in moral geography. The magnet draws him on ever faster and faster until it holds him paralyzed against the frozen iron:

> In those Hyperborean regions, to which enthusiastic Truth, and Earnestness, and Independence, will invariably lead a mind fitted by nature for profound and fearless thought, all objects are seen in a dubious, uncertain, and refracting light. Viewed through that rarefied atmosphere the most immemorially admitted maxims of men begin to slide and fluctuate, and finally become wholly inverted....
>
> But the example of many minds forever lost, like undiscoverable Arctic explorers, amid those treacherous regions, warns us entirely away from them; and we learn that it is not for man to follow the trail of truth too far, since by so doing he entirely loses the directing compass of his mind; for arrived at the Pole, to whose barrenness only it points, there, the needle indifferently respects all points of the horizon alike.[9]

Dualisms and Doublegangers

In the Sixth Book of the *Republic*, Plato distinguishes *dianoia*, or the understanding of mathematical objects, from that higher *noesis* which intuits the eternal Forms and alone deserves the name of knowledge (*episteme*). To classify "Mont Blanc" as an epistemological poem is to say no more than that it asks which, if either, of these faculties the seeker after truth can trust and whether either differs in kind from *eikasia*, the uncritical awareness of images. If we know anything at all, how do we know it? Many students of Shelley have tried to mine his answer from the monolith of "Mont Blanc," and in my opinion Earl Wasserman's judicious reading of the poem exhausts this approach.[10]

Critical concentration on the observer who speaks the poem has, however, slighted the object of his inquiry. Because it is after all a poem and not an ontological discourse, "Mont Blanc" remains in the realm of *eikasia*, not *episteme*. The dialectic it develops is one of tropes, not categories. These figures, approximate renderings of the object Power, are religious, and with one exception they have not been noticed before. I wish now to examine them in detail. Wherever the following remarks shift their emphasis from the poem's images to their skeptical observer, wider reference will be made to optics than to epistemology—for Power cannot, "as it really is," be known at all.

"One would think," Shelley wrote to Peacock immediately after the picnic on the *Mer de Glace*, "that Mont Blanc was a living being & that the frozen blood forever circulated slowly thro' his stony veins."[11] The Power that inhabits the mountain is impersonal and aloof and cares nothing for the happiness or misery of men:

> The works and ways of man, their death and birth,
> And that of him and all that his may be;
> All things that move and breathe with toil and sound
> Are born and die; revolve, subside, and swell.
> Power dwells apart in its tranquillity,
> Remote, serene, and inaccessible.
>
> (92–97)

Shelley tries in "Mont Blanc" to understand the "living being" he cannot, and in any case would not, propitiate. The poem never confronts its subject face to face; Power is inscrutable except through its outward emblems. But "*This*, the naked countenance of earth" and "these primaeval mountains" suggest the force informing them even as the experiential accidents of bread and wine lead "the adverting mind" to bleeding flesh, the substance they conceal from taste and eyesight (98–100).

The eucharistic analogy is Shelley's own, and it coincides with the predicate of the involuted first sentence of his second strophe. The poem's imagery has to this point (line 19) drawn the eye downward. In the first strophe the totality of "things," or their images, had tumbled through and lent splendor to the mind. The second strophe has continued the downward sweep of the eye by invoking the metaphor's delayed vehicle—"Thus thou, Ravine of Arve"—in terms of the "cloud-shadows and sunbeams" that sail *above* it (12, 15). Power "comes down" through this fissure and for a moment stands still: "thou dost lie" (16, 19). Images of effluence yield now to images of penetration. The eye no longer moves laterally or vertically, but concentrates. It becomes a pilgrim. It seeks to pierce the veil of the temple's inner shrine, there to confront "some" symbol which, though not "imageless," remains unseen and lies beyond the reach of plastic or verbal art:

> Thine earthly rainbows stretched across the sweep
> Of the aethereal waterfall, whose veil
> Robes some unsculptured image.
>
> (25–27)

The mood is literally dithyrambic, for the Presence is indicated only by the ritualistic swaying and the ancient anthem of its celebrants, the chorus of Titanic pines:

> thou dost lie,
> Thy giant brood of pines around thee clinging,
> Children of elder time, in whose devotion
> The *chainless* winds still come and ever came
> To drink their *odours*, and their mighty *swinging*
> To hear—an old and solemn harmony.
>
> (19–24)

The italicized words, with their buried reference to a censer, add to the gazer's quest a savor of the processional in the Mass: *introibo ad altare Dei*.[12] The trees and winds are acolytes. Their harmony lulls the scene and its observer to a "strange sleep" or "trance sublime and strange" like that which, "when the voices of the desert fail/ Wraps all in its own deep eternity" (27, 35, 28–

29). The voices in the wilderness are the poet's own and, of course, those of the fathers of all churches.

The most notorious feature of Shelleyan optics is the vagueness bred of his seeking "in what I see the manifestation of something beyond the present & tangible object."[13] But when he does try to view the object with a connoisseur's eye and as in itself it really is, he either screens the dominant image or takes its measure against a frame in the foreground. Most characteristically, he establishes perspective by looking *through* one thing *towards* another, and, as in the second strophe of "Mont Blanc," religious associations are rarely far to seek.

Shelley notes, for example, of a temple just outside the walls of Paestum, "Beside the outer range of columns it contains an interior range of column above column, & the ruins of a wall which was the screen of the penetralia."[14] On the mountainous road to Salerno, he was chiefly fascinated by "deep dark recesses which the fancy scarcely could penetrate."[15] A "magnificent spectacle" obtruded on him in the Temple of Jupiter at Pompeii: "Above & between the multitudinous shafts of the [?sunshiny] columns, was seen the blue sea reflecting the purple heaven of noon above it."[16] Again: "I see the radiant Orion thro the mighty columns of the temple of Concord."[17]

All these observations occur in yet another travelogue series to Peacock, recording a trip from Rome to Naples and back again in the winter of 1818–1819. They accompany reflections on proportional *trompe l'oeil* and on the symbolic intention of Hellenistic architecture; the Greeks, Shelley writes, "lived in harmony with nature, & the interstices of their incomparable columns, were portals as it were to admit the spirit of beauty which animates this glorious universe."[18] One wonders whether he felt his correspondent required descriptive fidelity, or whether Shelley's eye had simply been cleansed by a climb explicitly analogous to the Chamouni excursion. For these remarks begin with a report of Vesuvius, whose fires inevitably suggest ice: "Vesuvius is, after the glaciers the most impressive expression of the energies of nature I ever saw.... The lava like the glacier creeps on perpetually."[19]

The uncarved palladium hidden by the Mont Blanc waterfall also prefigures the "mighty darkness . . . Ungazed upon and shapeless" who fills "the seat of power" in *Prometheus Unbound* (II, iv, 2, 5, 3). Although the "veil has fallen," Demogorgon is forced finally to answer Asia in words that echo the passage we have been discussing:

> If the abysm
> Could vomit forth its secrets.... But a voice
> Is wanting, the deep truth is imageless;
> For what would it avail to bid thee gaze
> On the revolving world?
>
> (II, iv, 2, 114–118)

Asia has been asking for a naturalistic definition of God, just as Shelley, looking at Mont Blanc, has sought to know the Power in whose *likeness* the Arve descends from "the ice-gulfs that gird his secret throne" (17). But the concrete vehicle is only half the symbolic entity; if read inductively, if followed upward by the naked eye, it is no sure avenue to meaning, to the "secret," numinous source. Gazing upon "the revolving world"—upon the literal flux of the river—makes Shelley giddy, and he projects his vertigo onto the object from which it arose:

> Dizzy Ravine! and when I gaze on thee
> I seem as in a trance sublime and strange
> To muse on my own separate fantasy,
> My own, my human mind, which passively
> Now renders and receives fast influencings,
> Holding an unremitting interchange
> With the clear universe of things around.
>
> (34–40)

The transition effected in these lines shows that the quest has failed for the moment, that it is perforce double, and that it involves two logical steps, whose sequence Shelley has reversed.

The epistemologist should precede the theologian. We cannot say what we know until we know *how* we know. Do the graffiti scratched on the walls of the sensorium truly represent the "universe of things around," or are they idols? Can we elicit Deity from any design perceived by the bodily eye, or must we look *through* the natural veil to find nature's God? Shelley cannot divorce psychological from religious symbolism. For if in either case the brain casts the light it thinks flows into it—if it "renders" more valid "influencings" than it "receives"—then both the retinal image and the worshiped Presence are self-born and, to adapt Yeats's phrase, mockers of the poet's enterprise.

Glacier above and river below, the Arve conveys not only Power, but also, by virtue of the epistemological conundrum that comes down with it, Shelley's moral indecision with regard to that force. If the impressions that course through the mind are inaccurate, then the phenomena to which they refer—the "everlasting universe of *things*"—may not exist, and certainly do not exist as they are seen (1). Even more certainly, they lack any human value that the fancy has not imported into them. Looked at this way, impressions and notions may succeed one another as cause follows effect, but their tendency lacks purpose. The "vast river" of images "bursts and raves" over its rocks pulled only by gravity to a goal it cannot be said to seek (10–11). The telic cause of the cataract is not truth, but repose, and its efficient cause is Necessity. Mechanists abstract this principle from the flux subsisting in the material realm; skeptics assume it to rule the mental cinema of that realm.[20]

In the fourth strophe Shelley's temporarily necessarian speaker confuses the causative chain with what he will later call the Strength that governs thought. The sacramental vision of the second strophe has yielded to sensationalism, and the observer has lapsed into a psychological determinism that outstrips Godwin's restatement of Jonathan Edwards' objections to the freedom of the will. The poem's final question will correct these mistakes by asserting the autonomy of Imagination and showing that the "laws" of nature are neither a literal description of cause, as materialists claim, nor the scientific convenience—the pattern imposed on sequence—of the skeptics. Natural law is conscious, and it has intention. By aligning itself with that intention, the individual human will achieve its liberty. For the duration of the fourth strophe, however, the poet thinks of his mind as an automaton; it makes little difference whether we call it the Humean organ of habit or the Holbachian and Hartleian slave of "vibrations."

Once more the poet lifts his eyes to the summit, and this time he sees what Frankenstein and Walton saw:

>   there, many a precipice,
> Frost and the Sun in scorn of mortal power
> Have piled: dome, pyramid, and pinnacle,
> A city of death, distinct with many a tower
> And wall impregnable of beaming ice.
>
> (102–106)

Not jasper, sapphire, chalcedony or emerald: ice bastions this antitype of the New Jerusalem, which has replaced the tabernacle obscured by the waterfall. "And he showed me," reports Saint John the Divine, "a pure river of water of life, clear as crystal, proceeding out of the throne of God and of the Lamb" (Revelations xxii.1). Shelley too has seen water descend from the "secret throne" of Power (17). But the source is "ice-gulfs." The upper Arve remains frozen, and the solid waters of death smash through the worshiping pines:

> Yet not a city, but a flood of ruin
> Is there, that from the boundaries of the sky
> Rolls its perpetual stream; vast pines are strewing
> Its destined path, or in the mangled soil
> Branchless and shattered stand.
>
> (107–111)

The psychological corollary is clear. Information erodes the mind. The glacier of impressions gouges ever deeper ruts in the brain it will one day overwhelm. It typifies the mutability that granted to Blake and enabling Shelley to penetrate the waterfall's veil includes an act of will.

Sight in lateral extension and triple-dimensional insight work by turns for the speaker of "Mont Blanc." But in the latter case the object itself is not obscured by the imposition of meaning on the object. Double vision entertains both aspects at once. When the bodies of Tiresias, Oedipus, Samson and the speaker of *Paradise Lost* were blinded, the spiritual eye was unsealed. But Shelley's mountain never disappears. What the corporeal eye sees as *nature morte* (if anything can be called dead that has never been awake), the auxiliary, supersensory faculty guesses to be the vehicle of a metaphor whose tenor analogizes to a god. Coleridge's discursive Understanding translates Blake's "Single vision and Newton's sleep." *A Defence of Poetry* will call it Reason, the logical or analytic principle that enumerates quantities. Blake's second or imaginative level of vision (Coleridge's Reason) Shelley too will name Imagination, "the perception of the value of those quantities." The former stands to the latter "as the body to the spirit, as the shadow to the substance."[23]

Peacock's half-playful philistinism would not provoke this definition from Shelley until 1821. But even four years earlier it was to "Greeky Peaky," the most learned occultist he knew, that Shelley confided the symbolic intentions of "Mont Blanc" under a dark conceit. Or rather he did so *through* Peacock, the unnamed and thereby fictitious audience of Mary's *History of a Six Weeks' Tour* (1817). In revising the Chamouni journal-letter for publication in this little volume, Shelley emended the sentence quoted at the beginning of this section to read as follows: "One would think that Mont Blanc, *like the god of the Stoics*, was a vast animal, and that the frozen blood for ever circulated through his stony veins."[24] The simile seems idle, but in fact it names the Power who quickens Mont Blanc.

The Stoics saw subsisting in matter, known to them as "the Passive," certain active "laws" or "reasons," which they called *logoi*. The singular noun *Logos* denoted the sum of these principles and named the divine Personality. According to this sys-

Mont Blanc and the Magus Zoroaster

This doggerel fragment, entitled "Passage of the Apennines," immediately recalls the boat-stealing episode in *The Prelude*, which, of course, Shelley had not read. More pertinently, it demonstrates his habitual conversion of qualities of vision into qualities of light. This is not the textbook projection of subject onto object. The perceiving subject, in itself inexpressible, has been translated into the non-human energy that illuminates the object and through which the object must pass in order to be known. Here daylight and starlight respectively inform Blake's outward and inward vision. So Emily, the facultative Sun of *Epipsychidion*, complements the facultative Moon, which is to say that Reason, benighted, reflects Imagination. In *The Triumph of Life* the moonlike chariot of worldly intellect extinguishes the false Matilda's sun and rainbow of sensuous naïveté; these in turn trample out the stars, "heaven's living eyes" of poetic intuition.

The striding Apennine is neither the actual mountain nor a phantasm of the brain. The symbol exists in the *commerce* between thing and eye; it floats, as it were, in the middle air. For the starlight alone, and not the subject into whom it flows and dies, defines this moment in which empirical fact cannot be told from imaginative and moral truth. Yeats, writing of moonlight, assigned such moments to the "quarter where all thought is done." By that glare the "intellect no longer knows/*Is* from the *Ought*, or *Knower* from the *Known*."

Vision was fourfold in Blake's

> supreme delight
> And threefold in soft Beulah's night
> And twofold Always.[22]

The word "insight" implies depth, a dimension not noticeable unless we keep both eyes open. Stereopticon slides and the "3-D" movies of recent years annoyed us less by the banality of their premise—the interest of a "view" for its own sake—than by the optical virtuosity artificially imposed upon us. For we are ordinarily aware of length and breadth alone; we observe in depth only when we need or wish to. The simultaneity of perspectives granted to Blake and enabling Shelley to penetrate the waterfall's veil includes an act of will.

Sight in lateral extension and triple-dimensional insight work by turns for the speaker of "Mont Blanc." But in the latter case the object itself is not obscured by the imposition of meaning on the object. Double vision entertains both aspects at once. When the bodies of Tiresias, Oedipus, Samson and the speaker of *Paradise Lost* were blinded, the spiritual eye was unsealed. But Shelley's mountain never disappears. What the corporeal eye sees as *nature morte* (if anything can be called dead that has never been awake), the auxiliary, supersensory faculty guesses to be the vehicle of a metaphor whose tenor analogizes to a god. Coleridge's discursive Understanding translates Blake's "Single vision and Newton's sleep." *A Defence of Poetry* will call it Reason, the logical or analytic principle that enumerates quantities. Blake's second or imaginative level of vision (Coleridge's Reason) Shelley too will name Imagination, "the perception of the value of those quantities." The former stands to the latter "as the body to the spirit, as the shadow to the substance."[23]

Peacock's half-playful philistinism would not provoke this definition from Shelley until 1821. But even four years earlier it was to "Greeky Peaky," the most learned occultist he knew, that Shelley confided the symbolic intentions of "Mont Blanc" under a dark conceit. Or rather he did so *through* Peacock, the unnamed and thereby fictitious audience of Mary's *History of a Six Weeks' Tour* (1817). In revising the Chamouni journal-letter for publication in this little volume, Shelley emended the sentence quoted at the beginning of this section to read as follows: "One would think that Mont Blanc, *like the god of the Stoics,* was a vast animal, and that the frozen blood for ever circulated through his stony veins."[24] The simile seems idle, but in fact it names the Power who quickens Mont Blanc.

The Stoics saw subsisting in matter, known to them as "the Passive," certain active "laws" or "reasons," which they called *logoi*. The singular noun *Logos* denoted the sum of these principles and named the divine Personality. According to this system, which has been aptly described as a monism drifting towards dualism, the universe is a sacramental body whose phenomena are not in fact separable from the laws or Law informing them.[25] But because the ontologist possesses distinct terms for the rational and the material "components" of the world, he can assign syntactical priority to either. Is matter a mode of God, or is God a mode of matter? The Stoic progressionist watched the divine mind evolving throughout a continuously created nature towards more perfect self-expression; his mechanistic opponent viewed God as what Shelley called him in 1811: a completed entelechy, "a synonime for the *existing power of existence*," like gravitation or "the soul of a clock."[26] Blake's metaphor applies again: where the single eye of the materialist notes stasis and death, the binocular vitalist sees plasticity and purpose. The Stoics had to choose between *natura naturata* and *natura naturans*, or, in Shelley's imagery, between a walled city of impersonal Being and an evergreen, chanting landscape of Becoming; between characterless, directionless phenomena and those same things breathed through by their determining and uplifting essences.

Although the mountain itself does not change, the features selected for emphasis are, under either visual aspect, precise correlatives of the faculty used. The concrete object, in other words, embodies the cyclopean or two-eyed subject by whom it is known. The imagination or proto-imagination discovers like Job, not words, but the Word—not discourse or dogma but a symbol, reminiscent of Mercy on his seat within the ark, beyond the waterfall's cloud of seeming. But the unaccompanied rational eye detects no vitality in the gleaming, ruinous glacier. Reason's Leviathan merely *exists*, like Lowell's Moby-Dick, as "IS, the whited monster" who neither thinks nor grows.

The last metaphor is Shelley's too, and it is, of course, originally Scriptural. The Hebrew *leviathan* translates the Greek *ouroboros*, the perpetually constricting, tail-devouring snake of time and chaos who hopes to strangle creative Eternity. We shall see in Chapter Five that Jupiter, the snowbound emperor of all rational hatreds, metamorphoses into this dragon in the penultimate stanza of *Prometheus Unbound*. But there is already a hint of such symbolism in the fourth strophe of "Mont Blanc":

> The glaciers creep
> Like snakes that watch their prey, from their far fountains,
> Slow rolling on.
>
> (100–102)

The simile attracts special notice for two reasons. First, it is not generally accurate, though it may well have been so for the Arve in 1816. Glaciers tend to carve their own paths, to bowl over those obstructions which would force an unfrozen river into a winding course. And serpentine kames are mainly produced by ice-sheets, not valley glaciers. The lesson of hindsight is more useful; our experience of Shelley's later verse warns us never to assume that his snake-imagery is gratuitous. To understand it here we must look at yet another passage from the Chamouni journal-letter to Peacock:

> Do you who assert the supremacy of Ahriman imagine him throned among these desolating snows, among these palaces of death & frost, sculptured in this their terrible magnificence by the unsparing hand of necessity, & that he casts around him as the first essays of his final usurpation avalanches, torrents, rocks & thunders—and above all, these deadly glaciers at once the proofs & the symbols of his reign.[27]

In 1814 Peacock had abandoned his abortive epic *Ahrimanes*, whose title character, Zoroaster's principle of universal filth and darkness (*angrō mainyush* = *evil spirit*), will remain locked in nearly equal combat with Ormuzd (*Ahura Mazda*), the god of light and life, until the latter triumphs at the end of history. Shelley had read of this conflict in Barruel, but his and Peacock's serious interest in Persian dualism dates from the summer of 1813, when they conversed at Bracknell with John Frank Newton, vegetarian, syncretistic mythographer, and student of the Hindu Dendera Zodiac. According to this "Manichean Millenarian," as he was later dubbed in *Nightmare Abbey*, the hemisphere of

Ormuzd may be subdivided into the quarters of Creation and Preservation, which directly oppose the Ahrimanic segments of Destruction and Restoration. Newton's identification of Ahriman the Destroyer with Siva and Jupiter justifies the imaginal similarity between the aquiline skygods of *The Revolt of Islam* and *Prometheus Unbound*. Finally, Shelley learned from Count Volney's *Ruins of Empires* that the serpent stood for Ahriman in Persian iconography.[28] The figure's marginal appearance in "Mont Blanc" as a projection of single vision need not detain us. The emblem invites our attention mainly because Shelley will hereafter upset our expectations of it. *The Revolt of Islam* will assign the snake to Ormuzd, and three years later *Prometheus Unbound* will divide it against itself.

The third, fourth, and fifth stanzas of the Dedication of *The Revolt of Islam* detail the circumstances in which the shadow of Intellectual Beauty had fallen on the young Shelley and "burst/ My spirit's sleep." One May morning, outside what was presumably an Eton schoolroom, the boy began to weep without knowing why, and, as in the 1816 hymn to the Power dawning in him, "I clasped my hands." The children's voices that broke in on this trance sounded in one respect like that which sang to Saint Augustine, *tolle, lege*. For the young necromancer who had hitherto "called on poisonous names" (according to the "Hymn to Intellectual Beauty") was hereby converted to the "meek and bold" service of wisdom, justice and freedom. Henceforth he would take up and read occult literature as if it were the Scriptures, and would buckle it to him as Saint Paul and Spenser's Saint George had the whole armor of God:

> And from that hour did I with earnest thought
>   Heap knowledge from *forbidden mines of lore,*
> Yet nothing that my tyrants knew or taught
>   I cared to learn, but from that *secret store*
>   Wrought linkèd armour for my soul, before
> It might walk forth to war among mankind.
>
>   (37–42, my italics)

Shelley devotes this, his second epic (composed, interestingly enough, in Spenserian stanzas), to the rescue of Lucifer, Isaiah's "son of the morning," from the calumnies heaped on him by orthodox apologists for the Fall of Man.

The first Canto of *The Revolt of Islam* narrates a duel between an eagle and a serpent, " 'Twin Genii, equal Gods,' " who " 'o'er mortal things dominion hold' " (350, 347). At sunset the lacerated snake drops exhausted into the sea, swims ashore, and creeps into the bosom of a woman who tells the poet that the antagonists are disguised. In the beginning of the world they were meteors, " 'A blood-red Comet and the Morning Star' " (356). When the latter fell in combat, the " 'conquering Fiend,' " who is presumably Jehovah as well as Ahriman, changed the " 'starry shape' " of his immortal foe to " 'a dire Snake, with man and beast unreconciled' " (378, 368–369). But the woman has seen Ormuzd or Lucifer in sleep, when the " 'wingèd youth,' " who wears the Morning Star on his brow, bent over her and kissed her, just as Eros had covered Psyche (500). Shelley too beholds him—"Majestic, yet most mild—calm, yet compassionate"—enthroned in a great hall to which the woman transports him and where all three await the arrival of the martyred souls, Laon and Cythna (639).

The heavenly war of Canto One adequately accounts for the presence of evil in the world, but it does little more. A theodicy is not a theology, and Shelley's myth merely decorates the revolutionary chronicle it frames. Shelley would not vindicate this symbolism, nor would he rehabilitate Lucifer, until the dramas of 1818–1819 recast his epic matter in Gnostic terms. His *Essay on the Devil, and Devils* of the same year insists that we tell the serpent of Genesis from Isaiah's Lucifer and from the Satan of Revelations. The various Gnosticisms not only explicate these distinctions; unlike the non-Christian system of Zoroaster, they are casuistically as tricky and dogmatically as thoroughgoing as the Body of Faith they have always threatened. And because the heresiarchs were Platonists, they identified Lucifer, as Shelley wished to do, with an Eros who loves that which he desires to *know*. Whatever imaginative subtlety *The Revolt of Islam* may have lies not in its "philosophy" but in its emblematic irony.

If benevolence did not so often wear a loathsome shape, men would not need imagination. The bodily eye that recoils from Frankenstein's creature is the same vain organ that prejudges the fallen, ophidian Lucifer and thereby betrays the mind to the impostures of orthodoxy, which always sides with Ahriman. Conversely, the forces of malice masquerade as seraphs; they get at us through our enthusiasms and our lusts. The tusked and scaly tempter of ecclesiastical fresco is a dangerous priestly hoax. Shelley's point in transferring the emblem of Zoroaster's devil to his own Ormuzd-figure is thus far perfectly obvious. Why, then, is his symbolism so unstable elsewhere in the poem?

Canto Four equates the Serpent and the Dove (as do the Gospels) with Wisdom and Innocence (1584), but in Canto Two fear and lust are called twin serpents, as are hate and guile in Canto Ten (701, 4078). The King glares on Laon like "a toothless snake," Faith is "an obscene worm," and the Fear of Hell is a hydra who wields the Future "like a snaky scourge" (1941, 2168, 4290, 4302). Cythna compares Hate to Amphisbaena, whose sting is self-contempt (3386). In the revolutionary sunrise of the world, however, " 'From its dark gulf of chains, Earth like an Eagle springs' " (3693). And Laon says of America, " 'That land is like an Eagle' " (4423). Shelley has not forgotten that he turned the symbolic convention topsy-turvy in Canto One. In a fallen world, malevolence and hypocrisy will remind good men of the snake's cold eyes and forked tongue. For what has fallen is perception itself. Even the comparatively clear-sighted reformers of that world will launch the emblem of an eagle into the republican dawn of which they dream. Imaginal consistency is the hobgoblin of the *bien-pensant* poet, theosophist, or political liberator because images may or may not be faithful to worlds outside the sensorium of the individual witness.

Insofar as we trust images, Ahriman can scramble them to our confusion. Little Buttercup's point about jackdaws, peacock feathers, gilded farthings, and ambitious brill was Shelley's and

Blake's point too. Are the "stars" who "threw down their spears,/ And water'd heaven with their tears" the angels who have just lost, or those who have just won, the war between the Archfiend and the Son? Heaven and Hell look so much alike, according to Blake's satiric epithalamion, that "in the Book of Job, Milton's Messiah is call'd Satan." Even more terrifying is history's decree that the triumphant victim turn into the tyrant; Orc always ends as Urizen. The *Marriage* says again: "Know that after Christ's death, he became Jehovah."

The duplicitous emblems of *The Revolt of Islam* prepare the way for a transformation-symbolism as mercurial as Blake's in *Prometheus Unbound*, where pain equals hatred and the sickly consciousness determines the form of its own punishment. Prometheus tells the Furies:

> Whilst I behold such execrable shapes,
> Methinks I grow like what I contemplate,
> And laugh and stare in loathsome sympathy.
>
> (I, 449–451)

They explain in reply why this is so:

> from our victim's destined agony
> The shade which is our form invests us round,
> Else we are shapeless as our mother Night.
>
> (470–472)

Prometheus assumes that these "phantasms" derive "From the all-miscreative brain of Jove" (448). We shall see in a moment that dramatic irony could scarcely be more obvious.

Earth's account of her early history shows that Prometheus has unintentionally fathered present human misery. Joy quickened men at the birth of Prometheus, and his voice "uplifted/ Their prostrate brows from the polluting dust" (I, 159–160). His subsequent fall both coincided with and caused theirs, for his curse upon Jupiter is the spell enslaving them. All painful events in human society mirror the life-withering rancor within the Titan's brain, and the mother has become the type of the unregenerate son:

Mont Blanc and the Magus Zoroaster

> And in the corn, and vines, and meadow-grass,
> Teemed ineradicable poisonous weeds
> Draining their growth, for my wan breast was dry
> With grief; and the thin air, my breath was stained
> With the contagion of a mother's hate
> Breathed on her child's destroyer; ay, I heard
> Thy curse.
>
> (I, 174–180)

Prometheus' imprecation redounds upon his own beloved creatures because it feeds Jupiter. The Olympian torturer cannot exist independently of the hatred, terror, and remorse sprung from and battening upon the Titan's heart.

Jupiter emanates from perverted and denied imagination, and Prometheus' complaint, "I gave all/ He has; and in return he chains me here," is a tautology (I, 381–382). Jupiter personifies the hatred by which Prometheus binds himself. The Titan unsays his curse by commanding the Phantasm of Jupiter to repeat it. This is the lyrical drama's one tragic moment, since the hero had given way to the pity that will release him before articulating his forgiveness in his opening speech. Jupiter's specter prepares for its walk-on by making up its face to look as Prometheus had looked before he achieved *anagnorisis* and before the play began. Jupiter is himself the "loathsome mask" of Prometheus, and the Titanic false-face worn by his Phantasm affords the reader his single glimpse of the stiff-necked and arrogant fire-bringer:

> I see the curse on gestures proud and cold,
> And looks of firm defiance, and calm hate,
> And such despair as mocks itself with smiles.
>
> (I, 258–260)

Jupiter is literally the "sceptered curse," and the Phantasm of Jupiter is Prometheus' malevolent aspect, the ghost of his dead self risen from beneath the grave to mimic him for the last time.

To conduct the imagination to that nether world, Earth cites the experience of Zoroaster. This is his last appearance in Shelley's verse:

> Ere Babylon was dust,
> The Magus Zoroaster, my dead child,
> Met his own image walking in the garden.
> That apparition, sole of men, he saw.
> For know there are two worlds of life and death:
> One that which thou beholdest; but the other
> Is underneath the grave, where do inhabit
> The shadows of all forms that think and live
> Till death unite them and they part no more;
> Dreams and the light imaginings of men,
> And all that faith creates or love desires,
> Terrible, strange, sublime and beauteous shapes.
>
> (I, 191–202)

Those researchers who have probed Persian scripture and folklore for the source of this incident have, I think, misdirected their attention. The Zoroastrian allusions of "Mont Blanc" and *The Revolt of Islam* establish a context sufficient in itself to define the function of Earth's hagiograph. The Magian and Gnostic dualisms interested Shelley as matrices of emblematic ambivalence. Images do not change, but their tenors do. Single and double vision will gather antithetical meanings from the same figure. The world "which thou beholdest" and the wide womb of possibility perform a dialogue which is literally travesty: Jupiter and Prometheus, Ahriman and Ormuzd, Jehovah and Lucifer play-act each other, and the man who fails to scrape the scales of sensuous prejudice from his eyes will not detect the naked body of truth or menace beneath the frippery. The world under the grave is more rather than less "real" because dreams discover it, love desires it, and faith and "light" imagination create it. Prophets and revolutionists catch glimpses of it because their minds are at home in that extensionless realm of Becoming which the many misinterpret as a temporal "future." Laon and Cythna had to perish to enter it, and so did Zoroaster, who is emphatically Earth's *dead* child. Her living son cannot marry Asia, his erotic emanation, until she has like Orpheus undertaken a night-journey

Mont Blanc and the Magus Zoroaster

to "the depth of the deep" (II, iii, 81). Shelley is now fully aware that the imagination has a purpose of its own and that that will is suicidal. "No more let Life divide," pleads the speaker of *Adonais*, "what Death can join together." In *Prometheus Unbound* things as they commonly seem and things as they ought to be consummate their union below the tomb. "None," Marvell thought, "do there embrace," but only there will Zoroaster "part no more" from his daemonic image.[29]

It is just possible that Earth's parable influenced Blake. S. Foster Damon speculates that "Oxford, immortal Bard," the bit-player who reproves Albion in Plate 46 of *Jerusalem* and then faints dead away, is an allegorized Shelley.[30] Plate 48 contains the following lines, in which we may or may not wish to substitute Prometheus for Jerusalem and Asia or Earth for "Maternal Love":

Beneath the bottoms of Graves, which is Earth's central joint,
There is a place where Contrarieties are equally true:
(To protect from the Giant blows in the sports of intellect,
Thunder in the midst of kindness, and love that kills its beloved:
Because Death is for a period, and they renew tenfold.)
From this sweet Place Maternal Love awoke Jerusalem.[31]

The contrary experiences of the corporeal and the spiritual eye—of reason and imagination, Urizen and Los—may amount to the same thing in death's kingdom. But the interview between the two worlds does not regenerate the man who is unprepared for it, nor does his mirror-genius arise from a "Place" unequivocally "sweet." On 23 June 1822 Shelley surprised his own doubleganger strangling Mary in her bed at Casa Magni. We shall see in Chapter Eight that he knew what the encounter forebode. It was clear to him that, as Tekla remarks in Strindberg's *Creditors*, "he who sees his attendant spirit (*fylgia*) dies."

Wherever Shelley abandons the descriptive-meditative mode for abstract reflection in "Mont Blanc," he becomes hard to understand. The poem's cruxes testify to its technical immaturity; as discourse, it is not so well written as prose. But the criterion is irrelevant, not to say philistine. The basic linguistic unit of poetry, including the "poetry of statement," is the metaphor, as the category is that of philosophy. The obscurities in "Mont Blanc" are not examples of a confused metaphysics; they are simply weak figures. Our brief pursuit of the later fortunes of the symbolic system embryonic in 1816 should enable us now to penetrate two of these vexatious passages.

"Mont Blanc" ends with an exclamation and a question:

> The secret Strength of things
> Which governs thought, and to the infinite dome
> Of Heaven is as a law, inhabits thee!
> And what were thou, and earth, and stars, and sea,
> If to the human mind's imaginings
> Silence and solitude were vacancy?

The second sentence has incited many quarrels, despite the inescapable fact that the operative word, *imaginings*, is not a synonym for "reasonings" or for "thoughts" generally. If there is little Godwin in "Mont Blanc," there is even less Berkeley. Shelley does not state that the mountain would disappear if he closed his eyes or if his reason refused to admit the hypothetically needful but logically unprovable existence of things outside it. He asks a series of questions: do the *logoi*, the "laws" of the Stoics, truly inform nature, or does the imagination set up a sacrament in vacancy? Conversely, is the "hand" of Ahrimanic Necessity "unsparing" only because we arm it? Do the outward and visible signs of the mountain in fact point to anything inward and spiritual? *The Cenci* repeats these questions, and *The Triumph of Life* approaches with bitter and multiple irony what we can never know but may guess to be negative answers.

The second crux is much more troublesome, for the text itself is open to dispute:

Mont Blanc and the Magus Zoroaster

> The wilderness has a mysterious tongue
> Which teaches awful doubt, or faith so mild,
> So solemn, so serene, that man may be,
> [In such a] [But for such] faith, with nature reconciled;
> Thou hast a voice, great Mountain, to repeal
> Large codes of fraud and woe.
>
> (76–81)

The first phrase bracketed in line 79 appears in the Boscombe MS.; Shelley published the second in the *History of a Six Weeks' Tour*, and his widow reprinted it with the *Posthumous Poems* of 1824. The manuscript reading is straightforward enough, but it is also deistic. "As you mention Religion," Shelley had written to Janetta Philipps in May, 1811, "I will say, that my rejection of *revealed* proceeds from my perfect conviction of its insufficiency to the happiness of man.... My rejection of *natural* arises wholly from *reason*. I *once* was an enthusiastic Deist, but never a Christian."[32] The Shelley of 1817 read nature not as the finished though open record of Providential *magnalia*, but as the vehicle of a revelation (he had changed this much) struggling towards self-realization. Because he could no longer see the creation as the established text, the dead letter of natural religion, he corrected his *lapsus styli* and sent "Mont Blanc" to the press.

The alternative reading of line 79 is maddeningly ambiguous. The prepositional phrase contradicts the verb it modifies: a mild, solemn and serene faith would reconcile man with nature if he did not have such faith. Shelley has canceled wording dishonest to his present position; has he filled the lacuna with an absurdity? The circle of apparent illogic breaks when the substantive *faith* is detached from its modifiers. The noun is the object of knowledge; the adjectives are projectile and refer to the subject who knows. Insofar as faith produces mildness, solemnity and serenity in man, it persuades him to make up his quarrel with matter. But because those emotions refer to affect, because they define the believer rather than *what* he believes, the intellect cannot trust them. They are the accidents of cognition, not its substance.

The distinction is Lockean as well as Aristotelian, and we muddle it all the time. The man who says, for example, "This ice cube is cold," does not utter a tautology but a kind of metaphor. He imports his sensation of coldness into a rectangular solid composed of water molecules at a critical density. Whatever his motives for making such a remark, he is harmless. But his further inference that everything that tastes like bread must be bread and only bread would not at all moments in history have evoked the response due apparent truisms. Religion insists that we distinguish what we "feel"—sensations or sentiments—from that of which we have most certain knowledge. It blesses the person who has not seen and yet has believed, while it condemns him who mistakes *bien-être* for beatitude. Shelley warns the imaginative man that the Ahriman within him, his rebellious rational and lower faculties, fosters and exploits this confusion of primary and secondary qualities.

Process, the first article of the phenomenology urged here, implies imperfection. Matter is evil in this poem to the precise extent that it can and will improve, mendacious insofar as it enfolds a promise. The phrase, "But for such faith," condenses the moral paradox of *natura naturans*. Mont Blanc's "mysterious tongue" does not preach present reconciliation with the world of eye and ear. It calls for hope through an evolutionary creed which includes its opposite: "awful doubt" of elements yet unredeemed.

The mountain is a judge, the interpreter of *logoi*. Large, fraudulent codes shrink before its sentence of repeal. The "secret Strength of things" was for the Stoics in truth what it is in Shelley's simile: "as a law" to the infinite dome of heaven. We may now follow its fortunes as a collective and proper noun—as a Person named the Logos—through *The Cenci* and *Prometheus Unbound*.

IV
The Paterin Beatrice

Introduction

Mary Shelley's research into the most pessimistic of medieval heresies is an overlooked source of *The Cenci*. Even she no longer saw or understood this connection in 1839, when she coarsened her husband's theodicy in a gloss which critics who like to think him callow still quote against him: "Shelley believed that mankind had only to will that there should be no evil, and there would be none . . . that evil is not inherent in the system of the creation, but an accident that might be expelled."[1] The few direct pronouncements that Shelley risked upon this subject after 1813 severely qualify his wife's report. In *Prometheus Unbound*, for instance, imagination exorcises the imps of remorse, superstition, and vindictiveness, but "chance, and death, and mutability" persist, together with those other "clogs," the passions. Reason and will, though free, remain under house arrest until the hour of bodily death. Nor is there any guarantee, Demogorgon warns us, that the cycle of horrors will not come round again.

The "tired child" who in 1818 had longed to lie down and weep "Till death like sleep might steal on me" grew ever more despondent in the struggle to banish his wife's "accident" from nature and society and from the human heart. If we are too weak to expel the spoiler, we can at least cheat him of protracted pleasure by anticipating his final assault: "Die,/ If thou wouldst be with that which thou dost seek!" Susceptible at all times to momentary disgust with the realm of eye and ear, Shelley endured moods in which mortal birth seemed to him, as it seems to Beatrice Cenci, an "eclipsing Curse," and life in the world a contagion and "slow stain."

"According to Jesus Christ, and according to the indisputable facts of the case, some evil Spirit has dominion in this imperfect world."[2] And according to Shelley throughout the rest of this *Essay on Christianity*, the founder of that religion was a platonizing socialist who "represented God as the principle of all good, the source of all happiness, the wise and benevolent creator and preserver of all things. . . . Jesus Christ expressly asserts that distinction between the good and evil principle which it has been the practice of all theologians to confound."[3] Through Peacock, Volney, and John Frank Newton, Shelley knew of the Zoroastrian deadlock between Ahriman and Ormuzd, the personifications of the darkness and the light. If he had simply viewed the Gospel rubrics through the medium of Persian dualism, his position would have been exactly that of the flayed sage, Mani. We shall presently see that Shelley was theologically (and geographically) far closer to home. He was as confident as a Cathar *perfectus* that the amalgamation of the spirit of differentiating justice with the merciful Paraclete is an historical accident and a psychological absurdity. The monistic established churches apparently conceive of God as a literal extension of the *paterfamilias*, who ensures the directionless anguish of His children by demanding that they simultaneously fear and love Him. This to Shelley was a moral impossibility, however an orthodox Christian might modify the metaphor to that of a stern but kindly teacher who guarantees us all manner of joy beyond the asses' bridge of seeming illogic.

The Cenci was written between the Third and Fourth Acts of *Prometheus Unbound*. The tragedy of Beatrice will here be regarded as a pyrrhonistic exercise in aid of the affirmation celebrated by Shelley's lyrical drama. In *The Cenci* the whole creation is a syphilitic chancre and the god of this world (Shelley argues from design) a witty degenerate.

The Cenci

According to the manuscript "Relation of the Death of the Family of the Cenci,"[4] the Count was a multilateral sexual psychopath. Shelley takes up the story at the point where advancing age makes Francesco Cenci's bodily lusts yield to and unite in "spiritual" sadism:

> True, I was happier than I am, while yet
> Manhood remained to act the thing I thought;
> While lust was sweeter than revenge; and now
> Invention palls:—Ay, we must all grow old....
>   I the rather
> Look on such pangs as terror ill conceals,
> The dry fixed eyeball; the pale quivering lip,
> Which tell me that the spirit weeps within
> Tears bitterer than the bloody sweat of Christ.
> I rarely kill the body, which preserves,
> Like a strong prison, the soul within my power.
> (I, i, 96–99, 109–115)

The predestinarian Calvinist God has often been suspected by unbelievers of reveling in similar feelings. Encomia of an exercised, breathed, and uncloistered virtue notwithstanding, the moral oxymoron of *felix culpa* may seem cheaply sentimental to a man—not necessarily an infidel—in real and prolonged pain. One is unfortunately bound sooner or later to introduce the critical chestnut of Milton's Deity into any discussion of Shelley's demonology. The epic character of the Father, for all His Arminian tact and plain speaking, has at times appeared whimsical to readers innocent of or reacting against earlier religious training. Shelley willfully and even playfully misinterpreted *Paradise Lost* for the same reason that he would have despised *Wilhelm Meister* and Carlyle's notion of human existence as a *Bildungsroman*. The great Taskmaster's postponement of the inheritance of the Kingdom—if indeed He means to give it—is an unnecessary, cranky complication, "mere shamefacedness and coquetting."[5]

A bourgeois analogy may help to clarify Shelley's point: the mighty industrialist who insists that his heir earn his way up from the stockroom must, to make the trial morally meaningful, include the real possibility of failure. This could be interpreted as perverse and pompous egotism, if not something worse in its universal extension. Shelley's description of God in his essay, *On the Devil, and Devils,* echoes Cenci's just-quoted self-anatomization and was written at roughly the same time:

> But to tempt mankind to incur everlasting damnation must, on the part of God and even on the part of the Devil, arise from *that very disinterested love of tormenting and annoying which is seldom observed on earth except from the very old.* . . . The thing that comes nearest to it is a troop of idle, dirty boys baiting a cat; cooking, skinning eels, and boiling lobsters alive, and bleeding calves, and whipping pigs to death; naturalists anatomizing dogs alive (a dog has as good a right and a better excuse for anatomizing a naturalist) are nothing compared to God and the Devil judging, damning, and then tormenting the soul of a miserable sinner.[6]

Shelley's curious insistence in his Preface to *The Cenci* upon the Catholic setting of the story is partially explained by his emphasis in such millenarian writings as *Hellas* upon the extreme age of the enemy. Age makes tyrants cruel, and this cruelty stems from the fear attendant upon impotence. In *The Cenci* the Babylonian Whore overdresses to disguise her debility.

The comparatively legalistic character of the older religion is also important. A kind of cash-and-carry absolution flourished in the Papal Court by which the historical Cenci could and did buy pardon from Clement VIII for sins including that "not to be mentioned among Christians" and likewise passed over by Shelley. A chapel traditionally thought to have been built by Cenci to Doubting Thomas guarantees the eternal repose of his soul, as we are told in the Preface. There, also, a basic distinction is drawn between the faith of Rome and the quasi-Calvinist sects of modern England:

> But religion in Italy is not, as in Protestant countries . . . a gloomy passion for penetrating the impenetrable mysteries of our being, which terrifies its possessor at the darkness of the abyss to the brink of which it has conducted him. Religion coexists, as it were, in the mind of an Italian Catholic, with a faith in that of which all men have the most certain knowledge. It is interwoven with the whole fabric of life. It is adoration, faith, submission, penitence, blind admiration; not a rule for moral conduct. It has no necessary connection with any one virtue. The most atrocious villain may be rigidly devout, and without any shock to established faith, confess himself to be so.

The sacrament of Penance is the crux of this distinction. God does not care for merit, the service of "good works." Nor does grace abound upon the simple contingency of belief. When Shelley says that Roman Catholicism is not a rule for moral conduct, he means that a novena or a sum of money is a surer guarantee of salvation than are a tremulous conviction of sin and the simultaneous wish to reform one's behavior.

Another aspect of Roman legalism, the paternalism everywhere denounced in *The Cenci*, is hardly explained by our biographical knowledge of the spats with Sir Timothy. The tragedy's great developmental irony is Beatrice's growing awareness, uncompleted until the moment that the headsman waits for her around the corner, that Cenci, Clement, and Almighty God form a triple entente. Her father, *il Papa,* and *Pater Omnipotens* constitute a tacit hierarchy; each is plenipotentiary within his own sphere, concentric with the other two, and each serves his own interest with that of the others. Thus the Pope

> holds it of most dangerous example
> In aught to weaken the paternal power,
> Being, as 'twere, the shadow of his own.
>
> (II, ii, 54–56)

Camillo's attempted intercession for papal clemency is later refused in even stronger words:

> "Parricide grows so rife
> That soon, for some just cause no doubt, the young
> Will strangle us all, dozing in our chairs.
> Authority, and power, and hoary hair
> Are grown crimes capital."
>
> (V, iv, 20–24)

Cenci acts with assurance in destroying his family, for he knows that, "The world's Father/ Must grant a parent's prayer against his child" (IV, i, 106–107). Such is that lifted in imprecation against his sons and miraculously fulfilled by the collapse of a church upon the worshiping Rocco. The event is celebrated by a lavish supper at which Cenci elevates a bowl of wine in thanksgiving:

> Could I believe thou wert their mingled blood,
> Then would I taste thee like a sacrament,
> And pledge with thee the mighty Devil in Hell,
> Who, if a father's curses, as men say,
> Climb with swift wings after their children's souls,
> And drag them from the very throne of Heaven,
> Now triumphs in my triumph!
>
> (I, iii, 81–87)

The passage is critical for two reasons. First is the obvious profanation of the Eucharist, the consecration of the blood of the New Testament. This is paralleled later by the curse upon Beatrice, which perverts the command given with the older Covenant to Noah:

> That if she ever have a child; and thou,
> Quick Nature! I adjure thee by thy God,
> That thou be fruitful in her, and increase
> And multiply, fulfilling his command,
> And my deep imprecation! May it be

> A hideous likeness of herself, that as
> From a distorting mirror, she may see
> Her image mixed with what she most abhors,
> Smiling upon her from her nursing breast.
>
> (IV, i, 141-149)

Both these passages anticipate classic psychoanalytic theogony. Symbolic cannibalism and actual incest are Cenci's major sins, as they were for Freud two of the primitive, antisocial drives which religion was invented to repress. Christianity supposedly sublimates them into the doctrines of the Real Presence and *Mater Coniunx*.

Cenci's pledging of the devil in the first passage is problematical, but actually explains God's willingness to let His vicar invert the mysteries and give them what trusting humanity never suspected to be their real meaning. It is quite a joke. To bear children is to bring further capacity for suffering into the world. Spirit is daily crucified in flesh, devoured, and thus miserably perpetuated. These apparent contradictions are reconcilable only in the heresies that regard Christ as a rebel against Jehovah. Before considering them it is sufficient to know that in *The Cenci*, as in the essay *On the Devil, and Devils*, "God" and "Satan" are hypostases of a single Personality. Cenci wavers between thinking himself "like a fiend appointed to chastise/ The offences of some unremembered world" (IV, i, 161-162) and speaking of his ordained task as follows:

> My soul, which is a scourge, will I resign
> Into the hands of him who wielded it;
> Be it for its own punishment or theirs,
> He will not ask it of me till the lash
> Be broken in its last and deepest wound;
> Until its hate be all inflicted.
>
> (IV, i, 63-68)

Just before his death Cenci is entertained by prospects of the laughter in hell and lamentation in heaven over Beatrice's pollution. But he also knows that, "'Tis plain I have been favoured from above,/ For when I cursed my sons they died" (IV, i, 39–40). It does not matter what Cenci calls the Ruler of the world. The divine power is malevolent and will continue to pamper its servant, however inconsistent he may be in his catechism. The one thing it will not tolerate is publicity tending to compromise its own reputation or that of the Holy See.

Cardinal Camillo had warned Cenci in the opening speech of the play that if he kept on waving his dirty linen like a flag before "men's revolted eyes," Clement would find it impolitic to sell him any more mercy. The outward "glory and the interest/ Of the high throne" must be safeguarded at all costs. The divine power at last decides to liquidate Cenci for his public outrageousness. His dispatch would seem to be the embarrassing business of his immediate superior, the Pope. But Clement's legate does not arrive at Petrella until the moment after the murder. The dark spirit has rid itself of an indiscreet agent at the expense of his and its devoted victims, the Countess and the younger Cenci. The keeper of the keys can therefore vindicate the sacred paternal right with a clear conscience. Clement righteously condemns those who to his immense relief anticipated his mission. The *Realpolitik* of the unbeheld divinity is always economical.

If the god of this world is corrupt and sadistic, physical nature is at best indifferent. The off-stage thunderstorm which should accompany the destruction of Cenci in fact heralds news of the failure of the attempt. "Then wind and thunder," exclaims Giacomo, "Which seemed to howl his knell, is the loud laughter/ With which Heaven mocks our weakness!" (III, ii, 37–39). Shelley may be poking grim fun at the fallacy of all who in art as in moral judgment would open an appeal from God to His creation. The irony of this meaningless conjunction of *Sturm* and *Drang* doubtless seems cheaper today than it would have in 1819 to a Covent Garden audience expecting more in the pathetic vein of Lewis, Maturin, and Kotzebue.

Beatrice does not recognize the covenant existing among the three Fathers until the hour of her death. Her developing awareness of this contract makes her tragic as Vittoria Corombona, to whom she has been so often and so idly compared, is not. In the First Act she prematurely proclaims that "there is a God in Heaven" who will not allow Cenci's news of the deaths of Rocco and Cristofano to be true (I, iii, 52); in the next to last scene, when the verdict is in and the chance of appeal negligible, she still exhorts her family,

> Take cheer! The God who knew my wrong, and made
> Our speedy act the angel of His wrath,
> Seems, and but seems, to have abandoned us.
> Let us not think that we shall die for this.
>
> (V, iii, 113–116)

A moment earlier she had weakly taxed "the small justice shown by Heaven and Earth/ To me," but she has now recovered the faith that cheats her (72–73). Full *anagnorisis* is still to come.

Throughout the latter part of the play Beatrice names herself and the hired assassins "weapons" in the right hand of justest God. Her metaphor is mocked both by the event and by its echo of Cenci's boast that he has been appointed "God's scourge for disobedient sons" (III, i, 316). Beatrice's mental habits being what they are, her mendacity in the trial scene needs little explanation or excuse. She persuades Marzio to die under torture rather than implicate her because she does not see herself as what in the Count's words and in fact she is: "A rebel to her father and her God" (IV, i, 90). Beatrice considers herself orphaned and says as much several times. How can she then be guilty of the crime with which she is charged? "I am more innocent of parricide/ Than is a child born fatherless" (IV, iv, 112–113). Besides, God has armed her. His law invalidates that of the Papal Court, and fidelity to Him supersedes all oaths sworn therein. Him she thinks she serves despite all temptations to atheistic despair:

> Many might doubt there were a God above
> Who sees and permits evil, and so die:
> That faith no agony shall obscure in me.
>
> (III, i, 100–102)

This statement is doubly ironic. Though what is actually said contains only half her mixed-up meaning, Beatrice's words are literally true; God does permit evil. And her negatively implied faith in justice in God's good time is precisely what will later be obscured by the pain of her attempt to outface death's impudent leer with dignity.

Before Beatrice knew what crucifixion might really feel like, she had querulously paraphrased one of the Last Words: "Thou, great God,/ Whose image upon earth a father is,/ Dost Thou indeed abandon me?" (II, i, 16–18). After she has been raped she senses "A clinging, black, contaminating mist" about her which "eats into my sinews, and dissolves/ My flesh to a pollution" (III, i, 17, 21–22). Here again her words are ironically prophetic, for when she is almost in the article of bodily dissolution and Bernardo's last plea to the Pope has failed, tragic *anagnorisis* comes upon her for one moment (immediately half-repented) in this same shape. The material creation and its great Father are whimsically pernicious. The just God she thought she served was her own invention. For this grotesque mistake eternity's practical joke will be an unceasing, incestuous defilement, a caustic vapor thirsting for entrance at every orifice. Its caress will have teeth and nails of flame. The passage in question is deservedly celebrated:

> If there should be
> No God, no Heaven, no Earth in the void world;
> The wide, gray, lampless, deep, unpeopled world!
> If all things then should be ... my father's spirit,
> His eye, his voice, his touch surrounding me;
> The atmosphere and breath of my dead life!
> If sometimes, as a shape more like himself,
> Even the form which tortured me on earth,
> Masked in gray hairs and wrinkles, he should come
> And wind me in his hellish arms, and fix
> His eyes on mine, and drag me down, down, down!
> For was he not alone omnipotent

On Earth, and ever present? Even though dead,
Does not his spirit live in all that breathe,
And work for me and mine still the same ruin,
Scorn, pain, despair?

(V, iv, 57–72)

This paranoid misreading of Creation and of the revealed mysteries of the Church is not an isolated Shelleyan fancy. It is the most persistent of vulgar errors and has in all ages, under various names, constituted the gravest, because the most logical, of doctrinal threats. Wherever it has caught the popular imagination, as in the region of Albi, it has spread like fire and has proved eradicable only in the same element. In her second novel, *Valperga*, Mary Shelley gave it a name which, if rightly pondered, should help us see *Prometheus Unbound* and *The Cenci* as halves of a single religious poem.

Valperga

The most interesting character in *Valperga: or, the Life and Adventures of Castruccio, Prince of Lucca* (1823) is a girl named Beatrice. Her features are described when she first enters as forming "a picture such as Guido has since imagined, when he painted a Virgin or an Ariadne, or which he copied from the life when he painted the unfortunate Beatrice Cenci" (II, 17–18). Saintly at first, she is deflowered by Castruccio and then captured, subjected to unnamed varieties of sexual violation, and finally driven mad by a diabolical mage about whom "there was something that might be called beautiful; but it was the beauty of the tiger, of lightning, of the cataract that destroys" (III, 86–87). In time she forsakes her orthodox devotions and becomes what Mrs. Shelley calls a *Paterin* (III, 88). Her heretical creed is outlined by Beatrice in words whose echo of the verses last quoted leaves little room for doubt that she is modeled upon *la Cenci*. She explains to the novel's heroine (amusingly named Euthanasia) that,

you either worship a useless shadow, or a fiend in the clothing
of a god. Listen to me, while I announce to you the eternal and
victorious influence of *evil, which circulates like air about us,
clinging to our flesh like a poisonous garment, eating into us,
and destroying us.* . . . Then reflect upon domestic life, on the
strife, hatred and uncharitableness, that, as sharp spears, pierce
one's bosom at every turn . . . and all which man in his daily
sport inflicts upon man. . . . Oh! surely *God's hand is the
chastening hand of a father, that thus torments his children!
His children? his eternal enemies!*

(III, 43-45)

The Beatrice of *Valperga* will seem at a casual glance the first
of many nineteenth-century borrowings from Shelley's tragedy.
The most notable of these are Hawthorne's in *The Marble Faun*
and Melville's near the end of *Pierre*. But *Valperga* is actually an
analogue and in one respect a source of *The Cenci*. The connection between them has not to my knowledge been noticed before.

Although *Valperga* was not begun until 1820 and published
only the year after her husband's death, Mary Shelley started
thinking about her novel in 1817 at Marlow. She read and studied
for it at Naples in the winter of 1818–1819 while Shelley was
completing the First Act of *Prometheus Unbound*.[7] Shelley told
Peacock that *Valperga* was "raked out of fifty old books."[8] No
evidence exists that he read more than one of them with her, but
in that one, Simonde de Sismondi's *Histoire des Républiques Italiennes*, Shelley encountered, on or about 20 January 1819, the
following passages:

> It is not within the scope of this work to give an account of
> the entry into Europe of the Paulicians, a Manichean sect,
> who, hunted out of Asia by the persecutions of the Greek
> emperors . . . advanced slowly towards the West and scattered
> the first seeds of the Reformation among the Latin peoples;
> but since these sectaries, to whom Raymond, Count of Toulouse, granted a refuge in Languedoc, in the neighborhood of

Albi, multiplied also in Italy, where they were known under the name of *Paterini*, it is fitting that we give them some moments of attention.

The persecutors of the Paulicians and the Albigensians have consistently affirmed that the foundation of their doctrine was the dogma of the two principles, which has prevailed from all time in the East and is not completely foreign to the Jewish and the Catholic religions. . . . [These heretics] recognized . . . in the universe two creative powers: that of the invisible world, whom they called the Good God, and that of the visible world, whom they named the Evil God. This is the system of Manes, on the eternity of spirit and matter. To the first god they attributed the New Testament, to the second the Old Testament. And, to prove that the latter was indeed the work of the god of evil, they threw into relief all the crimes reported there and those qualities of the jealous, vindictive and terrible god which the Hebrews thought they saw in the Supreme Being. . . . [The Paulicians] believed that men were angels, fallen from their pristine grandeur, but that their souls, after some transmigrations, would return to their ancient glory.[9]

The name *Paterini* (or Patareni, Patrini, Paterelli, Patalini) was originally applied in the early eleventh century to the extreme reform party in the Milanese Church.[10] The word may derive from the Latin *patera* (cup) or from *pataria*, the Milanese ragmarket and hence a dialect term for any popular faction. By the end of the thirteenth century, when the historical Castruccio Castracani came of age, the name had been transferred by Italian writers to dualist heresies generally, and particularly to Bosnian and Dalmatian *Bogomilstvo*. "Paterin" was, like "Manichee" or the later "Jacobin," a name with which to conjure up a stock, uncritical response of pious horror. It was employed by the married clergy as an *ad hominem* answer to advocates of clerical celibacy, and an unseemly word, originally denoting the heresy's Bulgarian origins, has survived into modern English. Since reproduction was considered by the dualists a greater triumph for the devil than the momentary lapse of a *perfectus* into sensual pleasure for its own sake, sodomy may have been looked upon with relative toleration. Nature and natural law were indeed regarded by medieval heretics as the work and politics of our ancient foe, but the notorious chastity and suicidal fasting of the Albigensian Cathari, whose religion absorbed many Bulgarian elements, have inclined most historians to consider this imputation of Crying Sin the exaggeration of special pleading, if not outright slander.

The cry of "Manichee" is harder to discount. Used as a smear and with a canting fuzziness of definition, even in the Lateran Council's 1179 condemnation of the Paterini, it is none the less accurate. The Bogomils and Paterini were offspring of the Paulician heresy that had been drifting west from Armenia since the eighth century. Paulicianism can be traced back through Mani to the first Gnostic sects, which it links with the later Albigensian Gnosticism. Little is known of the heresy's dogma except through distorted orthodox refutations, as most Paulician literature was destroyed. We shall look at some of these refutations in the next chapter. For the moment it can be said, very roughly, that most of the medieval dualist sects denied the inspiration of the Old Testament and the divinity of Jehovah; they despised the symbolism of the Cross and subscribed to the Valentinian and Docetist notion that the spiritual Christ passed through the body of the Blessed Virgin like water through a pipe. Although they explicitly disavowed the apostleship of Mani, the Paulicians taught the essential evil of matter and the eternal hostility of Zoroaster's two principles.

Medieval dualism preserved in its mythology a corruption of Plato's doctrine (in the *Timaeus*) of an intermediary Demiurge, the shaper of the phenomenal world upon the eternal model or Paradigm above him. The Cathari identified this Craftsman with Jehovah, who has sadistically punished us and our friend the Serpent for seizing the forbidden knowledge by which we expose his pretension to omnipotence. Jehovah had tried to defraud men of their heritage by enclosing them in a prison of material pain and sensuous ignorance, but here too the eaten apple, the bringer of bodily death, has been the instrument of our release.

Mary Shelley's Paterin Beatrice does not behold the God above the Demiurge. Shelley's heroine too achieves insufficient *anagnorisis*. She recognizes the malice of the institutionalized goblin who is god of this world, but dies with no more than a vaguely intuited

> faith that I,
> Though wrapped in a strange cloud of crime and shame,
> Lived ever holy and unstained.
>
> (V, iv, 147–149)

Both Beatrices have descended to that nadir of despair which must precede all true awakening. But neither does awake. Their Paterinism lacks the sophisticated hope of its Gnostic parent and Cathar stepchild; it is "vulgar error" indeed. The Albigensian flowering in the high culture of Provence took root in a similar condition of cosmic paranoia among the starved and brutalized peasantry of the eleventh, twelfth, and thirteenth centuries. Such hatred of the world's Father, however natural in the serf with wit enough to detect the impostures of his parish priest, was not for the troubadours and Cathar *perfecti*, nor is it for Shelley, the final answer.

Beatrice and Prometheus

Beatrice Cenci is a less "poetical" though a more tragic version of Prometheus. She is in fact Shelley's Satan. He remarks in the Preface to *Prometheus Unbound* that "The character of [Milton's] Satan engenders in the mind a *pernicious casuistry* which leads us to weigh his faults with his wrongs, and to excuse the former because the latter exceed all measure. In the minds of those who consider that magnificent fiction with a *religious feeling* it engenders something worse." Both these responses—that of the secular rationalist and that of the devotee—are deliberately elicited in *The Cenci*. Shelley admits this in virtually the same words just quoted concerning readers of Milton: "It is in the restless and *anatomizing casuistry* with which men seek the justification of Beatrice, yet feel that she has done what needs justification; it is in the *superstitious horror* with which they contemplate alike her wrongs and their revenge, that the dramatic character of what she did and suffered, consists" (*The Cenci*, Preface). In other words, Shelley tells the reader that he has created a work of art to which the only valid responses are, paradoxically, illegitimate. In April of 1819 he had written three acts of *Prometheus Unbound* and thought the poem complete. We must now ask why he should have wished to follow it with such a child of the left hand.

Beatrice is marked by only one of "the taints of ambition, envy, revenge, and a desire for personal aggrandisement, which, in the Hero of *Paradise Lost,* interfere with the interest" (*Prometheus Unbound*, Preface). Yet that fault of vindictiveness far outweighs the other three. Prometheus has still to purge himself publicly of this single satanic vice as Shelley's lyrical drama opens. Revenge is renounced in the unsaying of the great curse upon Jupiter, and this recantation unbinds the Titan. Beatrice, on the other hand, never learns to forgive wrongs darker than death or night. She goes to her death in chains because she does not know that "the fit return to make to the most enormous injuries is kindness and forbearance, and a resolution to convert the injurer from his dark passions by peace and love. Revenge, retaliation, atonement, are pernicious mistakes. If Beatrice had thought in this manner she would have been wiser and better; but she would never have been a tragic character" (*The Cenci*, Preface).

Revenge is a carnal passion, implemented by the sense-fed understanding, which regards all moral questions *sub specie saeculi.* Beatrice Cenci not only arrogates to herself the Lord's prerogative of repayment, but also denies the imagination, which for Shelley combined the shaping power of the *vates* with the higher reason. In the purest Gnostic traditions the latter mental power, known to us as intuition, alone has power to tear the loathsome mask from the Demiurge. The two faculties together are roughly

The Paterin Beatrice

equivalent to the Logos, the Word as artificer, the Word itself made flesh, the Second Person of the Neoplatonic and orthodox Christian Trinity. Both the Logos and the Gnostic Jehovah stem directly from the Craftsman of the *Timaeus*, who is Plato's mythic personification of *Nous* or universal creative Mind. The Gnostics divided this power against itself; the Father was the Demiurge, whereas the epithet *Nous* denoted both the punished Serpent and Christ, the redeeming parricide.

In *The Cenci* Shelley plays off these opposed philological traditions (which we shall re-examine shortly) against each other and creates a dualism beyond the dualism. One version just misses canceling the other in this war of imagination upon superstition, this shadow-duel between twin emanations of a single potent monad. Beatrice is satanic rather than Christ-like because she is unsuccessful. And she is unsuccessful because she is blind to her clear function in an otherwise ambiguous universe of muddled theological syncretism.

When the imagination is denied, it has a nasty trick of returning as terror. As such it blazes in the frenzied mind of Mary Shelley's Paterin: " 'the fire that dwelt in my brain gave unnatural light to every object. . . . if imagination live, it is as a tyrant, armed with fire, and venomed darts, to drive me to despair' " (*Valperga*, III, 88, 102). Terror is an instrument of the Demiurge, the imagination perverted and stolen by him from the unseen God or Paradigm in order to mock human hope:

> "He, the damned and triumphant one, sat meditating many thousand years for the conclusion, the consummation, the final crown, the seal of all misery, which he might set on man's brain and heart to doom him to endless torment; and he created the Imagination. . . . the imagination, that masterpiece of his malice; that spreads honey on the cup that you may drink poison; that strews roses over thorns. . . . that apple of gold with the heart of ashes; that foul image, with the veil of excellence. . . ."
>
> (*Valperga*, III, 46–47)

Prometheus' recantation of the curse may seem too easy a conversion. The decision for forgiveness has in fact been made when the play opens; the Titan's dark angel, summoned up for the last time as the Phantasm of Jupiter, has already lost the match. Little is seen of the preceding spiritual struggle in which Prometheus must often have cried, with Mary Shelley's Beatrice, " 'Destruction is the watchword of the world; the death by which it lives, the despair by which it hopes: oh, surely a good being created all this!' " (*Valperga*, III, 48).

When Shelley paused between the Third and Fourth Acts of *Prometheus Unbound*, he was aware of this dramatic deficiency. He had created, as he says in the Preface, a purified Devil, a "type of the highest perfection of moral and intellectual nature." But he had not demonstrated the condition of sin that precedes conversion, the Fall from which men and Titans rise. To this end he made the satanically vengeful Beatrice, whom he clothed in the slough of religious ignorance already cast by his Prometheus. The Hell to which she goes, as the curtain obscures her march to the chopping block, is a crag in the Caucasus.

The crude Paterinism of the two Beatrices represents the human understanding *in extremis* as it wars unaided against the Demiurge. Paterinism is a protoreligion, a desperation, not a faith, for the imagination has not yet descended to heal the eye blinded in its own pride. As the Cathars recaptured the Valentinian and Marcionite vision obscured to the Paulicians, so Prometheus casts out Beatrice. The hymn that concludes Shelley's lyrical drama rises out of and over the choked scream of the senses, gnawing at the mesh of their drowning rattrap. Paterins die because they believe the Demiurge's lie that the Paradigm he attempts to hide and the Word he impersonates—both of whom will one day judge him—do not exist. The Logos, his beneficent doubleganger and brother under the fright-wig, has the strength to undo him utterly. Shelley is not making phrases when he reminds us in the Preface to *The Cenci* that "Imagination is as the immortal God which should assume flesh for the redemption of mortal passion."

V
The Ophite Demogorgon

And I thought of the albatross,
And I wished he would come back, my snake.
For he seemed to me again like a king,
Like a king in exile, uncrowned in the underworld,
Now due to be crowned again.

—D. H. Lawrence, "Snake"

Let us look now at the one character in *Prometheus Unbound* whose symbolic function has never been interpreted to general satisfaction. Who is Demogorgon, what does he do, and how?

Vulture and Serpent

Prometheus' single reference to the bird that lacerates him does not name its species:

> Heaven's wingèd hound, polluting from thy lips
> His beak in poison not his own, tears up
> My heart.
>
> (I, 34–36)

Mrs. Shelley's Note to the drama began the tradition that a vulture was meant. If she was right, then her husband deliberately perpetuated an iconographical mistake. He knew from Aeschylus that the bird of Zeus was an eagle, and so Apollo describes Jupiter (III, ii, 11). Shelley may not have known (and it makes little difference) that the modern association of Prometheus with a vulture comes from those sixteenth-century artists who confused the fire-stealer with Tityus. Rubens, for example, based his painting of Prometheus upon Michelangelo's drawing of the would-be rapist of Latona.[1] The "wingèd hound" is at all events not one, but three. Panthea calls the Furies "Jove's tempest-walking hounds,/ Whom he gluts with groans and blood" (I, 331–332). Nourished by carrion, they are rather vulturine than aquiline, as the Third Fury admits in a simile: "The hope of torturing him smells like a heap/ Of corpses, to a death-bird after battle" (I, 339–340). Their metaphoric nature is determined by the putrescence of their food. The substitution of the Titan's mortified heart for his liver needs no explanation.

In the moment of his fall, Jupiter compares the Power who drags him down and renews the heart of Prometheus to a serpent:

> Sink with me then,
> We two will sink on the wide waves of ruin,
> Even as a vulture and a snake outspent
> Drop, twisted in inextricable fight,
> Into a shoreless sea.
>
> (III, i, 70–74)

This duel of emblems is already familiar to readers of *Alastor* (227–237, 325) and *The Revolt of Islam*. Although Shelley had seen analogues in the *Iliad*, *Choephoroe* and *The Faerie Queene*, and had derived his special usage of the image, however indirectly, from Persian dualism, classical and Magian myth hold no monopoly upon it. It turns up, for instance, in Toltec art, where its contraction, the feathered snake Quetzalcoatl, figures even more prominently. Like the phoenix, it betokens endless increase within perpetual reduction. Hart Crane evokes the native American form of the trope from the ashes that remain of Maquokeeta's dance in flames:

> Now is the strong prayer folded in thine arms,
> The serpent with the eagle in the boughs.

In *Prometheus Unbound* Shelley recasts the iconography of a monism closely related to the system of Zoroaster. For the moment we need notice only that the ugly snake, born in the dark earth and belly-creeping upon it, circumstanced too by libidinous and Satanic connotations, is here the principle of love, beauty, liberation, and the Light of the good God.

The most important parallel to Jupiter's metaphor occurs in Chapter 3 of Shelley's abortive romance, "The Assassins" (1814). Albedir discovers a quasi-crucified stranger who has just fallen from Heaven and whom Newman White called the Wandering Jew "half-way metamorphosed into a benevolent Promethean champion."[2]

> A young man, named Albedir, wandering in the woods, was startled by the screaming of a bird of prey, and, looking up, saw blood fall, drop by drop, from among the intertwined boughs of a cedar. Having climbed the tree, he beheld a terrible and dismaying spectacle. A naked human body was impaled on the broken branch. It was maimed and mangled horribly; every limb bent and bruised into frightful distortion, and exhibiting a breathing image of the most sickening mockery of life. *A monstrous snake had scented its prey from among the mountains—and above hovered a hungry vulture.* From amidst this mass of desolated humanity, two eyes, black and inexpressibly brilliant, shone with an unearthly lustre. Beneath the blood-stained eye-brows their steady rays manifested the serenity of an immortal power, the collected energy of a deathless mind, spell-secured from dissolution.[3]

The serpent and the vulture flee at the approach of Albedir, but they would surely have returned later in the completed story. For although they are enemies, together they constitute the two-handed engine by whose means the Assassin intends to purify the world at large and to make it resemble his own secluded demi-Eden. He yearns to feed "holy liars," "parasites," and "the respectable man" to the ravens. "The Assassin would cater nobly for the eyeless *worms* of earth, and the *carrion fowls* of heaven."[4] Human progression lies beyond the dialectical ministry of these brute contraries. Just so the intertwined fall of Jupiter and Demogorgon drowns with them the old Adam and baptizes the fallen Garden in a "shoreless sea" of ruin:

> Let hell unlock
> Its mounded oceans of tempestuous fire,
> And whelm on them into the bottomless void
> This desolated world, and thee, and me,
> The conqueror and the conquered, and the wreck
> Of that for which they combated.
>
> (III, i, 74–79)

The serpent has a still deeper ritualistic function for the Assassins. Albedir brings the proto-Prometheus to his paradisiacal dwelling, with which the stranger appears familiar: "Albedir's habitation seemed to have been his accustomed home."[5] There they find the children of Khaled and Albedir " 'by the waterside, playing with their favourite snake.' . . . They sate beside a white flat stone, on which a small snake lay coiled . . . they arose and called to the snake in melodious tones, so that it understood their language. . . . Then they ran round and round the little creek, clapping their hands, and melodiously pouring out wild sounds, which the snake seemed to answer by the restless glancing of his neck. . . . The girl sang to it, and it leaped into her bosom, *and she crossed her fair hands over it, as if to cherish it there.*"[6]

These Assassins are evidently a sect of snake-worshipers. If the story had been finished, the serpent might have been identified with the Demogorgon-like powers whom Shelley credits with ordering the rise and fall of empires and religions, breathing "the decrees of their dominion from a throne of darkness and of tempest."[7] We are told more specifically that many of the Assassins' beliefs "considerably resembled those of the sect afterwards known by the name of Gnostics. They esteemed the human understanding to be the paramount rule of human conduct."[8]

The puzzling thing about all this is that the historical Assassins were not Christian Gnostics, but Ismaili Muslims. The one contemporary study of them, Joseph von Hammer's *Geschichte der Assassinen*, was published in 1818 and not translated into English until 1835. If Shelley ever discovered his mistake, he did not do so until the spring following the composition of his fragmentary romance. On Saturday, 8 April 1815, as he neared the end of a complete reading of *The Decline and Fall of the Roman Empire*, he entered in his wife's *Journal* the following paraphrase of a note in Gibbon's sixty-fourth chapter: "All that can be known of 'The Assassins' is to be found in 'Memoires of the Academy of Inscriptions,' tom. xvii, pp. 127–170."[9] This is presumably a reference request to Mary, who had visited the British Museum to see "all the fine things" the day before. If she returned to it before 10 May, however, it would have to have been on Wednesday, Thursday, or Friday of the week following Shelley's notation; the *Journal* pages for those days have been torn out. Shelley could, of course, have searched or meant his wife to search elsewhere.

What Shelley actually had in mind when he wrote "The Assassins" was a Gnostic sect known alternatively as Ophites and Naassenes (from the Greek *ophis* or Hebrew *nahas*, both meaning "serpent").[10] The question is how he knew of them. The only detailed source available in the early nineteenth century was the thirtieth chapter of the first book of Saint Irenaeus, *Adversus Haereses*, "Quae est Ophitarum et Caianorum Irreligiositas et Impudentia et unde Conscripta Ipsorum." If Shelley saw this hostile summary before writing his romance, its absence from the received list of his reading is easily accounted for. Our main source for Shelley's reading after the Notes to *Queen Mab* (1813) is Mary's *Journal*, which was begun by Shelley on 28 July 1814, the day of their elopement from England. Mary's first entry is dated 8 August, and "The Assassins" was started on 25 August, the same evening that Shelley, Mary, and Claire Clairmont, overwearied with continuous travel, settled into their "ugly house" at Brunnen for what they thought (until the following afternoon) would be six months.

Shelley may have seen J. L. Mosheim's epitome of *Adversus Haereses* in the sixty-second chapter of the second volume of the

German theologian's *Commentaries on the Affairs of the Christians Before the Time of Constantine the Great*. Cadell and Davies' publication, in 1813, of the first English translation of this Latin work was at least timely. Or the poet may have been referred to Saint Irenaeus by Peacock, whose interest in and knowledge of esoterica, Hermetica and exploded theologies generally was unsurpassed among Shelley's close friends. The Zoroastrian dualism of which Peacock had just finished writing in 1814 meets and marries Christian Gnosticism in the system of Mani.

The possible influence of Thomas Taylor should not be discounted. Shelley may have met him with Peacock in 1812 or in London in the summer of 1814.[11] Taylor's translations of Plato were in any case familiar to the poet, as were the introductions and footnotes in which Taylor discussed Orphic and Alexandrian systems and interpreted Plato's theology by the smoky light of Proclus' commentaries. Although he was far from sympathetic with such Judaized forms of Neoplatonism, Taylor must have known Gnosticism well. After writing "The Assassins" Shelley encountered Gnostic allusions in Wieland's *Peregrinus Proteus*[12] and elsewhere, and he can hardly have missed Gibbon's specific reference to Saint Irenaeus.[13] Additional study of the subject is altogether likely in the summer of 1817, when Shelley and Peacock, both living at Marlow and seeing each other frequently, were respectively writing *The Revolt of Islam* and preparing to write *Rhododaphne*.[14]

Finally, Shelley may never have read Saint Irenaeus at all. It makes little difference. He had learned the essential article of Ophite belief by the summer of 1814, if only through conversation. By September, 1818, he also knew at least one of the finer details. Before going further, we must glance at the crude mechanics of the system as a whole.

The Ophite Genesis

The Ophite heresy was distinguished from other forms of Gnosticism by its concentration upon Original Sin. Whereas its Valentinian parent emphasized the Incarnation and Passion of Christ, the leading event of the snake-worshipers' mythology was the seduction of Adam and Eve. Most other minor sects resembled Ophitism in deriving their names not from those of their founders (e.g., Marcion, Valentinus, Paul of Samosota), or from cognates of *gnosis* (e.g., the Mandaeans from the Aramaic *manda*), but from the Scriptural personages or events central to their doctrine and ritual. Cainites, Sethians and Sodomites flourished contemporaneously with the Ophites.

All Gnosticism makes a primary distinction between *pistis* and *gnosis*, which is very roughly that between belief and absolute knowledge, or pure cognition.[15] The object of human gnosis is the Pleroma, or eternal overworld of purely spiritual beings. Here dwells, say the Ophites, "a kind of first Light in the Power of the Deep, blessed, and incorruptible . . . this is the Father of all, and is called the First Man. And his thought coming forth they call the Son of him who sends it forth: and say that this is the Son of Man, the Second Man. And that beneath these is the Holy Spirit."[16] This much of Saint Irenaeus' report recalls countless Christian and Neoplatonic readings of the triad of the *Timaeus*. Plato's "soul of the world" was traditionally identified with the Holy Ghost, as was his "intellect of the soul of the world" with the Logos, or second Person of the Trinity.[17] Here all resemblance ends.

The First and Second Men fall in love with the Holy Spirit, or First Woman, and impregnate her with the Light, causing her to give birth to Christ from her right side. At the same time she boils over on the left, spilling an emanation of light and virtue into the Sea of Matter, from which it assumes a body. This emanation is called Sophia (Wisdom), the Left, and Prunicos (the Whore). The mediatrix between spirit and matter, Sophia longs to be reabsorbed into the higher Light whence she fell; she ascends at last, but not before producing a son, Ialdabaoth.

Saint Irenaeus goes on to relate that Ialdabaoth rebelliously creates a son of his own, who in turn generates another son; the process continues to the completion of a hebdomad. These Heavens, Excellencies, or Virtues (known in other Gnostic systems as Archons or Aeons) perch on the seven spheres of the material cosmos, each fainter in worth and power as he is posterior in generation and more distant in space from the everlasting Light. The power by which they rule the earth is referred to in most Gnostic theology as *heimarmene* (universal Necessity) and is equivalent to natural and Mosaic law. Their leader and ancestor Ialdabaoth turns up in the Old Testament as Jehovah. Because of his position in the seventh sphere, he may also be regarded as Saturn, Kronos-Chronos, Father Time; more frequently he is identified with the upstart Olympian Jupiter, present chief of the pantheon.

Ialdabaoth's six offspring begin at once to quarrel with him for first place,

> upon which Ialdabaoth in grief and despondency looked upon the dregs of matter lying beneath, and fixed his desire thereon: whence they say a son was born (*which was Mind itself* [Nun] *twisted into the form of a serpent*): and afterwards spirit and the soul, and all worldly things: whence were generated all oblivion, and wickedness, and jealousy, and envy, and death. *And this serpentlike and crooked Mind they say did yet more overthrow their father by his crooked ways....*
>
> Whereupon Ialdabaoth, exulting, boasted of that all he had under him, and said, *I am Father and God and none is above me*. But his mother [Sophia] hearing cried against him, "Lie not, Ialdabaoth; for there is above thee the father of all the first man, and Man the Son of Man." And all being troubled at the new voice, and unimaginable name, and inquiring whence the cry came, Ialdabaoth, they say, said, *Come let us make man after our image*.[18]

The six Virtues or Archons, deceived by Sophia into thinking that man will aid them and Ialdabaoth against the unknown God above them all, create in concert a gigantic Adam. But Sophia, by unspecified and presumably obscene sleight of hand, drains Ialdabaoth of his power as he breathes life into Adam's nostrils. Men

The Ophite Demogorgon

thereby gain "Mind and Conception" (*nun et enthymesin*), through which they intuit and give thanks to the First Man instead of to their makers. These gnostic faculties, known generally as the *pneuma*, or divine spark, are distinct from the *psyche*, or seven "soul-vestments" (each given by an Archon), which together with the body are subject to heimarmene, and within which the Archons hope to imprison the pneuma. In later religious history Jesus Christ descends to rescue Nun (the Greek *nous*) and restore it to its eternal home in the Light of the Pleroma.

Gnosticism offers two plans for destroying the work and defeating the designs of the Archons in this world. Since the natural and the moral laws affect only the body and psyche, the "pneumatic" man may be ascetic or he may be nihilistic and libertine.[19] The emphasis upon murder and sexual novelty in the names of many Gnostic sects reflects the latter way and accounts for their swift and thorough extirpation.

As the creative and obstructive intermediary between the true God and man, Ialdabaoth-Jehovah-Jupiter is an obvious perversion of Plato's *demiourgos agathos*. The serpent, the crookedly incarnated Nun or Mind itself, becomes his antagonist in the Ophite reading of the second and third chapters of Genesis. Sophia Prunicos now plots by means of this snake

> to transgress the command of Ialdabaoth. And Eve as being told this by the Son of God [the serpent deceiving her for her own good] easily believed it, and persuaded Adam to eat of the tree, of which God [Ialdabaoth] had said he should not eat. And they say that they eating knew the virtue which is above all, and departed from those [the Archons] who had made them. And that Prunicos seeing that they are overcome even by their own work, uttered great joy, and again cried out, that whereas the Father [the First Man] was incorruptible, this one [Ialdabaoth] did of old lie in calling himself the Father.[20]

Ialdabaoth punishes the serpent by casting him down into a lower world, where he rages against men for having gained their freedom by his ministry and to his loss. Death enters Eden, and with it a beneficial sense of sexual shame, teaching men to despise the flesh. And Adam and Eve "were patient, knowing that their body is put on them for a time."[21]

The later Peratae identified Jesus as a "pneumatic" principle with the serpent itself. Mani in the third century simply substituted Jesus for the snake in the Paradise story. Saint Irenaeus reports that some Ophites even "say that Wisdom [Sophia] herself was made a serpent; and was therefore contrary to the maker of Adam, and introduced knowledge among men; and that therefore the serpent is called wiser than all."[22] For present purposes we may accept Hans Jonas' summary of the significance of the Gnostic version of the Fall: "It is the first success of the transcendent principle against the principle of the world, which is vitally interested in preventing knowledge in man as the inner-worldly hostage of Light: the serpent's action marks the beginning of all *gnosis* on earth which thus by its very origin is stamped as opposed to the world and its God, and indeed as a form of rebellion."[23]

The Prometheus legend lends itself naturally to Gnostic interpretation, either favorably or unfavorably for the Titan as the mythographer concentrates upon his refusal to serve or his gift of fire. The Stoics considered this element, in Cicero's words, "the bearer of cosmic reason"; for the Valentinians it symbolized demiurgical or "ignorant" reason. Similarly the Heraclitean "everliving fire" became the Gnostic "death and corruption."[24] The alchemist Zosimos, on the other hand, made the sons of Iapetos prototypes of all "philosophers" (by which he meant "pneumatic" men) who are above heimarmene, or material fate:

> Hermes [Trismegistus] and Zoroaster have declared that the race of philosophers is superior to heimarmene, meaning that they take no delight in the "happiness" which comes from it. Ruling their pleasures, they are not then injured by the evils

The Ophite Demogorgon

caused by heimarmene. Living always in their inner conscience [i.e., by pneuma], they do not accept the pretty gifts which it offers, since they see in them an unlucky end. For this reason Hesiod (*Works and Days*, v. 86) shows us Prometheus advising Epimetheus: "What is the happiness which men judge greatest of all? A beautiful woman, some say, with lots of money." Prometheus declares that he himself takes no gifts from Olympian Zeus, but rejects them, thus teaching his brother that he ought to refuse, in the name of philosophy, the gifts of Zeus, that is to say, the gifts of heimarmene.[25]

Ialdabaoth-Jehovah is clearly equivalent to Shelley's Jupiter, against whom both his Prometheus and his Christ rebel. As Ialdabaoth is conditioned by the factious heimarmene of Archons through whom he expresses his unstable power, so Jupiter is the enthralled administrator of "Fate, Time, Occasion, Chance, and Change," the material Necessity of this world as it flows. Demogorgon tells Asia, "All spirits are enslaved which serve things evil:/ Thou knowest if Jupiter be such or no" (II, iv, 110–111).

All things are subject to heimarmene but eternal Love. Prometheus' forgiveness, which is a form of *willed* love, activates the pure human love in Asia, who by this means forces Demogorgon upwards from his throne. Love in its eternal aspect is the "Almighty" and "Merciful God," the First Man unknown to Jupiter, who "reigns" but for a time (II, iv, 11, 18, 28). Love and Light, syntactically linked many times throughout the play, are two distinct but hypostatically indivisible persons of the One. The connection implies that God must be known both emotionally and cognitively, by human love acting in concert with human wisdom. Neither way is sufficient in itself. Asia must marry Prometheus before total gnosis can be achieved.

Prometheus, "nailed to this wall of eagle-baffling mountain" (I, 20), is meant to resemble Christ, "a youth/ With patient looks nailed to a crucifix" (I, 584–585). The misrepresentation of Christ and the distortion of His doctrine by the established churches was one of Shelley's favorite themes, as it has been from the beginning and remains today for all militant heretics. Shelley's admiration of the character and moral teachings of the historical Jesus did not extend to the theological tradition that has grown up around him. The single element of Christian myth accepted by Shelley is the premise from which all Gnostics start. It colors the entire *Essay on Christianity* and is worth quoting again, for it is baffling in the larger Shelleyan context without some knowledge of the Gnostic influence upon him: "According to Jesus Christ, and according to the indisputable facts of the case, some evil Spirit has dominion in this imperfect world."

The temptation to equate Asia with Sophia Prunicos should be resisted. Wisdom the Whore enters modern literary tradition through a Tyrian prostitute with whom the "auspicious" (*faustus*) Simon Magus traveled about and whom he tried to pass off as the reincarnated Helen, the female "Thought of God" to his own "First Man." Although a liaison of wisdom of sorts with love, if bought, this will obviously not fit Prometheus and the demure, rather schoolgirlish Asia. Nor is the information that Sophia in her unfallen state—the Ophite Holy Spirit, the Barbeliote Ennoia—becomes the "moon-, mother-, and love-goddess of Near Eastern religion" particularly helpful.[26] These *Magnae Matres* are indistinguishable in effect from the Neoplatonic *Venus Coelestis*. Such an identification would also make Jupiter and the Christ-Prometheus the children of Asia's right and left hands respectively.

Sophia Prunicos takes her body from the Sea of Matter, and Asia is a "daughter of Ocean." So too Demogorgon assumes the aspect of a snake through his sea-nymph mother Thetis, reminding us of the birth of the Ophis from the lust of Ialdabaoth after "the dregs of matter lying beneath." But the detailed parallel with wave-born Aphrodite (II, v, 20–30) prevents the ascription of a specific source for Asia, and the sea in *Prometheus Unbound* is clearly a symbol of thought, not matter. "Heaven's ever-changing Shadow, spread below" (I, 28), its passions mirror tempest and calm in both macrocosmic and microcosmic intelligence. The evaporation and precipitation of freshened water follow the upward and downward movement of hope and fear, desire and despair. "Oracular vapour" signals the awakening of Demogorgon, as does the tidal ascendance of a "gusty sea of mist" (II, iii, 4, 43). Conversely, Jupiter's curses, "Like snow on herbless peaks, fall flake by flake" (III, i, 12); he does not see in this poised and trembling mass a portent of his own impending downfall. The movement of water in *Prometheus Unbound* figures by images of accumulation and dissolution the revolution predicted for the actual, political world by Shelley in his Preface: "The cloud of mind is discharging its collected lightning, and the equilibrium between institutions and opinions is now restoring, or is about to be restored."

Any attempt to cram the whole of *Prometheus Unbound* within the inelegant framework of Gnostic theology would vulgarize Shelley. The two myths are independent organisms; if in certain major aspects they look very much alike, many minor features cannot be reconciled. Shelley took from Ophitism what he could use and no more. The psychological antagonisms are roughly the same, and the conflict between the demiurgic Ialdabaoth and the First Man affords striking parallels to that of Jupiter with the One, Eternal Light and Love. I shall now try to show that Demogorgon is the Gnostic Ophis overlaid with the mythography of Plato.

The Demiurgic Imagination

... the Eternal, the Immortal,
  Must unloose through life's portal
The snake-like Doom coiled underneath his throne.

(II, iii, 95–97)

This is the first of two similes in *Prometheus Unbound* which associate Demogorgon with a snake. The other is of course Jupiter's metaphor of himself and his destroyer as a vulture and a serpent. The latter image assumes such importance elsewhere in Shelley's work that I have taken neither comparison to be gratuitous here and both to be susceptible of precise interpretation.

"The dreaded name of Demogorgon" probably entered modern literature by way of a scribal error for the *demiourgos agathos*, Plato's beneficent artificer of the cosmos upon an eternal pattern (*Timaeus*, 28-40). Preserved as such in the *Genealogia Deorum Gentilium* (which Shelley quite possibly knew),[27] the demiurge has degenerated linguistically and functionally into a primal force who dwells in a dark abyss and so terrifies mortals that his name cannot be uttered.[28] Peacock summarized Boccaccio's description of Demogorgon in a note to *Rhododaphne* (1818): "He was the Genius of the Earth, and the Sovereign Power of the Terrestrial Daemons. He dwelt originally with Eternity and Chaos, till, becoming weary of inaction, he organized the chaotic elements, and surrounded the earth with the heavens."[29] Boccaccio goes on to speak of the aged goddess Eternity. A *socia* of Demogorgon, she sits surrounded by the tail-chewing snake of the annual cycle; the snake is not, however, related in any way to Demogorgon. Nor does Plato mention a serpent in connection with his Craftsman. And the only character with a clearly demiurgic station in *Prometheus Unbound* is Jupiter, even though it is finally not he but "Merciful God" who "made the living world" (II, iv, 18, 9).

Reference to *Adversus Haereses* may unperplex us. The serpent of the Ophites is called Nun or "Mind." Saint Irenaeus' translator has Latinized the Greek *nous*, which normally stands for the higher cognitive faculty. Aristotle, for example, opposed *theoretikos nous* (the Platonic *noesis*) to *dianoia*, or "understanding" (*De Anima*, II, iii). The word was roughly translatable as "thought," "intellect," or "mind" in Attic philosophy until Anaxagoras made a revolutionary application of it to the principle ordering the elementary particles of the world. Plato then personified *nous* with this double meaning as his Demiourgos, the power who creates the cosmos upon higher models, which it perceives by rational intuition. These models are in eternity; the Demiourgos, like Shelley's Demogorgon, is responsible to no other realm of being. "Now if so be," Plato says, "that this Cosmos is beautiful and its Constructor good, it is plain that he fixed his gaze on the Eternal [*aidios*]; but if otherwise (which is an impious supposition), his gaze was on that which has come into existence. But it is clear to everyone that his gaze was on the Eternal."[30]

The demiurgic Nous of the *Timaeus* is a precise analogue to the Imagination of *A Defence of Poetry*. Combining Kantian *Vernunft* with the plastic or synthetic *to poiein*, Shelley's Imagination creates images upon eternal patterns as Artificers shape worlds.[31] The poet is literally a "maker," and his craft is defined as " 'the expression of the imagination.' "[32] Nous enters *Prometheus Unbound* disguised as the Ophite Nun, "Mind itself twisted into the form of a serpent." Shelley deliberately preserves the degraded name of its mythic personification, the name garbled anonymously, recorded as such by Boccaccio, Ariosto, Spenser, Marlowe and Milton, and handed down still further by Peacock. Shelley retains "Demogorgon" for the same reason that he follows the Renaissance iconographical error with regard to the vulture, the snake's dialectical antagonist. These degenerate emblems and the psychological qualities they represent must cancel each other out if the Garden is to revive.

Demogorgon is the Imagination, and his work is the poetry of Creation itself. When he is read as such back into the text of the play, the equation proves so natural that it becomes difficult to see how the currently accepted identification of him solely with Necessity ever gained ground.[33]

Demorgon is the only character capable of seeing the pattern of eternal Love above the material necessity expressed by and limiting Jupiter. The information that there is a superior, "Merciful God" comes from him. Asia is puzzled by his answers because she lacks his intuitive *nous*; Prometheus too thinks Jupiter omnipotent over all save his own titanic will. It is up to Demogorgon to strip the loathsome mask from the Olympian, who, obstructive but not creative, is not even a true demiurge. As temporal hatred's "thought-executing ministers" turn human reason against itself, so eternal Love works by means of its servant Imagination, which must first be awakened by human love.

Love and Imagination were for Shelley the Presence and the vehicle of a single mighty sacrament:

> The great *secret* of morals is love; or a going out of our own nature, and an identification of ourselves with the beautiful which exists in thought, action, or person, not our own. A man, to be greatly good, must imagine intensely and comprehensively; he must put himself in the place of another and of many others; the pains and pleasures of his species must become his own. The great *instrument* of moral good is the imagination; and poetry administers to the effect by acting upon the cause.[34]

Demogorgon is the instrument of the great secret which he has just now told Asia as he rises from Love's "awful throne of patient power" (IV, 557) to cleanse, free, and remake the world. When Jupiter asks who he is, he replies, "Eternity. Demand no direr name" (III, i, 52). The agent calls himself by one hypostasis of the Trinity he represents. This is irony, directed against Jupiter, but it has misled literal-minded readers. Himself "eternal" and "immortal," the imaginative Demogorgon is (in the words of the Preface to *The Cenci*) "*as* the immortal God," Eternity herself, and he has assumed the flesh of the snake for the redemption of mortal passion. He redeems the Spirit of the Hour, who now perceives intuitively the eternal Light beyond heimarmene's veil, which the Spirit himself has helped to tear: "My vision then grew clear, and I could see/ Into the mysteries of the universe" (III, iv, 104–105).

This work of dethronement and clarification done, the second or "poetic" aspect of demiurgic Nous begins to be revealed. The world breaks into flower and song, Prometheus is unbound, and man recovers the heritage of which Jupiter-Jehovah-Ialdabaoth cheated him at the Fall. The Garden is *re-created* through the agency of the beneficent Artificer. Perpetual spring returns as the "King of Hours," "the Father of many a cancelled year," is locked in the depths of the sea (IV, 20, 14). Mortality is humanized, and the mind of man, no longer storm-vexed, seems "an

The Ophite Demogorgon

ocean/ Of clear emotion" (IV, 96–97). Man, once "a many-sided mirror" distorting the shapes of things as they are, has been harmonized and smoothed to "a sea reflecting love" (IV, 382, 384).

Both functions of imaginative *nous* are simultaneously awakened in Prometheus and Asia; they behold *and* they synthesize the "gathered rays which are reality," hitherto fragmented by the prism of Fate, Chance, Change and Occasion, which has now itself been shattered (III, iii, 53). The veil falsely called life had appeared "painted" (III, iv, 190) because the Light was refracted in its passage through matter, through the body's eyes and those ills of the flesh which superstition arose to justify and in some small measure to palliate. Truth's scattered beams are reconstituted into the primal blankness only when the Imagination has been liberated by love from the tyranny of clay. So too "the rays" of Panthea's "thought" had been "slowly gathered" earlier in the drama as she felt in dream the Titan's affectionate presence upon her (II, i, 86–87). In Demogorgon's "void abysm" alone "the air" had been "no prism" at that time (II, iii, 72, 74).

The redemption of earth first becomes evident in the second scene of Act III, as Apollo describes to Ocean the fall of Jupiter. The setting for this brief dialogue is an example of Shelleyan irony at its most pedantic. "Ocean is discovered reclining near the Shore" of the most fortunate of islands sacred to him. This is Atlantis, which the reader is meant to recall from the *Timaeus* (24e ff.) and its companion *Critias* as among the first and fairest artifacts of the Demiourgos; it is Plato's urban Eden. This "work" and all that follow are "called the Promethean" (IV, 158) rather than the demiurgic or "Demogorgonic" because the agonized pity of the Titan is ultimately responsible for the release of the forces of re-creation.

The problem with which this discussion began can now be solved. Why should Shelley wish to dress Demogorgon in a costume of Gnostic "snake-like Doom," extracted from what is presumably a literary make-up kit stored "underneath his throne"? The parallel to the Genesis story is important, but neither this nor the various Aeschylean reminiscences—Clytemnestra's dream, for example—is in itself a sufficient explanation. Demogorgon lives in the depths of the earth, and chthonic deities are conventionally serpentine in classical myth. Why, then, are Shelley's Furies, the underground powers *par excellence,* but once described and briefly at that as having the traditional "hydra tresses" (I, 326)? A Freudian critic might argue that phallic Demogorgon is the id to Jupiter's superego and that their mutual cancellation and fall into the Sea of Mind represents the reintegration of Promethean personality, the restoring harmony of titanic ego. The analogy though vulgar is quite plausible, for the Imagination—divine or human, cosmogonical or mythopoetic—is not unnaturally rendered by sexual figures. Shelley's symbolic snake contains many such meanings, but our final reading must be from the text of the poem itself.

In the fourth scene of Act II Demogorgon replies that "God: Almighty God" made "thought, passion, reason, will,/ Imagination" (10–11). A few lines later Asia asks "who made terror, madness, crime, remorse," to which Demogorgon will only answer "He reigns" (19, 28). Reference to the larger Shelleyan context will show that the poet used chiasmus here, reversing the order of catalogued opposites to avoid a too mechanical parallelism. If the first set of terms is read backwards against the second, "imagination" appears as the divine antithesis of Olympian "terror," and "madness" consists of the paralysis or distraction of "will" and the subversion of "reason." "Crime" was for Shelley the abuse of "passion"; in his essay, *On the Punishment of Death,* the criminal is described as a person "of energetic character" whose basic "coarseness of organisation" allows him to pervert that energy to selfish or at least antisocial ends.[35] Finally, "remorse" is always furious "thought," here Jove's thought-executing hounds who feed upon the devastated heart that engendered them. So Actaeon's hunting-pack, in Shelley's most obsessive autobiographical image, tore their metamorphosed master to shreds.[36]

Imagination assumes the flesh of terror for the moment only.

The Ophite Demogorgon

Like the "creative faculty" which, according to the *Defence*, manufactures images, but is itself imageless, Demogorgon normally is "shapeless; neither limb,/ Nor form, nor outline" (II, iv, 5–6). Nous is the shapeless Shaper as the eternal Love it serves is the unmoved Mover. Imagination becomes a Doom for one revolutionary Hour by taking the twisted body of the Ophite Nun. It is a love in desolation masked and will continue to trick the eye so long as it is beheld in the refracting and inverting glass of matter and is measured by what Blake called a "ratio" of the five senses. Imagination cannot appear *in propria persona* until it has finished its work of liberation. Panthea therefore watches the embodied Demogorgon float upwards as "That *terrible* shadow"; the coursers of the Spirit of the Hour likewise "fly/ *Terrified*" (II, iv, 150, 153–154). Panthea has not yet been baptized with her sister Asia by that love, "common as light," which literally "makes the reptile equal to the God" (II, v, 40, 43).

Jupiter has "begotten a strange wonder" upon Thetis. He expects this "fatal child" to be "that awful spirit unbeheld," Demogorgon himself, rising now from his "vacant throne" and "clothed" for the occasion in "the dreadful might of ever-living limbs," in order that he may "redescend, and trample out the spark" of human resistance and aspiration (III, i, 18–24). Yet Jupiter fails to recognize the incarnated Demogorgon when he arrives: "Awful shape, what art thou?" (51). The entire speech opening this scene is another fine example of Shelley's dramatic irony. Jupiter speaks of his child as "the *terror* of the earth" (19), not knowing Prometheus' secret that this "prodigy" will be the "detested" and terrible instrument of his own downfall. He cannot know this, because he cannot comprehend the One of which Imagination is the agent. He is like Ialdabaoth ignorant of the Pleroma above him.

Jupiter is the anthropomorphic projection of the blind hatreds and materialistic lusts for whose justification men have crucified themselves. When someone like Jupiter calls Imagination to his aid (here by the sexual act), he will clothe it in the flesh of its inverse manifestation, terror, and the terror will destroy him.

This much of *Prometheus Unbound* mythologizes the moral lesson of *Caleb Williams*. The Platonic Demiourgos liquidates the false Gnostic demiurge. These two degenerate emblems—the vulture of thought turned against itself and the imaginative Nous twisted into the serpentine Nun of deicidal terror—plunge knotted together into the Sea of Mind, as had Laon and Cythna's Ormuzd and Ahriman before them. The murderous dialectic has been necessary for revival. For now that Time, Jove's sibling, has sunk annihilated by an emanation of eternal Love, the human love of the sea-born Asia rises to cancel *spatial* atomism and dissociation. Asia's marriage to Promethean wisdom restores to human intellect its exiled sensibility. In his own proper figure as the highest cognitive and only re-creative power—the Imagination *agathos*, the mind as Artificer—Demogorgon of course survives his involved fall. He has shed the skin of the snake and will cap the triumph that ends the play by uttering a final oracle to the newly constituted "great Republic" of being.

Nous and Logos

Language becomes in the new Eden

> a perpetual Orphic song,
> Which rules with Daedal harmony a throng
> Of thoughts and forms, which else senseless and shapeless were.
> (IV, 415–417)

This harmony is poetry, and it memorializes in the name of its plastic strength that of yet another mythical artificer, who wrought, among other things, a dancing ground, the golden comb of Aphrodite, and the wings of human aspiration towards the Light. The drama's central analogy from the Imagination to the Power that made the spheres is not frivolous—or if it is, then so is the opening paragraph of the Gospel according to Saint John. The poet's words marry the Word in the Logos. The "Ophite Demogorgon" is not finally heretical. Shelley's dark conceit masks the most catholic symbol ever known.

The Logos of "Mont Blanc" was not so complex. Shelley in

1816 had not yet passed through the syncretism of Philo Judaeus, nor had he needed to. Philo, whose life overlaps that of Christ, fused the Stoic *logoi* with the Platonic Forms (*ideai*) and employed either term interchangeably with the Pythagorean Numbers or Limits, the Scriptural Angels, and the Daemons of vulgar mythology.[37] Like that of the Stoics, his Logos represents God's creative energy, but it also signifies the archetypal model which that energy copied when it built the mundane replica in which we live. The Reason, Will, and Word of God, Philo's Demiurgic Logos contains the Paradigm it projects and unites in a single Godhead ultimate Mind and its agent. The Apologetic notion of the hypostatically Triune stems from this reconciliation of the *Timaeus* with the corporate theism of the Stoics and the monotheism of the Old Testament.

Thanks to Philo, who took Plato to mean that there is at most one God, the Nous of the Academy reappeared in time as the Evangelist's Logos and still later as the first Christian dogma, that of the manifested Son of God. By the opening decades of the fifth century, the orthodox position on the three-personed Deity was that of Saint Augustine, who authorizes us to express the Creative relationship of Father to Son to Holy Ghost as a broken but continuous sentence: God made the world/ by means of the Word/ because it was good. The divine Persons also correspond to the division of philosophy into physics, logic, and ethics. These sciences in turn elaborate the primal verbs by which man declares himself to be the image of the Trinity: *sum; cogito; amo*. I exist; I know I exist; I love my existence.[38]

Just as Prometheus "purifies" Satan, Demogorgon competes with the Logos whom Milton, like Shelley, stationed at the numinous center of his greatest poem. "And thou," says God the Father,

> my Word, begotten Son, by thee
> This I perform, speak thou, and be it done:
> . . . ride forth, and bid the Deep
> Within appointed bounds be Heav'n and Earth.
> (*P.L.*, VII, 163–164, 166–167)

Although Tasso's possibly apocryphal statement that God and the poet equally deserve the title of Creator would have enraged Milton, his epic equation of the Old Testament Logos—"Let there be light"—not only with the newly-revealed Christ, but also with the imaginative illumination of the otherwise darkling wordmonger could not have escaped so careful a reader as Shelley.

Pope's elevation of literary vulgarity to the rank of sacrilege also anticipates Shelley's equation of the Imagination with the Logos. Dulness, the Mighty Mother of *The Dunciad*, treads out the "*human* spark" and "Glimpse *divine*" invoked by Milton. The language profaned by Grub Street expands to the undoing and undone Word in the apocalypse that ends the poem. The illiterate Goddess, compared at first to Sin sprung from the brow of Satan and even more bitterly to the Paraclete who impregnated Milton's vast abyss, returns as Antichrist. The demiurgic daughter of the "great Anarch" heaps mountains of casuistry upon the head of skulking Truth, deprives philosophy of its telic cause, and reduces Mystery to mathematics. She personifies the "uncreating Word" she utters and the Chaos she restores. "*Art* after *Art* goes out" like a candle as universal Light expires before her triumph. The mock chiliasm of Pope's and Shelley's last major poems debases a common symbol: Christ the illuminator or, if we will, the firebringer. The goddess Life stands in the same perverted relationship to Demogorgon that Pope's Logos bears to Milton's. Dulness' sable throne reappears in 1822 as a blindingly bright chariot driven by a monster with eight dead eyes.

The cosmos of Shelley's drama seems to have room for two Christs: the crucified Prometheus and Demogorgon the Artificer. The apparent duplication is in fact a delayed identity. As we saw in Chapter Three, Shelley's doubleganger-symbolism everywhere aids dramatic economy. Few playwrights have compressed the so-called unities more tightly: the "action" of *Prometheus Unbound* elaborates aspects of a single act of forgiveness, performed just before the rise of the curtain; the simultaneous "time" of the first three acts shifts to eternity in the last; "place" extends throughout the mental landscape of Prometheus, who is strictly speaking the only character. His is the "human mind" from whose "operations" and "external actions" the other *dramatis personae* and the imagery are drawn. The Olympian sky-god and the wraith who repeats the curse are both phantasms of Prometheus' miscreative brain; Demogorgon personifies the faculty that presides over its re-creation. Both Jupiter and the Logos lurk in the underworld of the Titan's consciousness until, flushed into the sunlight by love, they battle to a therapeutic death. Jupiter, Prometheus' dead self, rises from "underneath the grave" at the same moment of recantation in which the "fatal child" of a new hour flies upwards from his "gray void abysm" to liquidate the enthroned specter or—if one may say so—the sublimation of the buried demon who had been custodian of the curse. The Father of Jealousy melts before the suddenly incarnate power—"terrible" only to the terrorist—of a new dispensation of spirit. The First Person makes way for the Second, grace supplants the Law, and the living Word shouts down the killing letter of the covenant of wrath.

Neither Demogorgon nor Prometheus "is" Christ in the mechanical sense of simple allegory. Shelley abominated the doctrine of the atonement, but the Titan at first thrives on it; in his vanity he regards himself as a type of Jesus, the scapegoat of the code of Moses. He cannot redeem nature and society until he has been cleansed of this flattering error. He must be regenerated by the destructive agency of that chthonic emanation who is the Generator of all things, the Logos, the philosophers' Christ, upon whom the churches hold no monopoly.

If Jupiter and Demogorgon are the Paternal and Filial identities of Prometheus, who is the Paraclete? The Shelleyan intellectual's discovery that his "passion for reforming the world" fails to include forgiveness for his enemies soon learns the dreadful corollary that he does not cherish his friends. He lacks sympathy with the men he seeks to benefit because he cannot imagine that which he knows. The horror of this revelation chains his will to the rock of its own obduracy, and that paralysis turns his medicine to poison:

> The wise want love; and those who love want wisdom;
> And all best things are thus confused to ill.
>
> (I, 627–628)

This breach cannot be healed until Prometheus' third hypostasis awakes to disinfect the world. Asia is to the Titanic whole what the Holy Spirit was to Saint Augustine's Trinity: the principle who saw and loved the goodness of the projected Creation and thereby unleashed the potency of the Logos. Painters traditionally surround Aphrodite with doves as she steps out of the ocean; Asia replaces the Dove who presided at Jordan over the baptism of the chosen Son.[39]

One last analogue needs to be pointed out. Los, the fourth Zoa who dwells in the depths of every man, stands for Imagination in Blake's facultative pantheon. He is the eternal Poet who hammered out the material cosmos on his blacksmith's forge and refined it in seven furnaces. "But thou, My Son," Tharmas commands him, "Glorious in brightness, comforter of Tharmas,/ Go forth, Rebuild this universe beneath my indignant power."[40] These instructions clearly echo those delivered to Milton's Christ. And Albion tells Jesus, "I see thee in the likeness & similitude of Los my Friend."[41] It is usually said that Los takes his name from an anagram of "sol," the sun he re-creates each morning. I would suggest instead that he is the Logos, contracted.

Ophis and Uroboros

> And if, with infirm hand, Eternity,
> Mother of many acts and hours, should free
>   The serpent that would clasp her with his length;
> These are the spells by which to reassume
> An empire o'er the disentangled doom.
>
> (IV, 565–569)

This passage has always caused two-fold difficulty. What is the serpent and what is the sex of the speaker? Demogorgon is first called "the Eternal, the Immortal" who sits upon "*his* throne."

The Ophite Demogorgon

Then he names himself "Eternity" at Jupiter's insistence. He speaks of Eternity finally as a "Mother." In all save the first instance, the other characters indicate Demogorgon by the neuter personal pronoun, and the Greek neuter nominative singular inflection survives, however fortuitously, in his name. All this has inevitably led to critical talk of a hermaphroditic Demogorgon.[42]

The Spirits whose song ends the third scene of Act II know that Demogorgon is male. Panthea refers to him as "it" because she is incapable of seeing more than a shapeless, "mighty darkness" (II, iv, 2) or a "terrible shadow." Demogorgon is called eternal and immortal, but never Eternity, except by himself with ambassadorial irony and in preference to a "direr name." Demogorgon's concluding statement that the triune God, Eternity-Light-Love, is in fact our Mother will scrape upon orthodox sensibilities, but we should remember that the "idol of my thought"—Intellectual Beauty, the Morning and Evening Star, Urania, the Mighty Mother—was always female for Shelley. It is absurd to suppose that Demogorgon here refers to himself ("herself") in the third person and ends this scene of triumph with a confession of his own infirmity.

The extricable doom mentioned by Demogorgon is more problematical. Saint Irenaeus' Ophis turned enemy to man after being cast down to the nether world as punishment for his aid to Adam, but the resemblance is specious. Demogorgon could hardly be warning the listening earth that he will wreck it if his Mother gives him half a chance. The beneficent nemesis coiled beneath the throne of immortal Imagination cannot be equated with that which surrounds and strives to strangle unlocalized Eternity except by violence to the decorum of character and to the letter of Shelley's images. The distinction between the two snakes can be illuminated by one final reference to Ophite doctrine.

Origen details in his *Contra Celsum* an Ophite diagram consisting of either seven or ten detached circles "*held together by a single circle, which was said to be the soul of the Universe and was called Leviathan.*"[43] The Hebrew *leviathan*, Origen explains, translates the Greek *ophis*, but his own word for "soul of the universe" is *psyche*. This "psychic" dragon must be distinguished from Saint Irenaeus' "pneumatic" Nun; the human body and psyche were, we remember, under the control of Ialdabaoth and heimarmene. Leviathan is the world-surrounding chaos itself, and he seeks to sabotage the whole Creation. The *Pistis Sophia*, which was unknown in Shelley's time, contains this analogue: "The outer darkness is a great dragon with his tail in his mouth, being outside the whole world and going round all the world."[44] Hans Jonas has found further Gnostic parallels in the apocryphal Syriac *Acts of the Apostle Thomas*, the Jewish *Acts of Kyriakos and Julitta*, and in the Mandaean system, where "this Leviathan is called Ur and is the father of the Seven [Archons]. The mythological archetype of this figure is the Babylonian Ti'amat, the chaos-monster slain by Marduk in the history of creation."[45]

This symbol, the *drachon ouroboros*, is by no means exclusively Gnostic. Analogues exist in Mithraism, Egyptian magic, and Hermetic alchemy.[46] It reached Shelley partially through the writings of Count Volney, Lord Monboddo, Spenser, and of course Boccaccio. The tomb of Clarissa Harlowe is a fifth possible source, hitherto unnoticed. Belford writes to Lovelace, "The principal device, neatly etched on a plate of white metal, is a crowned Serpent, with its tail in its mouth, forming a ring, the emblem of Eternity." Mary Shelley read Richardson's novel in 1815 and 1816 and attempted it again in Italian translation in 1818.

Shelley mentions "the vast snake Eternity" (non-surrounding) in *The Daemon of the World* (I, 100) and "the snake/That girds eternity" in *The Revolt of Islam* (IV, iv). The essay, *On the Devil, and Devils*, contains the information that, "In Egypt the Serpent was an hieroglyphic of eternity."[47] A canceled fragment of *A Defence of Poetry* equates poetry itself with "the Serpent which clasps eternity."[48]

Contra Celsum was written around A.D. 247. It predates Professor Notopoulos' *locus classicus* for the Uroboros, the *Hieroglyphica* of Horapollo, by anywhere from fifty to one hundred and fifty years. The symbol is morally neutral in Boccaccio,

The Ophite Demogorgon

Volney, Monboddo, and Richardson, as it is everywhere in Shelley except in *Prometheus Unbound* and in the Bodleian prose fragment, where it is auspicious. Horapollo, moreover, interprets it later in his first book as a pneumatic rather than a psychic principle (*Hierogl.*, I, 64). Only the Gnostics, so far as I have been able to determine, oppose the maleficent, chaotic, psychic Uroboros to the beneficent Nun who liberates the correspondent pneuma within men. Shelley's imaginative, demiurgic Nous, the snake who has shed his skin, is clearly warning the world in his final speech of that other serpent, anti-creation personified, who is in fact the fallen, psychic Jupiter compared earlier by Thetis to the poisonous "Numidian seps" (III, i, 40). The Uroboros seeks to undo the work which has just been brought to pass and to murder the true God as Demogorgon has canceled the false.

Shelley's first mention of the Uroboros in *The Daemon of the World* establishes definite dates for his hearing or reading of the antithetical Ophite serpents. Shelley published the original version of *Queen Mab* in the summer of 1813, almost exactly one year before his elopement with Mary, when the *Journal* reading list was started and "The Assassins" was composed.

It is most unlikely that Shelley ever met William Blake or read his work, though most survivors of the radical salon that had forgathered in Joseph Johnson's bookshop a quarter of a century earlier would have heard of Godwin's astonishing son-in-law. If Shelley's letters to Blake turned up tomorrow in the ruins of 17 South Molton Street, the critic would have to redouble his guard against facile analogies. The two symbologies look so much alike that one is all too likely to manufacture false parallels. With this caveat in mind, let us glance at the Ophis-Uroboros dialectic of *The Four Zoas*.

Orc, the "generate" body of the thorn-crowned and crucified Luvah, stands for the external reform of social evil as his father Los represents spiritual revolution. Los and Orc are to each other as the converted to the unreconstructed Prometheus. "I well remember," Orc brags to Urizen, "how I stole thy light & it became fire/ Consuming."⁴⁹ It is not Urizen, significantly, but Los whose jealousy chains Orc to a rocky mountaintop: as in Shelley's drama, rebels are bound by their corrupt Imagination, not by the Reason they have pilfered. The "Cold hypocrisy" of Urizen's Malthusian economics shatters Orc's fetters, and he sinks at once, like Beatrice Cenci and the obdurate Titan, to the state of error called Satan. Imagination has so thoroughly degenerated into rage that Orc cannot use Urizen's light properly. Reason becomes the dark flame that devours him, "turning affection into fury, & thought into abstraction."⁵⁰ He metamorphoses into the Serpent of the Garden and climbs the Tree of Mystery, to which Christ will soon be nailed.

Blake consistently associates the terrible and terrified Urizen, as Shelley did Jupiter, with whiteness and with frozen water: hail, icicles, wastes of snow. Zeus and Jehovah at once, the "King of Light" recapitulates his antagonist's fall into Satan the very next night. But whereas Orc becomes the Tempter of Genesis, Urizen turns into the chaotic *drachon ouroboros*, the Covering Cherub, the Leviathan of Revelations. The serpentine alpha and omega touch at last, and when the cycle ends, Orc has changed to Urizen. Thus Blake affirms the hypostatic identity of a demon-Jesus and a demon-Father.

Is it possible that religion's most potent symbols spontaneously and continuously renew themselves? The scholar can deal with Blake's snake-imagery in many ways. But if, having abandoned his search through Blake's library for the "sources" Shelley used (the Ophis-Uroboros enmity is *not* in the Bible), he chooses to believe where he cannot prove, he may be tempted to assume that the germ of the double metaphor floats in the seminary of every man's preconscious mind. And even if his search has been successful—even if the hypothetical excavator of South Molton Street has dug up Origen—he will still need to grant the latter alternative in Shelley's sense that the poet and the prophet must imagine that which they know. If psychologists cannot settle the question of archetypes, the literary critic had better shy away from it. But since it has been mentioned, one may as well end this section by offering as food or as poison for thought an excerpt from Jung's reflections on the Son of God:

> The agent [of the Logos] is an animate, autonomous being, the *serpent*. It appears spontaneously or comes as a surprise; it fascinates; its glance is staring, fixed, unrelated; its blood cold, and it is a stranger to man: it crawls over the sleeper, he finds it in a shoe or in his pocket. It expresses his fear of everything inhuman and his awe of the sublime, of what is beyond human ken. It is the lowest (devil) and the highest (son of God, Logos, Nous Agathodaimon). . . . Like the fish, it represents and personifies the dark and unfathomable, the watery deep, the forest, the night, the cave. . . . The snake is not an allegory or metaphor, for its own peculiar form is symbolic in itself.[51]

Natural Gnosticism: Godwin and the Shelleys Once More

For Marsilio Ficino, the discursive *ratio* that distinguishes mankind from the beasts was a faculty lower than *mens* or "mind" itself, the *intellectus humanus sive angelicus* which we share with God. *Ratio* is not strictly a compound of intuition and the senses, but it is torn by conflicting desires towards the material and the formal worlds. Although it can be defeated and enslaved by sensation, the converse is impossible; "reason" will never triumph in a vision of the Godhead towards whom it yearns. Ficino's Prometheus is the emblem of this faculty. His curiosity, like that of Caleb Williams, is the active function of the understanding that defines him; it is his torture too. Only the intuitive *mens*—Shelley's imaginative *nous*—beholds beatitude. Shelley did not read *Quaestiones quinque de mente*, but his interpretation of the unconverted Titan closely resembles that offered by Ficino:

> Nothing indeed can be imagined more unreasonable than that man, who through reason is the most perfect of animals, nay, of all things under heaven . . . should be the least perfect of all with regard to that final perfection for the sake of which

the first perfection is given. This seems to be that most unfortunate Prometheus. Instructed by the divine wisdom of Pallas, he gained possession of the heavenly fire, that is, reason [*ratio*]. Because of this very possession, on the highest peak of the mountain, that is, at the very height of contemplation, he is rightly judged the most miserable of all, for he is made wretched by the continual gnawing of the most ravenous of vultures, that is, by the torment of inquiry. This will be the case, until the time comes when he is carried back to that same place from which he received the fire, so that, just as he is now urged on to seek the whole by that one beam of celestial light, he will then be entirely filled with the whole light.[52]

Much has been written of the indirect and "natural" Neoplatonism of Shelley;[53] this like all labels, including Gnosticism, prejudices the eye of the reader as often as it clarifies the text. The approximate emblematic identity of the Ficinian with the Shelleyan Prometheus illustrates this point. A Neoplatonist and a quasi-Gnostic Platonist have made independent glosses on the same myth, and the results are hard to distinguish. When the legendary matter is as much Scriptural as classical—the undying worm *et in Arcadia*—discrimination becomes virtually impossible. Shelley never read Plotinus or Ficino, and we cannot be even remotely certain that he knew more of Gnostic myth than the Ophis and the Uroboros. How much of *Prometheus Unbound* is Judaized Platonism and how much is Neoplatonized Christianity? How much, for that matter, is German? Shelley knew a little Fichte and had read Drummond's *Academical Questions*. He absorbed Schelling's absolute idealism indirectly from a reading of *Biographia Literaria* in 1817. Can we begin to disentangle all these strands of "influence"? Beyond a certain point it is pedantry even to try. Shelley's characteristic and obsessive imagery is no more peculiar to him than it was to the antimaterialist poets and cosmographers of Germany, an earlier England, Alexandria, Asia Minor, and Athens, and presumably to the first illiterate shaman who ever suspected that the sky was but a larger cave and wondered what happened to it all when he blinked his eyes.

Maria Gisborne noted in her journal for 22 August 1820 that Godwin "has not seen the Prometheus, and does not think he shall read it through, for he hates to read books that are full of obscurities and puzzles."[54] Godwin had enjoyed *The Cenci*, but he knew perfectly well what to expect from his son-in-law in a more exalted mood. Omnivorous to the last, however, he attempted the first act of Shelley's lyrical drama on 19 September, rapidly became bored, thrust it aside forever, and went back to revising his answer to Malthus.[55] For all their mutual misunderstanding, Godwin, his daughter, and her husband are in their metaphysics the closest of families. And for all their deviation from the main course of Christian and post-Christian imaginative writing, they belong to a literary tradition at least as ancient and deep as that associated with our inherited nominalism and with the established churches.

The heretical bent of the Godwin-Shelley family is that of "a celebrated North Country apostle" and of Saint Irenaeus' unnamed and probably unknown adversary. The heresy is antinomian; it rejects the moral law insofar as that law's exactions pretend to constitute, if paid in full, a kind of afterlife-insurance. Gnosticism also disregards grace *ex machina* and insists that every believer bears the responsibility for his own salvation, which can only be achieved intellectually. The Ormuzd or Christ of its dualist forms possesses only slightly greater power than the dark Ahriman or Satan over whom the Light will someday triumph. The purer Gnosticisms suppose a sadistic demiurge to whom the First Man has virtually abandoned us. Either form has the apparent logical advantage over orthodoxy of attributing the origin and persistence of evil to the limitation or the comparative indifference of God. The Gnostic was not forced with Tertullian to embrace absurdity as transcendence or to celebrate the moral oxymoron of *felix culpa*. His theodicy comforted the sick and hungry serf who argued the insanity of Creation from its design as plausibly as the opposite reading was later derived from his own ambiance by many a leisured Deist essayist—by Timothy Shelley's "Palley," for instance.

The heresy has occasionally appealed to refined sensibilities as well. The troubadours were Cathars, and their phantoms still sang clearly enough in the winds above Avignon for Petrarch to hear them and to launch a lyrical genre often called Platonist, though the man who idealized Laura never read Plato. The Gnostic heresies were fully as catholic as the faith of the European theocracy into whose heart they had struck when all the fires of Innocent the Third failed to consume them quite. It remains a rationalization of pain, a paranoid cosmic view, a superstitious predisposition as natural and ubiquitous as human misery itself. It will spontaneously regenerate itself if it has to, for it has survived the burning of most of its books, evangelists, and theurgic grandmothers.

The seeming logical advantage of traditional or natural gnosticism is also the secret of its limitation. The unspectacular triumph of orthodoxy throughout Europe was no more an historical accident than was the blaze that consumed Montsegur. There are no historical accidents. In the absence of ritual, prescribed moral obligation, and prayer except as supererogation, the burden of responsibility placed upon each man for his own salvation is nothing short of terrifying. Gnosticism, like the Categorical Imperative, exacts formidable courage, however quixotic, and this the Albigensians had. But it also requires supreme arrogance, for the Gnostic or gnostic believes that his intellect will save him, that he has outwitted the surly mechanic who jerry-built the spheres. Most first-class minds go beyond the gnostic as Godwin, for all his notorious vanity, went beyond Samuel Newton.

The great developmental paradox of Godwin's philosophy is that the Sandemanianism he rejected was, despite superficial correspondencies, less Gnostic than the position towards which he moved. Newton believed that "God works to save or damn a man but according to the right or wrong judgment of his understanding." This is the discursive understanding, dependent upon the senses; it can learn only what the Lord of the material creation wants it to know. The quasi-Calvinist Jehovah to whom the Sandemanian presents this service is not surprisingly represented by Godwin as one who will have his little joke. He is like Ialdabaoth a divine buffoon, and the service, if acceptable, is presumably offered with a smirk. When terror vanquishes the understanding of Caleb Williams, Imagination does not take over. But he has learned to wonder, to respect the heart's affections and to despise the body's pride. Caleb is pre-gnostic and stands on the threshold of mystery, not yet ready with Shelley to forgive the flesh its infirmities and personified Matter its obstructionism.

The egotism of Frankenstein should be taken as a corollary to Caleb's. If vanity in mechanical invention is combined with trust in the sensory lower reason, the result is a materialistic, psychic, Archontic mockery of Shelley's pneumatic Imagination, which, as we have seen, performs the double cognitive and creative function of Platonic *nous*. Caleb and the artificer Frankenstein together make up Shelley's emblematic Prometheus before his Gnostic conversion, which further improves upon the tradition of this heresy by adding humility.

The Gnostic Marcion referred to the total material cosmos—world and flesh—as *haec cellula creatoris*, that is, as Ialdabaoth's dungeon.[56] The numberless analogues to this metaphor include, pre-eminently, the "prison bars" of the body in Plato's *Phaedo*, the "prison house" of Wordsworth's *Ode*, and Ficino's complaints "of the terrestrial world as a 'prison' where the pure forms or ideas are 'drowned,' 'submerged,' 'perturbed,' and 'disfigured beyond recognition.' "[57] The opening of Marvell's "Dialogue" details the comparison:

> O who shall, from this Dungeon, raise
> A Soul inslav'd so many wayes?
> With bolts of Bones, that fetter'd stands
> In Feet; and manacled in Hands.

Mary Shelley knew that the monstrous body could hide the innocent soul and in time chafe its inmate to the ragged and inhumane texture of the walls themselves. Frankenstein's creature is her extroversion of the satanic convention of hell carried about everywhere—"nor am I out of it," explains Faustus' tempter. So too Caleb Williams can break jail but not the body it symbolizes. Godwin near the end of his life restored to the metaphor its traditional theological significance:

> The human mind is a creature of celestial origin, shut up and confined in a wall of flesh. We feel a kind of proud impatience of the degradation to which we are condemned. We beat ourselves to pieces against the wires of our cage, and long to escape, to shoot through the elements, and be as free to change at any instant the place where we dwell, as to change the subject to which our thoughts are applied. . . . This is the original sin upon which St. Augustin [sic] and Calvin descanted.[58]

Jehovah is born when we regard fleshly decay as the emblem of our depravity; if we try through the will alone to discount the near-omnipotence of pain, we will end in that "dark idolatry of self" against which Shelley warned, the "rebellious self-idolatry" which Coleridge called "Satanic pride."[59] Prometheus is chained by bodily reasoning and the eyeless hatred inseparable from it. When he pities Jupiter, the outward and visible sign of his slavery, he forgives his own body. This relaxation of the spirit enables the play to end with a marriage, cancels the "beneficial" shame of the Gnostic Eden, and prevents the phallic Demogorgon, his work of liberation done, from becoming our archenemy as the snake had in the original Ophite myth. Shelley's Imagination is released by the human type of the eternal Love it serves. There was Light in the Gnostic Pleroma, but not Love; the Power of the Deep was quite unconcerned with us. In coming to gentle terms with the soul's treacherous envelope under the shadow of the spread wings that heal the world, Shelley approaches the more nearly orthodox solution of Milton. In surpassing the arrogance of the loveless Ophites and of both Beatrices, he raises his pagan and heretical syncretism to catholic stature.

VI

Orpheus and the West Wind

" 'This is a fine, clever fellow!' " Hogg said to himself after his first conversation with Shelley, " 'but I can never bear his society; I shall never be able to endure his voice; it would kill me. What a pity it is'! I am very sensible of imperfections, and especially of painful sounds,—and the voice of the stranger was excruciating: it was intolerably shrill, harsh, and discordant; of the most cruel intension,—it was perpetual, and without any remission,—it excoriated the ears."[1]

When modern readers complain of Shelleyan "shrillness," they do not mean that they have heard cacophonies in the verse itself. They refer to "tone," which may be defined as the emotional quality of a speaker's relationship to his primary auditor. This listener is almost never the reader. To borrow Mill's aphorism, the reader, by "overhearing" the auditor, catches ironies that qualify or even subvert the tone. Only lyric and dramatic utterances properly have tone, and lyrics have it only insofar as they *become* dramatic by including two persons: "I" and the object addressed, Peele Castle, Euphrosyne, Stella, a cuckoo, or God. No reader confuses himself with these objects, but unless he is careful, he will on the other hand mistake the poet's persona for the poet himself. The writer may encourage the neglect of this distinction by painting the mask to resemble his own face, but always, as Rimbaud remarked, *je est un autre*. Childe Harold is no more Lord Byron than Porphyria's strangler is Robert Browning. Thus we hardly need to be told that the young man who sings,

> Oh lift me from the grass!
> I die! I faint! I fail!

is a Champak-drunk East Indian; he could not in any case be P. B. Shelley.

To take a less obvious example, the moth who recites quatrains to the star is not Shelley writing mash-notes to a woman of flesh and blood. One might, he said, as well look for a leg of mutton in a gin-shop as come to him for "human or earthly" articles.[2] The inferior, passive, and weakly yearner who speaks most of these lyrics is Eros himself, the homeless and ugly offspring of Poverty and Plenty, who desires what he does not have, the Beautiful. Heavenly Love and Beauty reside in the third Neoplatonic Heaven, the sphere of Hesperus or the Venus Coelestis. Whoever condemns this metaphor as sentimental should know that he rejects Plotinus and Ficino with it, and through them, at either end, Sidney's Astrophel and the *Symposium*.

A poem's existence, then, depends upon four persons: the author, the speaker, the object addressed, and the reader. The posture called "tone" is a form of narrative irony. If, reading Shelley, we forget these axioms, the Amelia Curran portrait and Arnold's even more disastrous caricature will flash before our sight, and we shall find little in the tone of these lyrics but shrillness. By this we shall mean effeminacy, self-pity, and Ozymandiac arrogance. Interpreting the mask according to our notion of the man, we shall lose Shelley's voice in a whine of our own fancying.

The theological dimensions of Shelley's doctrine that Love is to the Imagination as the "great secret" is to the "instrument" of moral good were explored in the last chapter. This formula also contains a pragmatic truth of literary criticism: if we dislike a poem, we shall probably misread it. Dr. Leavis' failure to make out the grammatical sense of "Lines: 'When the lamp is shattered'" exactly illustrates this fruitless clash of sensibilities.[3] Suppose further that a reader sophisticated enough to register disgust at André Maurois' epicene cartoon in *Ariel* is just naïve enough

Orpheus and the West Wind

to confuse the speaker of the "Hymn to Intellectual Beauty" with its author. What will he make of the poem's epiphanic climax?

> Sudden, thy shadow fell on me;
> I shrieked, and clasped my hands in ecstasy!

If Saint Teresa or Saint John of the Cross were credited with those lines, we would know at once what was meant. "Ecstasy," from the Greek word for "derangement," is the mystic's precise term for his loss of outward sense and voluntary motor control in the presence of his God. When wings come between Shelley and the sun, his reaction is traditional: he shrieks and clasps his hands in what looks like prayer. He does not squeal, or giggle, or skip about the room. And yet we smile, for we had heard of the plaster Cupid, "beautiful but ineffectual," before we read the poem.

Douglas Bush's stigmatization of Shelley's heroes and martyrs as "variations on the portrait of himself as an effeminate romantic idealist" is a *locus classicus* of the biographical fallacy. "It is painful," Professor Bush writes, "doubly painful when we remember that Christ is in the background, to think of the Aeschylean god in terms of 'pale feet,' 'pale wound-worn limbs,' 'soft and flowing limbs And passion-parted lips.' "[4] A note follows to Shelley's description of Correggio's Christ, whose lips are parted (like those of many a Mannerist John the Baptist) in ambiguous if not indecent warmth. But we can spare ourselves all that pain if we will look only at the words themselves. Shelley did not decorate his text with a facing reproduction of Correggio's model; he used the word "passion" in a general Christic context, where it can only mean "suffering," the Passion of Our Lord. As for the pallor of the Prometheus-Christ's feet and lacerated limbs, the continued gnawing of a man's heart by a vulture will, like crucifixion, cause him to lose great quantities of blood.

Shelley's three major self-portraits appear in "Ode to the West Wind," *Epipsychidion*, and *Adonais*. A close reading of these passages will not only distinguish the persona from the man, but will also show that the persona's character and the tone of his grief are dictated in each case by the myth common to all three poems. The myth is again occult, though nominally classical. It tells of the first lyrist, whose mangled body was a blood sacrifice to his songs. The myth is that of Orpheus, poet and priest, and of the vegetative deities whose worship he reformed and whose annual slaughter and resurrection his words, by imitation, celebrate.

In the last three years of Shelley's life, the idiosyncrasy that had determined his choice of the most recondite symbologies research could yield invaded his prosody as well. Dante's chain-rhyme is the classic vernacular scheme for a purgatorial dream-vision; *The Triumph of Life* was therefore composed in tercets. Spenser's stanza, whose languid conclusion perfectly suits an elegiac mood (Latin elegy alternates pentameters with hexameters), was selected for *Adonais* at least partly because the poem is a parabolic variation on the "Garden of Adonis" episode in the Third Book of *The Faerie Queene*. Shelley had always insisted that his non-political verse was directed to a small and highly-educated audience. Today that audience necessarily consists of students of literary history. An awareness of the technical antecedents of Shelley's poems alone can trigger a full response to the thematic ironies implicit in them and suggest the mythological ancestors of their personages. In this sense Shelley may be called an academic poet.

The rhyme-scheme of "Ode to the West Wind" conforms to the larger numerological pattern within which Shelley develops his chief images. The historical connotations of terza rima take second place to certain overall ritualistic correspondences, which we shall now examine at some length.

The "Ode" is divided into five sections, each of which contains fourteen lines and ends with a couplet: the rhyme scheme is *ababcbcdcdedee*. If the tercets were not visibly separated on the page, the reader would not know until the end of the sixth line, when the *b*-rhyme repeats once too often, that the poem was to be something other than a sequence of Shakespearean sonnets. The obvious question—why, having fourteen lines to work with, a poet should confine himself to five rather than seven rhymes—leads nowhere. Shelley shared with Keats, Byron, and Wordsworth a distaste for the English sonnet, but not, significantly, their devotion to the tighter, four- or five-rhyme Italian form. He wrote comparatively few sonnets, almost none of which adheres to a strict pattern. Even the pallid, ostensibly Petrarchan "To the Nile" (1818) is spoiled by two feminine endings and two forced rhymes. "Ozymandias" (1817) follows the scheme *ababacdcedefef*, and the *e*-rhyme of the "Sonnet to Byron" (1821) dangles in isolation. "Lift not the painted veil" (1818) and "England in 1819" both reverse the normal order of octave and sestet; the first six lines (*ababab*) are succeeded by the equally mechanical alternation of *c*- and *d*-rhymes in the final eight. Such sloppiness is freakish in Shelley and indicates nothing less than boredom with the form. It forces the reader to presume that the contrasting intricacy, strength, and consistency, from section to section, of the "Ode" stanza conceal a more typical symbolic intent.

That symbolism has venerable antecedents. The Romantic renascence of Petrarch's sonnet coincided with the importation from Germany of a transcendentalism that revived, by restating, older "platonizing" habits of mind. When, for example, a Tudor Laura was something less than chaste, the opposition of octave to sestet adumbrated, no less than did the words themselves, the half-remembered but inescapably formative tension between Urania and Pandemos. So Keats measured his reactions to the brevity of sexual climax and to the *tristitia* that follows it against the "steadfastness" of the Pole Star. Mutability, armed with a bending sickle and envious of smooth complexions—"indifferent in a week," says Auden, "to a beautiful physique"—also reappeared with the genre, but mainly as the ravisher of statuary and architecture. These are "too weak," Shelley says of Rome's ruins, "The glory they transfuse with fitting truth to speak." Wordsworth in "Mutability" subjects a weed-crowned tower to that abstraction's "unimaginable touch," and Keats in another sonnet mingles "Grecian grandeur with the rude/ Wasting of Old Time."

The Italian form imposes Ciceronian syntax on the poet: octave and sestet reinforce, for example, the "when . . . then" construction which, surviving in Shakespeare, strengthens his looser framework. If the sonnet is broken down further into two quatrains and a sestet, the sentiment fits naturally into a pattern determined by, say, an "if . . . then . . . but" sequence of clauses. Syntax is logic, and the logic of romantic irony perfectly suits the sonnet's periodic structure.

Shelley and Byron, of course, preferred other Italian stanza forms as vehicles for their wry sense of the light years separating Heavenly Love from the Yeatsian complexities of mire or blood. A canceled passage of *Epipsychidion* pays tribute to Shakespeare's sonnets, but the poem itself imitates the first canzone of the *Convivio* in memorializing the poet's "rash" search for a mortal form of his "idol"—the One Venus, emblematically rendered by a fusion of the Pole and Evening Stars. Byron's ottava rima builds loosely to a terse and epigrammatic final turn whose inevitability invites flippancy. For six lines the intertwined arms and legs of Juan and Haidée writhe and glisten on the twilit beach; the dry, weary, and faintly pitying accents of the aging voyeur break in with the couplet. Connoisseurship ("a *group* that's quite *antique,*/ Half naked, loving, natural, and *Greek*") establishes distance and a worldly-wisdom against which there is no argument, for it hints the truth: that these lovers will degenerate into voluptuaries as soon as they move indoors.

If Shelley's tercets were not run-on, his "Ode" stanza and the Shakespearean sonnet, with its three discrete quatrains, would be roughly similar in effect. The English has one emblematic advantage over the Italian form. Because the quatrains are independent degrees by which the speaker climbs to an emotional *aperçu*, they can be taken to represent the rungs of Eros' ascent towards a glimpse of the beautiful Idea. Sir Philip Sidney, for example, rejects in an opening line the love that reaches "but to dust"; his mind, aspiring to "higher things" and the "light" of a vaguely Christian "heaven," rises to the perception and direct address of "Eternal Love" in the couplet. In his great cycle he writes, like Shelley, as star-lover to star. The same accommodation of sense to structure has, of course, been attempted within the Petrarchan pattern. Thomas Wyatt, called by "Senec and Plato" from the "baited hooks" of profane love, proclaims in a final line that he will no longer climb the "rotten boughs" of any worldly copy of the *Symposium*'s ladder. But the formal correlative of his steps to this renunciation is more shadowy, though visible, than it would be if the octave were clearly broken in the middle.

Shelley rejects this entire tradition. The gnostic and Platonic tendencies found elsewhere in his work have been excluded from the "Ode," whose stanza mimics only the Wind. The enjambment of most tercets combines a double effect of momentum and suspension, of unchecked onrush and escape, with a piling up of pressure, a gathering of breath, for each final explosion: "oh, hear!"[5] Although the Wind literally informs all the elements of the poem, it is not, as we shall see, one of them. For these we must look once more at the rhyme-scheme.

The special virtue of terza rima or of any chain-rhyme is its perpetual instability. Typography imposes an apparent unit of three lines, but "terza" more properly should denote the triple occurrence of each rhyme than the spurious tercet—spurious because it does not exist in the ear. Each sequence, beginning with the *b*-rhyme, perfects itself in five lines, the fourth of which disrupts the pattern otherwise nearing completion by introducing the next sequence. This discordant-concordant opposition of *visible* three to *audible* five not only underpins the tension between impetus and stasis enforced in this case by enjambment, but also establishes a numerological configuration that determines the poem's overall structure and its symbology. Before examining the total geometry, we should note a further tension between the 3:5 pattern and that of *four* tercets against *one* couplet (yielding both 4:1 and 4:5—which in the end will prove identical) in each stanza.

The first three of the "Ode's" five stanzas describe the action of the Wind upon three of the essences of ancient natural philosophy: earth, air and water. The fourth essence—destroyer, cleanser, regenerator, and therefore the element proper to the poet as a political reformer—is held in reserve until the end:

> Scatter, as from an unextinguished hearth
> Ashes and sparks, my words among mankind!

Insofar as these purely descriptive stanzas can be detached from the last two, which convert uneditorialized observation into personal metaphor, the "Ode's" structure magnifies the eye-ear ratio of three against five. It should be noted in passing that three and five are among the possible dimensions of the Golden Rectangle. Also, as neighbors in the Fibonacci series (1:2:3:5:8:13:21:34, and so forth), they recur as a clockwise-counterclockwise proportion throughout nature, from the seeds of conifers to the chambers of the nautilus.

The opening of the fourth stanza recapitulates the established imagery in epitome:

> If I were a dead leaf thou mightest bear;
> If I were a swift cloud to fly with thee;
> A wave to pant beneath thy power ...

Shelley's speaker then prays the Wind to deal with him as with the grosser elements ("Oh, lift me as a wave, a leaf, a cloud!"); he also implies that he craves liberation from them. They smell of mortality and change and are subject to the "heavy weight of hours" which has "chained and bowed" him too; they suggest the "thorns" on which he falls.

The amalgamation of all subigneous essences into the clay that composes breathing but unenlightened flesh (including the dormant poet's) has been long in preparation. The Wind's "stream" in the second stanza has recalled the forest and anticipated the sea:

> Loose clouds like earth's decaying leaves are shed,
> Shook from the tangled boughs of Heaven and Ocean.

Orpheus and the West Wind

So too the Mediterranean has drowned "old palaces and towers,"[6] now "overgrown with azure moss"; even farther below the surface the speaker imagines

> The sea-blooms and the oozy woods which wear
> The sapless foliage of the ocean.

The poem's conclusion reveals the Wind to be something other than the lightest of the three lower elements: not air in motion but the force that drives the air. It can be addressed in the second person without license because like the skylark it is alive. This fact explains the pictorial vagueness so often objected to in the second stanza. How could the poet represent the Wind behind the wind, the agency of Spirit upon corporeal air, without confusion? He chose instead to let clouds stand for the atmosphere which supports them, although he knew remarkably well (see, of course, "The Cloud") that they consist of tiny drops of water. He also rendered their interaction with the sea from which they rose in terms of the forest. And he had no choice. When Shelley tangled the "boughs of Heaven and Ocean," he tangled the imagery too, but he saved the larger metaphor. The fifth stanza confirms that the Wind is literally a fifth element interpenetrating the others. It is the Pythagorean ether, the *Quinta Essentia*. This information justifies the secondary structural ratio of four tercets against a total of five stanzaic elements (the fifth, again, being the couplet) and proves it the same as 4:1. For the Wind is consubstantial with all.

As fire quickens with intelligence the tenement of clay, so the Quintessence informs mineral and vegetable nature. It evaporates water and condenses vapor; every spring it arouses "the wingèd seeds," each "like a corpse within its grave," from "their dark wintry bed." Equivalent like Brahma to the universe it perpetually creates, this "Wild Spirit" is Siva and Vishnu as well—"Destroyer and preserver"—and thus a trinity.[7] It had killed William Shelley in June, and now in late October Mary was in her ninth month of pregnancy with the only son who would survive the poet. That ecology is the theme of this completely syncretistic and—one might as well say it—completely Christian poem:

> Thou fool, that which thou sowest is not quickened, except it die. . . .
> So also is the resurrection of the dead. It is sown in corruption, it is raised in incorruption:
> It is sown in dishonor, it is raised in glory: it is sown in weakness, it is raised in power.
>
> (I Corinthians xv. 36, 42–43)

A taste for numerology and medieval chemistry seems queer in a poet with an advanced aesthetic and years of laboratory experience; the connection between such lore and Orphic ritual will seem even more capricious until we recall a tradition usually neglected in the study of post-Renaissance English literary culture. Francesco Giorgio's *De Harmonia Mundi* (1525) measured the universe according to the fifth (*diapente*) and octave (*diapason*) of music. Through such transmitters as Robert Fludd (1574–1637), his work eventually influenced the cosmology of Milton. Giorgio was a Neoplatonic friar and a dabbler in the Kabalah, but his "Musical Philosophy" derives ultimately from Pythagoras. It appealed to a fascination with the mystical significances of numbers, which was as widespread in the sixteenth century as it had been in Dante's and remains prominent in *The Faerie Queene*. All such systems of cosmic harmony—popularly known as the "music of the spheres"—were wedded to occult learning generally, and especially to a concern with the writings then ascribed to Orpheus and Hermes Trismegistus.

Ficino claimed in his translation of the *Corpus Hermeticum* (1463) that these pseudonymous teachers were the doctrinal ancestors of Pythagoras, who thus emerges as a mathematician grafted onto an adept. If Désirée Hirst is right, Agrippa, Paracelsus, and the Florentine and French academicians handed down their syncretistic occultism through Boehme and the Philadelphians, Henry More and the Cambridge Platonists, William Law, Swedenborg and later eighteenth-century "enthusiasts" to William Blake, who purged it of the vulgarities it had picked up along the way, and whose mythological symbolism is in many respects startlingly like Shelley's.[8] In 1813, Fabre d'Olivet's translation, *Les Vers dorés de Pythagore*, gave new life to a pre-Revolutionary fad for numerology. Shelley's own interest in such systems grew out of his long-standing practice of "the Orphic and Pythagoric system of diet."[9] Let us look first at the Musical Philosophy in "Ode to the West Wind" and pass through it to Orpheus.

Pythagoras' great contribution to physics was his discovery that, in Arthur Koestler's words, "the pitch of a note depends upon the length of the string which produces it, and that concordant intervals in the scale are produced by simple numerical ratios (2:1 octave, 3:2 fifth, 4:3 fourth, etc.)."[10] His disciples adopted the Orphic belief in metempsychosis, which they feared, and worshiped number as the secret strength of all things, but the Renaissance received as doctrine only the sect's extension of their master's acoustics to cosmic sound. As the planets revolve through the upper air, fixed to concentric spheres, they produce tones which differ according to the length of the orbit of each and yield a chord of eight notes, a celestial concert which, if heard, would paradoxically be judged a dissonance. In his *Utriusque Cosmi . . . Historia* (1617) Fludd illustrates this "harmony" by the *monochordus mundanus*, a guitar-like instrument whose frets are formed by the intersection of planetary orbits (and the regions of the sublunary elements) with a single string, tuned in the drawing by an angelic hand. But the more common analogy is to Orpheus' own instrument: a gigantic lyre whose strings have been bent into circles.

Shelley urges the West Wind to make him

> thy lyre, even as the forest is:
> What if my leaves are falling like its own!

The germ of this metaphor had been present five years earlier. "Hark! whence that rushing sound?" Shelley had asked as the chariot of the Daemon of the World began its descent:

> 'Tis like a wondrous strain that sweeps
>   Around a lonely ruin
> When *west winds* sigh and evening waves respond
>   In whispers from the shore:
> 'Tis wilder than the unmeasured notes
> Which from the unseen *lyres of dells and groves*
>   The genii of the breezes sweep.
>
> (I, 48–55)

Although daemonic influence is rather a property of Neoplatonic panpsychism than of the Pythagorean Quintessence, the action of "genius" here is startlingly like the Wind's.

The mythological connotations of the metaphor become even more explicit in the dramatic lyric "Orpheus" (1820). The chorus leader describes a stand of cypresses and a cave,

>   from which there eddies up
> A pale mist, like aëreal gossamer,
> Whose breath destroys all life . . .
>
> (19–21)

until the breeze scatters it. Meanwhile the "weak boughs" of the cypresses "Sigh as the wind buffets them, and they shake/ Beneath its blasts" (32–34). Because Eurydice is dead, the air carries pestilence, and the wind-harp of the grove cries out in pain. All this changes the moment Orpheus begins to play:

> *Chorus.* What wondrous sound is that, mournful and faint,
> But more melodious than the murmuring wind
> Which through the columns of a temple glides?
>   *A.* It is the wandering voice of Orpheus' lyre,
> Borne by the winds, who sigh that their rude king
> Hurries them fast from these air-feeding notes;
> But in their speed they bear along with them
> The waning sound, scattering it like dew
> Upon the startled sense.
>
> (35–43)

The winds clearly stand for poetry itself, that is, for "making" and unmaking. What one breeze kills, the other mourns. But Orpheus' song, by purging his grief, renews the natural world, which falls silent with love. The trees and animals crowd in to hear him, and the wind resumes its normal neutrality (as regards the immediate felicity of man) in its third appearance, a dialectically necessary epic simile from "mighty poesy" to "a fierce south blast" which tears

> through the darkened sky,
> Driving along a rack of wingèd clouds,
> Which may not pause, but ever hurry on,
> As their wild shepherd wills them.
>
> (86, 88-91)

"Ode to the West Wind" exists on three levels of myth. Orpheus' music once tamed wild beasts, caused trees and stones to start from their places, and arrested the flow of rivers. Even so the Quintessence forces the grosser elements it interpenetrates to dance to the numbers of a celestial harmony, from birth through corruption to regeneration. The "plastic stress" of this divine Afflatus sweeps through the "dull dense world" of *Adonais* and compels form to follow form there in "new successions." Finally, the poet is himself a variant of that Romantic commonplace, the Aeolian lyre.[11] The world's soul, as it breathes through the Orphic mouth, performs a Promethean work of ordering and illumination:

> Language is a perpetual Orphic song,
> Which rules with Daedal harmony a throng
> Of thoughts and forms, which else senseless and shapeless were.
>
> (*P.U.*, IV, 415-417)

Shelley wrote in *A Defence of Poetry* that "the mind in creation is as a fading coal, which some invisible influence, like an inconstant wind, awakens to transitory brightness."[12] The West Wind scatters "ashes and sparks" from this ember. Insofar as they are revolutionary, the poet's enlightening "words among mankind" are incendiary too. The fire can only catch outside the poem, for the voice that fans the blaze must expire in doing so. The "unextinguished hearth" must be blown out. The mind itself must be offered in sacrifice.

The "Ode" contains only one classical allusion. The cirrus clouds, portending storm, are metamorphosed into a rout of ecstatic Thracian women:

> there are spread
> On the blue surface of thine aëry surge,
> Like the bright hair uplifted from the head
>
> Of some fierce *Maenad*, even from the dim verge
> Of the horizon to the zenith's height,
> The locks of the approaching storm.

Shelley visited the Florentine galleries, notebook in hand, at least twice in the week before he began the "Ode." He was not impressed by the statue of "A Bacchante with a Lynx," but jotted down a description of it anyway: "*The effect of the wind partially developing her young and delicate form upon the light and floating drapery, and the aerial motion of the lower part of her limbs are finely imagined.*"[18] Then he saw "A Statue of Minerva," which shocked him because it stood on an altar to Bacchus, decorated with the skulls of goats and, in moderate relief, the figures of four Maenads. His note on this group is as impressionistic as the earlier one, recording a concrete, wind-blown effect, had been photographic; it establishes that analogy from storm to the hair and clothing of the Dionysiac celebrant which within a few days would become the dominating metaphor of the second stanza of "Ode to the West Wind":

> The tremendous spirit of superstition aided by drunkenness and producing something beyond insanity, seems to have caught them in its *whirlwinds*, and to bear them over the earth *as the rapid volutions of a tempest bear the ever-changing trunk of a waterspout*, as the torrent of a mountain river *whirls the leaves* in its full eddies. *Their hair loose and floating*

seems caught in the tempest of their own tumultuous motion, their heads are thrown back leaning with a strange inanity upon their necks, and looking up to heaven, while they totter and stumble even in the energy of their *tempestuous dance*.[14]

Shelley goes on to condemn this "monstrous superstition," which inflicted on Roman art and morals "a deep injury little analogous to its effects upon the Greeks who turned all things, superstition, prejudice, murder, madness—to Beauty." And yet the Bacchantes call up favorable suggestions wherever they appear in the poems of 1819 and 1820. According to the "Ode to Liberty" (1820), Rome sucked "the milk of greatness" from Athens' bosom, "Like a wolf-cub from a Cadmaean Maenad" (92-93). And Panthea compares the mists rising from the portal of Demogorgon's cave to the "oracular vapour"

> Which lonely men drink wandering in their youth,
> And call truth, virtue, love, genius, or joy,
> That maddening wine of life, whose dregs they drain
> To deep intoxication; and uplift,
> Like Maenads who cry loud, Evoe! Evoe!
> The voice which is contagion to the world.
>
> (*P.U.*, II, iii, 4-10)

Asia replies that the "contagion" is liberty and a refreshed awareness of the splendors of nature. Finally, the Moon sings as she traces the circle of her mating dance with Earth:

> I, a most enamoured maiden
> Whose weak brain is overladen
> With the pleasure of her love,
> Maniac-like around thee move
> Gazing, an insatiate bride,
> On thy form from every side
> Like a Maenad, round the cup
> Which Agave lifted up
> In the weird Cadmaean forest.
>
> (IV, 467-475)

How does Shelley justify the use of symbols condemned in his notebook? The apparent conflict between the poet and the moralizing connoisseur can be resolved by an examination of two of the many competing versions of the death of Orpheus.

The first and less popular version came down to Shelley through the *Periegesis* of Pausanias.[15] In the course of his wanderings over Greece, Orpheus established the Mysteries of Hecate, of the Subterrene Demeter, and especially of Apollo, who had given him his lyre in the first place. Too enthusiastic a proselytizer, Orpheus gave away so many holy secrets that Zeus, as a security measure, blasted him with a thunderbolt. The first of the Bixby-Huntington Notebooks contains a fragment of terza rima (generally agreed to be connected with the "Ode"), whose canceled opening reads as follows:

> And what art thou presumptuous boy who wearest
>   The bays to mighty Poets only due?
> The ivy tresses of Apollo's fairest
>   Prophaning . . .[16]

Shelley admits that he wears the poisonous, "false laurel," not "that which bound Milton's immortal hair." He is none the less exultant:

>   And that I walk thus proudly crowned withal
> Is that I know *it may be thunderstricken*
>   And this is my distinction, if I fall
> I shall not creep out of the vital day
>   To common dust nor wear a common pall
> But as my hopes were fire, so my decay
>   Shall be as ashes covering them. Oh, Earth
> Oh friends, if when my   has ebbed away
>   One spark be unextinguished of that hearth
> Kindled in [. . . .][17]

These lines may or may not echo Pausanias. In either case they were soon abandoned.

The second account is Ovid's, who reports that after Orpheus

Orpheus and the West Wind

had lost Eurydice the second time, he forswore heterosexual love, sang such tragic amours as that of his father Apollo for Hyacinth, and converted the men of Thrace to pederasty:

> ille etiam Thracum populis fuit auctor amorem
> in teneros transferre mares citraque iuventam
> aetatis breve ver et primos carpere flores.
>
> *(Metamorphoses, X, 83–85)*

The Maenads, understandably vexed by this development, spotted Orpheus one day from a hilltop. The first of the women to recognize their disparager shrieked out against him and, *her hair streaming in the wind*, hurled a spear straight at his mouth:

> e quibus una leves iactato crine per auras,
> "en," ait "en, hic est nostri contemptor!" et hastam
> vatis Apollinei vocalia misit in ora.
>
> *(Metam., XI, 6–8)*

After bloodying him with stones, the Maenads ripped Orpheus to pieces with hoes and mattocks. The birds and beasts mourned the dismembered poet, the rivers swelled with their own tears, and the trees *shed their leaves as if tearing their hair* in grief:

> te carmina saepe secutae
> fleverunt silvae, positis te frondibus arbor
> tonsa comas luxit.
>
> *(Metam., XI, 45–47)*

Orpheus had taught the Dionysiac Mysteries to the Athenian Eumolpus and to Midas, the king of Phrygia. Bacchus therefore did not suffer his priest's murder to go unavenged:

> Non impune tamen scelus hoc sinit esse Lyaeus
> amissoque dolens sacrorum vate suorum . . .
>
> *(Metam., XI, 67–68)*

Before leaving Thrace forever, he turned the Maenads into oak trees. Their offending arms changed to branches, and their wind-tossed hair became leaves.

Shelley's debt to Ovid is clear.[18] Both poets manipulate their imagery in such a way that mourning and murder, the depilated leaves of the trees and the transformed hair of the Maenads, blend into one symbol. Comparison of the "Ode" with its source adds still greater value to the "tangled boughs" of the second stanza, explains away what had seemed Shelley's ethical confusion with regard to the Maenads, and, most important of all, underscores the paradox which in the end defines the tone. The Maenads are votaries of Dionysus, and Orpheus is his hierophant. If mourner and murderess are identical, so are priest and victim.

Proclus, commenting on Plato, reports that "Orpheus, because he was the principal in the Dionysian [*sic*] rites, is said to have suffered the same fate as the god."[19] In some versions of the story—including as we shall see, *Adonais*—Orpheus is an incarnation of Dionysus, and his death recapitulates the Titans' dismemberment of the newly born, horned god. Each year at the summer solstice the priests of the Dionysiac rites re-enacted this murder in the *omophagia*, their highest mystery, by tearing a bull apart and eating its flesh raw. Various horned animals, representing the god's metamorphoses in this struggle to escape the Titans, sometimes replaced the Thracian bull in other Greek lands. The Cretans substituted a wild goat and merged the ceremony with the cult of Zagreus. Wherever a stag was used, Dionysus became confused with Actaeon, as he does in *Adonais* and as Orpheus does in the poem that bears his name:

> Awhile he paused. As a poor hunted stag
> A moment shudders on the fearful brink
> Of a swift stream—the cruel hounds press on
> With deafening yell, the arrows glance and wound,—
> He plunges in: so Orpheus, seized and torn
> By the sharp fangs of an insatiate grief,
> Maenad-like waved his lyre in the bright air,
> And wildly shrieked "Where she is, it is dark!"
>
> (46–53)

The identification of Orpheus with the Bacchantes is subliminally present in the "Ode" as well. When the speaker begs to be dealt with as the forest—"What if my leaves are falling like its own!"—he is not straining a metaphor. He refers neither to incipient baldness nor to the pages of his book—even though "the leaves of the tree" are, in the words of Saint John of the Apocalypse, "for the healing of the nations." He wears the bays of Apollo's bard, the vine leaves of Bacchus, and the Maenads' crown of oak and ivy. He celebrates a feast in which he is at once the minister, the eaten god, and the human devourer, fulfilling thereby the triple function formulated by the terrible figure at the center of every Eucharist: *hoc est enim meum corpus*. In the passage last quoted, Orpheus cannot decide whether to take up his lyre or to drown himself. The singer of "Ode to the West Wind" need not so choose, or rather has no choice to make. The trumpet of his prophecy will awaken earth *by virtue of* the death he embraces. In the hair of the Maenads—"the locks of the approaching storm"—we recognize that obsessive image of the sailor's suicide which will recur to the Orphic-Actaeontic speaker of *Epipsychidion* and *Adonais*.

Priest, divine victim, and ravenous communicant, Orpheus is first and last a singer of songs. The leaves run before the Wind "like ghosts from an *enchanter* fleeing," and, "by the *incantation* of this verse," the Wind also scatters the evangel of a human spring. Shelley borrowed the pun from Milton:

What could the Muse her self that Orpheus bore,
The Muse her self for her *inchanting* son
Whom universal nature did lament . . .

The diction of "Lycidas" and "Ode to the West Wind" reaches back beyond *canere* ("to sing or prophesy") and *cantare* ("to sing or bewitch") to the Indo-Germanic KAN or HAN ("to sound").[20] It evokes memories of the birth of language itself, the "perpetual Orphic song," and of villages where music had the potency of magic and the lyrist and the shaman were a single person. Shelley's poem concerns the human voice, which sets stones dancing and echoes the spheres; it concerns the *vates* who immolates himself for the regeneration of his fellows and of the god who possesses him. "That which thou sowest is not quickened, except it die." That is why the poet must fall and bleed, and why the poem takes the "tone" it does.

VII
Actaeon, the Phrasemaker

*Prima nepos inter tot res tibi, Cadme, secundas
causa fuit luctus, alienaque cornua fronti
addita, vosque canes satiatae sanguine erili.
at bene si quaeras, Fortunae crimen in illo,
non scelus invenies; quod enim scelus error habebat?*
(*Metamorphoses*, III, 138–142)

The "Epipsychidion" I cannot look at; the person whom it celebrates was a cloud instead of a Juno; and poor Ixion starts from the centaur that was the offspring of his own embrace. If you are anxious, however, to hear what I am and have been, it will tell you something thereof. It is an idealized history of my life and feelings. I think one is always in love with something or other; the error, and I confess it is not easy for spirits cased in flesh and blood to avoid it, consists in seeking in a mortal image the likeness of what is perhaps eternal.
(Letter to John Gisborne, 18 June 1822)

Epipsychidion dramatizes the speculation which is the second of Shelley's heresies: if the book of nature is so corrupt that no moral lesson can be drawn from it and no anagoge read into it, symbolic language must be a sham. The vehicle of any metaphor is necessarily concrete, but if the world of eye and ear to which it is anchored does in time "betray the heart that loved her"—if the phenomenal realm is mindless, as it sometimes seems in "Mont Blanc," or the province of that malicious daemon who tortured Beatrice Cenci—then what Wordsworth called "the language of the sense," from which every figurative utterance borrows its vocabulary, is reduced to vacuous or mad gibberish. The poet makes phrases, not metaphors. He engages in an enterprise which does not befit the human mind and may, as we shall see, prove murderous. Shelley's most perfect lyric, "Ode to the West Wind," invokes an immanent deity; the gnostic *Epipsychidion* wrecks itself in the attempt to flesh transcendence in words. The greatness of *Epipsychidion* is commensurate with the banality of its tropes, for any poem that takes as its theme the inadequacy of poetry and ends by demonstrating that "the deep truth" is, as Demogorgon said, "imageless" can only achieve an inverse success. Its failure must be, in fact, the measure of that success. "These words inefficient and metaphorical," Shelley noted to his early essay, *On Love*. "Most words so—No help!"[1]

Marriages and Metaphors

What, precisely, is an *epipsychidion?* Editors have debated whether Shelley's title should be taken to mean the "soul out of my soul" mentioned in line 238 of the poem or the tiny "soul within the soul" of line 455. Both camps have forgotten that the prefix *epi* normally means "upon." Carlos Baker has even invented a "psyche-epipsyche strategy," which he defines as an analogue to that motion of *eros* towards the Beautiful which "may be found under explicit discussion in the *Symposium* and *Phaedrus* of Plato. . . . in Shelleyan terms, the mind (psyche) imaginatively creates or envisions what it does not have (epipsyche), and then seeks to possess epipsyche, to move towards it as a goal."[2] The compound *epipsyche* exists in nobody's Greek but Baker's. He is punning, as Locock did before him, on the cycle and epicycle of Ptolemaic astronomy.[3]

All such philological legerdemain assumes that the poem was named for its specific subject rather than its literary class. Shelley's title is thematic only insofar as it is generic. Neville Rogers' query very nearly hits the mark: "if you may have an *Epinikion* for a Triumph-song and an *Epithalamion* for a Marriage-song, why should you not have an *Epipsychidion* for a Soul-song?"[4] Shelley's foible of paranomasia warrants our taking this suggestion one step further: an epipsychidion is to souls what an epithalamion is to bodies and bedchambers. It is a hymn for the marriage of minds, and Shelley's poem is the first of the genre. As Spenser composed his *Epithalamion* in the six-rhyme, eighteen-line stanza Dante had used for the second canzone of the *Convivio*, so the last lines of Shelley's 1820 translation of the first canzone (*Voi, ch'intendendo, il terzo ciel movete*) preface his own nuptial song, an improvisation upon that poem and upon the *Vita Nuova*.[5] The *Commedia* supplied the rhyme-schemes of "Ode to the West Wind" and *The Triumph of Life*, as well as the latter's dream frame and manner of portraiture. *Adonais* of course employs Spenser's habitual stanza. In *Epipsychidion* Shelley imitated both masters of his Italian period at once.

Epipsychidion asks Emilia Viviani the question Aeneas blurted out when he failed to recognize his mother Venus: *quam te memorem, virgo?* But the hero's answer—*o dea certe!*—does not come so easily to the poet, whose task is to create a metaphor of a metaphor. Emily actually embodies the "One," the Aphrodite Ourania, whom the day- and folding-star, Lucifer-Hesperus, merely emblematizes here and in Shelley's other verse. He thinks that in this mortal form he has found no mere "Metaphor of Spring and Youth and Morning" (120), but something holier still: the absolute symbol of the goddess, the "shadow of that idol of my thought" (268). The identity must be proven, however, in strictly poetic terms. The desiderated *primary* symbol, in which Emily will convey the One, must rest upon lower figures, upon a stratum of *secondary* metaphors for Emily and Urania as each is in herself.

The venture succeeds by the back way of apparent disability. To explain, for instance, why "Young Love"—the poet himself—cannot "teach Time, in his own gray style,/All that thou art,"

Shelley calls his mistress the "Sweet Lamp" at which his "moth-like Muse has burned its wings" (53–56). Like most of the poem's secondary tropes, the Lamp is affective; it reveals the agent only as she strikes the patient. In other words, the observer's inadequacy alone defines the girl. Shelley refurbishes the metaphor eight paragraphs later to carry the history of his childhood pursuit of Intellectual Beauty:

> Then, from the caverns of my dreamy youth
> I sprang, as one sandalled with plumes of fire,
> And towards the lodestar of my one desire,
> I flitted, like a dizzy moth, whose flight
> Is as a dead leaf's in the owlet light,
> When it would seek in Hesper's setting sphere
> A radiant death, a fiery sepulchre,
> As if it were a lamp of earthly flame.
>
> (217–224)

Epipsychidion is clumsiest where the "Newton among poets" juggles astronomy to get the similes he wants and will have at any price in the reader's literal assent. The mixed figure, Hesper-Polaris, foreshadows the sea-voyages that conclude this poem and *Adonais*. Sailors steer by the North or lodestar, but Platonists yearn for the morning-star of Aphrodite; the referential fusion is unavoidable. A caviler might be answered that there is always an appeal open from nature to art.

To return to the main question, this passage is one of many which help to establish through repeated secondary metaphors a primary identity to which the "gray style" of discursive argument would be inadequate. Shelley clothes his invisible Lady in the secondary trope already suggested for Emily. The suicidal moth who speaks the poem becomes as well its figurative node, the one point of tangency between lamp and star, Emily and the One; he is the catalyst in a dialectic of secondary metaphors whose synthesis will hopefully prove the assertion: *o dea certe!*

"Secondary metaphor" is not another name for circumlocution, but in this poem it is always periphrastic:

> I measure
> The world of fancies, seeking one like thee,
> And find—alas! mine own infirmity.
>
> (69–71)

The first five paragraphs of *Epipsychidion* address Emily as a "captive bird" and a "Seraph of Heaven"; a "Benediction," a "Veiled Glory," a "Moon beyond the clouds" and a "Star above the Storm"; a "Form," a "Wonder," a "Beauty," a "Terror" and a "Harmony"; a "Mirror" and a "Lamp"; a "Smile . . . a gentle tone . . . a belovèd light"; a "Solitude, a Refuge, a Delight"; a "Lute"; a "buried treasure"; a "cradle of young thoughts" and a "violet-shrouded grave of Woe." Shelley rummages through the rag-bag of his habitual vocabulary for the *mot juste*, the password that will permit him to move on to the more important business of the next part of the poem. These shopworn images and scraps of phrases—most of which he has handled with great scruple in earlier poems—here are pasted together any which way on the desperate chance that they will add up to a picture. They do not. When Shelley unveils his finished representation, we see nothing, unless abstraction can be seen. The canvas is blank, for the metaphor subsumes not one concrete image:

> See where she stands! a mortal shape indued
> With love and life and light and deity,
> And motion which may change but cannot die;
> An image of some bright Eternity;
> A shadow of some golden dream . . .
>
> (112–116)

All the secondary metaphors have failed; they reveal neither the girl herself nor the "deity" with whom she is "indued." But the primary metaphor—Emily *as* Venus—remains sound, if incorporeal. She was the intelligence who guided Dante's *terzo ciel*, but now her "Splendour" leaves "the third sphere pilotless" (116–117). She becomes in a double manifestation the fixed reckoning-point towards which, as helmsman, she steers Shelley's

"Fate/ Whose course has been so starless!" (130–131). He can now "dare" the poem's second and more difficult task, which is to illuminate the woe that is in marriage, to "beacon the rocks on which high hearts are wrecked" (147–148).

"I am not thine," Shelley had asserted, "I am a part of *thee*" (52). The concluding four hundred and fifty-odd lines of *Epipsychidion* attempt to prove through metaphor that lovers' souls can merge into one. The Trinity is a similar mystery, and neither would necessarily have seemed absurd to an amateur chemist in the age of Dalton and of Avogadro's Law (1811).[6] The poem's chief myth owes far less, of course, to religion and science than it does to the *Symposium*. Shelley's self-portrait as a passive and weakly desirer clearly copies Diotima's Eros, the houseless son of Poverty and Plenty, who yearns for what he does not possess, the Beautiful. But the bridegroom's quest for a symbol of hypostatic identity with his bride—"Would we two had been twins of the same mother!" (45)—comes down to Shelley from the hermaphroditic egg, with four arms, four legs, and two backs, of which Plato makes Aristophanes speak. This primal man was split into sexed halves when the world fell. That day inaugurated the marriage chase and all our woe (one could venture that it saw the birth of comedy too). Socrates rejects the pretty story, even as a parable, perhaps because metaphors are only as strong as their concrete correspondents. And it is observably untrue that the copulation of bodies or of minds blends them or heals the sundering of nature for our sins.

Epipsychidion is literally and abundantly a *romantic* exercise in that it exploits all the conventions hatched from Aristophanes' egg and nurtured by the troubadours, the singers of the *dolce stil nuovo*, and the courtly recasters of degenerated epic. The poem's "failure" to preserve these conventions immediately suggests some nasty questions which lurk just beneath its surface and which are left to its readers to ask out loud. Yeats's Bishop deludes himself in believing that the "heavenly mansion" of which he prates is anything other than Crazy Jane's "foul sty."

Actaeon, the Phrasemaker

How, then, do Oisin and Niamh, Crane's Faustus and Helena, or, for that matter, Laon and Cythna improve upon the frogs, spawning in a ditch? Will the angel ever get rid of the ape and tiger, or will his struggles breed monsters to mock him with a family resemblance? A centaur, Shelley wrote to John Gisborne, was the offspring of the embrace which is *Epipsychidion*.

The grand attraction of the Muslim Paradise is the absence of irrelevancies: the houris have no souls. The West, however, muddles sentiment with sex. Though women still suffer the vestiges of that social subjugation and intellectual disdain against which the mother of Shelley's wife protested so tragically, Christendom has always granted them spiritual equality to men. We like to think of love as an essence that is shared and of the act of love as a mingling of two immortal subjects. Our grammar reflects this preference. All seemly English verbs of coition are intransitives that govern prepositions. "Dirty words" offend some people not because they are onomatopoeic, or because the living language preserves its old snobbishness against Anglo-Saxon derivatives (*screw*, for instance, is French in origin), or because these verbs were plow-, spear-, or tool-words once, or because they were born in violence (*ficken* = to beat or strike). They are dirty because they take a direct object:

> For never did thy Beauty since the day
> I saw thee first and wedded thee, adorn'd
> With all perfections, so inflame my sense
> With ardor *to enjoy thee*, fairer now
> Than ever, bounty of this virtuous Tree.
>
> (*Paradise Lost*, IX, 1029–1033)

The woman is a thing. Adam's diction shocks us, for all its high breeding, because we are dualists who invade another's person not as a possession or prize, but gently, as befits so fragile a vessel, and reverently, for it contains the Holy Ghost. Grammar, I have said, is logic, and a nation's logic, the workaday tool of its philosophy, is the index of its prejudices.

Shelley copied into the same notebook in which he composed

much of *Epipsychidion* this crucial sentence from the *Convivio*: "Amore ... non è altro che unimento spirituale dell' anima e della cosa amata" (III.ii.16).[7] The first line of the poem offers sisterhood as an example strong enough, for the moment, to carry this definition. " 'The love a sister bears towards a sister,' " Shelley had told Hogg years before, " 'is unexceptionable.' " The friends were strolling then through a garden near Oxford and pretending that it was overseen by two spirits. These guardians could not be man and mistress, for " 'the love of the sexes, however pure, still retains some taint of earthly grossness.' " Nor could mother and child exercise such tutelage. The latter's very existence would poison the atmosphere with the remembrance of carnal passion. Brothers would not be suitable, for the masculine temperament is independent and aggressive. Only sister nymphs could maintain the self-effacing intimacy required of garden geniuses.[8]

The marriage on the garden-island at the end of *Epipsychidion* differs from this reverie—which obviously prefigures *Rosalind and Helen* (1817–1818) and *The Sensitive Plant* (1820)—in one important respect: Emily's soul is not only the "sister" of Shelley's "orphan one," but its "spouse" as well. Shelley insists that their love, unlike that of the siblings Laon and Cythna, is in no way fleshly, but he does not deprive their spirits of sexuality. He plays with overtones of incest as he deals directly, elsewhere in the poem, with the idea of adultery, thereby injecting the criminal conventions of romance and the early vernacular lyric into his private experiment with inherited metaphor. Courtly love is by definition adulterous, and Dante chose *incestuous* adultery, pimped to by a book *di Lancialotto come amor lo strinse*, to convey the full pathos of lovely and mortal sin: Francesca can never escape the embrace of Paolo Malatesta, the brother of her husband Gianciotto. Dante's longing for Signora de' Bardi and Petrarch's for Laura were less criminal than the desires of Tristram and Lancelot du Lac only because they despaired of fulfillment. Shelley begs the question when he insists upon the "purity" of his infatuation with Emilia Viviani; the conclusion of this chapter will argue that his technical innocence was no innocence at all.

Actaeon, the Phrasemaker

Shelley and Emily set sail at last for an eastern island, "Beautiful as a wreck of Paradise" and bright as the star that guides them, Aphrodite's planet, "that wandering Eden Lucifer" (423, 459). Such voyages to the Hesperides and their antipodes haunted Shelley's imagination throughout his career like "echoes of an antenatal dream" (456). Here the island becomes a metaphor of Dante's "spiritual union of the soul with the beloved object," the Phoenix riddle by which, in Donne's words, "to one neutral thing both sexes fit" and, rising after death, "prove/ Mysterious." As "the blue heavens bend . . . to touch their paramour," the sea, and as "Earth and Ocean seem/ To sleep in one another's arms," so the poet and his bride hope to decay, blend, and

> become the overhanging day,
> The living soul of this Elysian isle,
> Conscious, inseparable, one.
>
> (544–545, 509–510, 538–540)

Prince Athanase, whose soul resembled "Vesper's serene beam" and who "had wedded Wisdom," learned "Plato's words of light . . . the story of the feast" in a tower overlooking the sea (61, 31, 224, 227). Prometheus and Asia consummate their marriage in "a cave,/ All overgrown with trailing odorous plants" (III, iii, 10–11). These images, ubiquitous in Shelley's verse, are of course sexual in origin. Tower and cave merge in the "pleasure-house" inherited by the lovers of *Epipsychidion* from a "wise and tender Ocean-King," who reared it "for delight" and made it "sacred to his sister and his spouse" (491, 488, 487, 492). " 'Tis not," Shelley emphasizes, "a tower of strength, though with its height/ It overtops the woods." Nor is it a cave, exactly, although it lifts itself "from the living stone . . . in caverns light and high" (486–487, 496–497). It looks like both at once and stands not for Donne's riddle of one organ *in* the other, but for a higher mystery, a hermaphroditism by which the distinction of parts is lost and the egg of Aristophanes restored.

The pretty artifice is as frigid as the Galatea-Emily of lines rejected from *Epipsychidion:*

> some guess right,
> And others swear you're a Hermaphrodite;
> Like that sweet marble monster of both sexes.[9]

Another Hermaphrodite, bright as the "shape of vital stone/ Which drew the heart out of Pygmalion," ballasts the boat of the Witch of Atlas but inadequately accompanies her artistic solitude (xxxv, 328). The symbolism of *Epipsychidion*'s bower is similarly sterile. Throughout the honeymoon passage, the imaginative dialogue between the poet and the poem degenerates ever further into whimsy.

The island paradise fails finally when the poet sees that words do not do justice to his conception, that the conception itself is inadequate to his desire, and that the literary relationship of craftsman to artifact poorly counterfeits an embrace. Thirty lines before the end of the poem proper and the beginning of the *tornata*, Shelley predicts the cessation of speech at the limits of formulable meaning:

> And we will talk, until thought's melody
> Become too sweet for utterance, and it die
> In words, to live again in looks, which dart
> With thrilling tone into the voiceless heart,
> Harmonizing silence without a sound.
>
> (560–564)

The lover realizes that he must hold his tongue, and moments later the poet stops talking too, or stops talking as a poet. He abandons the forms of utterance which distinguish his craft from that of the reasoner. Symbolic language gives way once more to discursive statement and abstract assertion:

> We shall become the same, we shall be one
> Spirit within two frames, oh! wherefore two?
> One passion in twin-hearts . . .
>
> (573–575)

Actaeon, the Phrasemaker

Epipsychidion achieves one last, vague figure: the lovers are meteor-like, tangent spheres "instinct" with "expanding flame." The poet's diction then casts off concreteness and soars unballasted out of sight. Metaphor is deserted entirely, except for the marriage-emblem of the verse itself, that yoking of disparate elements which is the couplet:

> One hope within two wills, one will beneath
> Two overshadowing minds, one life, one death,
> One Heaven, one Hell, one immortality,
> And one annihilation. Woe is me!

(584–587)

At the end of the *Paradiso* Dante was struck dumb by the sight of God: "A l'alta fantasia qui mancò possa." His tongue lacked force to declare his high imagination. But nothing more remained to be said, for he had penetrated the infinite, and where there is no boundary, there can be neither transgression nor failure to go the limit. When the former question had arisen at the end of the *Purgatorio*, Dante had simply pulled back on the rein, *lo fren de l'arte*. But the terms of Shelley's experiment demand that he exhaust his materials and, if need be, crack his instruments:

> Woe is me!
> The wingèd words on which my soul would pierce
> Into the height of Love's rare Universe,
> Are chains of lead around its flight of fire—
> I pant, I sink, I tremble, I expire!

(587–591)

The ruin of the poem is the success, albeit negative, of the demonstration. To paraphrase the *Defence*, Shelley has proved that metaphors are at best the hierophants of an inspiration which remains unapprehended. He has shown too that symbols no more truly wed essences than the marriage service makes man and wife one flesh. It remains to examine the wreckage incidental to his researches and to doubt, as he did, the morality of the quest.

Quod enim scelus error habebat?

Dante outlines four levels of literary interpretation in his exegesis of the poem *Epipsychidion* imitates, the first canzone of the *Convivio*. We have looked at the lowest and highest meanings, the literal and the anagogical. Shelley's image of himself as a bleeding and cornered stag opens up the two remaining areas. Allegory, Dante says, combines personal symbolism with secular "prophecy"; tropology points a moral.

> In many mortal forms I rashly sought
> The shadow of that idol of my thought.
> And some were fair—but beauty dies away:
> Others were wise—but honeyed words betray:
> And One was true—oh! why not true to me?
> Then, as a hunted deer that could not flee,
> I turned upon my thoughts and stood at bay,
> Wounded and weak and panting; the cold day
> Trembled, for pity of my strife and pain.
>
> (267–275)

Shelley's stricken deer conveys all the bafflement, loneliness, and guilt of Cowper's famous figure, but here the guilt is neither religious nor squarely faced. Its dissolution is one purpose of the poem, and its cause must be sought in the life to which the "letter" of this spiritual autobiography so clearly points. Reference to the parallel passage in *Adonais* will begin to bring out the significance of remorse in *Epipsychidion*.

Adonais operates within a myth of the seasonal cycle, but unlike "Ode to the West Wind" it contains two rival vegetation gods, the dead poet and his chief mourner. Shelley enters carrying the thyrsus of Dionysus and the Maenads:

> a light spear topped with a cypress cone,
> Round whose rude shaft dark ivy-tresses grew.

He also resembles one of the three wild forest cats variously said to have drawn Bacchus' war-chariot to India: "A pardlike Spirit beautiful and swift." Shelley paints himself as Dionysus for the same reason that he calls himself "frail," "a dying lamp, a falling shower,/ A breaking billow." He expects to share the death of the poet-priest he mourns. Like the Syrian Tammuz and the Egyptian Osiris, Adonis was killed by a boar, and Diodorus Siculus reports (I.23) that the cult of Dionysus took its liturgy from the sacrificial rites of Osiris, as plagiarized by Orpheus and reinstituted at Cadmean Thebes.[10] Shelley further enforces the connection with his subject by describing himself as so weak that he "can scarce uplift/ The weight of the superincumbent hour" and by coloring his face with the consumptive's hectic flush:

> On the withering flower
> The killing sun smiles brightly: on a cheek
> The life can burn in blood, even while the heart may break.

Thus he renders in verse the clinical facts, as he had received them, of Keats's death:

> Hunt tells me that in the first paroxysms of his disappointment *he burst a blood-vessel; and thus laid the foundation of a rapid consumption*. There can be no doubt but that the irritability which exposed him to this catastrophe was a pledge of future sufferings, had he lived. And yet this argument does not reconcile me to the employment of contemptuous and wounding expressions against a man merely because he has written bad verses; or, as Keats did, some good verses in a bad taste. *Some plants, which require delicacy in rearing, might bring forth beautiful flowers if ever they should arrive at maturity*.[11]

Shelley takes pains to suggest the likeness of Keats to himself because he writes as one who "in another's fate now wept his own."

We saw in the last chapter that the ritual murder of the bull Dionysus was confused in antiquity with the death of the stag

Actaeon. The self-portrait of *Epipsychidion* is partially unriddled by the revival of the muddled icon in *Adonais:*

> he, as I guess,
> Had gazed on Nature's naked loveliness,
> Actaeon-like, and now he fled astray
> With feeble steps o'er the world's wilderness,
> And his own thoughts, along that rugged way,
> Pursued, like raging hounds, their father and their prey.

The naked, lovely "Artemis" is in both poems Urania, the great genetrix of Nature with whom Adonais "is made one." Mistress and "mighty Mother" together, she prefigures the most powerful of all *matres coniuges*, the Blessed Virgin, and serves Shelley, as she did Milton, in the role of Heavenly Muse. She reigns in *Epipsychidion* as a "veiled Divinity" over the

> world within this Chaos, mine and me . . .
> The world I say of thoughts that worshipped her.
>
> (243-245)

When the vision of this Being fades, the "thought" or "thoughts" of which she is the "idol" (*eidolos*) turn into the hounds of memory, who lacerate the poet with that sense of separation and contrast which is one aspect of romantic irony. The true One is incomparable and irrecoverable, and the best of "many mortal forms" cannot so much as "shadow" her. Or so it seems at this point in the poem. But loss is not guilt, and Actaeon was punished for a genuine if involuntary transgression. When he stumbled upon Diana bathing with her nymphs, he committed a capital offense, which one may, as one wishes, call a crime or, with Ovid, a mistake, *scelus* or *error*. What outrage has Shelley committed? Does he merely glamorize his situation, tarting it up in the borrowed rags of legend? One last look at *Adonais* will clear the allusion to Actaeon of the taint of melodrama.

When Urania asks the Shelley-Dionysus figure who he is, he makes no reply,

Actaeon, the Phrasemaker

> but with a sudden hand
> Made bare his branded and ensanguined brow,
> Which was like Cain's or Christ's . . .

or the Wandering Jew's. But Ahasuerus, though like his descendant Cain "companionless/ As the last cloud of an expiring storm," killed no brother. And here, represented by Shelley, the Wanderer does not mock the Saviour with whom he links himself. The equation of Cain to Christ reminds us that Prometheus would not utter the name that "hath become a curse"—that a despairing Jesus hangs and wails throughout history "for the faith he kindled" into flames of persecution—that the religion of brotherly love has become a code of intolerance and fratricide (*P.U.*, I, 604, 555). Shelley's description of himself as a "Love in desolation masked" recalls the earlier anatomy of "Ruin" as "Love's shadow" and the Furies' exhibition of Christ as an emblem of

> those who do endure
> Deep wrongs for man, and scorn, and chains, but heap
> Thousandfold torment on themselves and him.
> (*P.U.*, I, 780, 594–596)

Shelley ties his own benevolent intentions and their pernicious effects to those of Christ. To invert what Goethe's archfiend says of himself, both are spirits who always affirm: part of the force that wills the good yet ever creates evil.

The scar of infamy on the forehead of Cain-Christ-Shelley is hidden by a crown of "faded violets," the flowers of chastity or dead virginity, and of "overblown" pansies (*pensées*).[12] "That's for thoughts," Ophelia tells us, and it will presently appear that his thoughts torture Actaeon by reminding him not only of the One, but also of mortal injury done in her name to the brother—or sister—he meant to keep. Prometheus' Furies had been hellhounds:

> ministers of pain, and fear,
> And disappointment, and mistrust, and hate,

And clinging crime; and as lean dogs pursue
Through wood and lake some struck and sobbing fawn,
We track all things that weep, and bleed, and live.

(I, 452-456)

But Shelley first employed Actaeon as the type of *remorse* (and the myth perfectly renders the tearing jaws of *mordere*, the word's Latin root) in the context of parricide, which Giacomo Cenci repents too late:

O, that the hour when present had cast off
The mantle of its mystery, and shown
The ghastly form with which it now returns
When its scared game is roused, cheering the hounds
Of conscience to their prey!

(V, i, 5-9)

The speaker of *Epipsychidion* deludes himself that he worships his "Spouse! Sister! Angel!" innocently so long as he does not go to bed with her (130). Copulation was a social necessity among the children of Adam and Eve, but even there, in the first dwelling built on the east of Eden, incest reflected fratricide as *eros* reverses *thanatos*. Byron developed this mirror-identity as the double theme of *Cain* (also written in 1821) and many of his earlier plays and Oriental Tales. Manfred, as we have noted, seduces and destroys his sister Astarte. The mirror connects incest with fratricide in the still fuller sense that both are born of self-love. Narcissus presses his lips to the looking-glass; Cain smashes it with a rock. The "wise and tender Ocean-King" who built the bower which the poet of *Epipsychidion* will usurp married his sister "ere crime/ Had been invented, in the world's young prime" (488-489). Can the sibling affection of Shelley and Emily be so free of peril? The poem's concluding section fails metaphorically partly through discomfort with its own false logic. The lovers' yearning for a prelapsarian home proves that they are fallen. Their need to escape history and society by sailing from their present selves to an island in the new and ancient golden world shows that they are not worthy of "America," which, Goethe's Lothario knew, is "here or nowhere."

If the density of souls is so slight that they can marry as twins within a single egg, or as rarefied gases permeate each other, they must be infinitely divisible too. The health of the loving spirit, who expresses her affinity for her sister in the diction of incest, depends upon a converse eclecticism, a selective outbreeding that is easily misread as promiscuity:

> True Love in this differs from gold and clay,
> That to divide is not to take away.
> Love is like understanding, that grows bright,
> Gazing on many truths. . . .
>   Narrow
> The heart that loves, the brain that contemplates,
> The life that wears, the spirit that creates
> One object, and one form, and builds thereby
> A sepulchre for its eternity.
>
>   (160–163, 169–173)

If man were naturally monogamous, he would not require laws to keep him so. "If the prisoner is happy," Shaw's Don Juan asks, "why lock him in? If he is not, why pretend that he is?" Shelley considered possessiveness in love the heart's most withering obduracy, and exclusiveness the vilest clause in "the code/ Of modern morals" (153–154). Those "poor slaves" who indenture themselves to it

>   travel to their home among the dead
> By the broad highway of the world, and so
> With one chained friend, perhaps a jealous foe,
> The dreariest and the longest journey go.
>
>   (155–159)

The Notes to *Queen Mab* condemn marriage as "the despotism of positive institution" over "the indisciplinable wanderings of passion." The hypocrisy that surrounds this commercial contract clamps "fetters on the clearest deductions of reason" and breeds prostitution as its "legitimate offspring."¹³ Marriage was for Shelley, again in the words of Shaw's misogynist, "the most licentious of human institutions."¹⁴ E. M. Forster's "extraordinarily civilized" Rickie Elliott flirts with his own ruin when he ignores Ansell's warning that "you want and you need to like many people, and a man of that sort ought not to marry. 'You never were attached to that great sect' who can like one person only, and if you try to enter it you will find destruction." Lines 149–173 of *Epipsychidion* speak of the loving soul as an organism that learns as it grows, but which festers and blights others the moment further change is forbidden it. And yet this libertarian passage—perhaps the most straightforward moral utterance in all of Shelley's mature verse—awoke noxious memories that crippled the autobiographical section he wrote next. It raised ghosts whom neither remorse nor the spells of metaphor were potent enough to lay to rest.

When Shelley refuses to

> select
> Out of the crowd a mistress or a friend,
> And all the rest, though fair and wise, commend
> To cold oblivion,

he advocates a community of love which is anything but democratic (150–153). Emilia and Mary will be

> Twin Spheres of light who rule this passive Earth,
> This world of love, this *me* . . .¹⁵
>
> (345–346)

But the twins do not heat and enlighten the poet with equal vigor. Emilia is like "an Incarnation of the Sun," and Mary is rather insultingly compared to the "cold chaste Moon," which "warms not but illumines" (335, 281, 285). Each rules the same number of hours in a different degree of intensity:

> So ye, bright regents, with alternate sway
> Govern my sphere of being, night and day!

Thou, not disdaining even a borrowed might;
Thou, not eclipsing a remoter light . . .

(360–363)

Shelley also marks the vacant orbit of a drowned "Planet," probably his first wife Harriet, and includes as an eccentric side-runner and casual visitor to his cosmos a "Comet beautiful and fierce" (Claire Clairmont?), who is at the same time Venus, "Love's folding-star":

The living Sun will feed thee from its urn
Of golden fire; the Moon will veil her horn
In thy last smiles; adoring Even and Morn
Will worship thee.

(368, 374–378)

There is no getting around the banality of this extended trope. The harmony of worlds in *Epipsychidion* is flat by comparison with the song of the Moon's mating-dance around the Earth in *Prometheus Unbound*. Illogic jars the concert too. Emilia, who had been a vision of the One, the star of dawn and dusk (*and* the Pole Star), becomes the Sun; a disruptive Comet now steps, with surpassing awkwardness, into her role as mover of the third sphere. The emblematic confusion is not excused by the possibility that the Comet represents the Pandemos, the lower Aphrodite of sexual passion. These "disasters" are incidental to the passage's chief vice, its dishonesty. Why, if Emilia unveils the long-withheld Divinity, does Shelley need any light but the Sun's? How, if she personifies the youthful Vision whose "Spirit was the harmony of truth" itself, can her lover's understanding grow any brighter by continuing to gaze "on *many* truths" (216, 163)?

Shelley's love ethic contradicts both itself and the practice it seeks to excuse: the marriages, the affairs, the sharing of Mary with Hogg in 1815. *A Defence of Poetry* calls the *Vita Nuova* "the idealised history of that period, and those intervals of [Dante's] life which were dedicated to love";[16] just so, Shelley wrote Gisborne, *Epipsychidion* "is an idealized history of my life and feelings." And the Advertisement claims that "the present Poem, like the *Vita Nuova* of Dante, is sufficiently intelligible to a certain class of readers without a matter-of-fact history of the circumstances to which it relates." If *Epipsychidion* adhered with any fidelity to either its literary or its "matter-of-fact" source—and the two are markedly similar—reference to the latter would be superfluous. Insofar as Emilia is the absolute and exclusive target of desire, Harriet and Mary resemble those ladies of "disguise"—*schermo* or *defensione*—who screen Dante's love for Beatrice from the stares of the vulgar (here they would veil her from Shelley's eyes too). Or we might say that the poet uses each of his mistresses as Dante, after the death of Beatrice, used the "lady of the window"; each consoles him for the retreat of the Vision.

We know, however, from Shelley's letters that he was always "in love with something or other"—that Harriet and Mary had each in her turn been embraced as the embodiment of all truth, virtue, and beauty—that Saint Augustine's quandary, quoted as the epigraph to *Alastor*, remained Shelley's to the end of his days: "Nondum amabam, et amare amabam, quaerebam quid amarem, amans amare." Shelley had subscribed himself "inviolably, eternally," "unalterably," "imperishably" and "indissolubly" the soulmate of Elizabeth Hitchener, the schoolteacher who, after she accepted his invitation to join a spiritual menage quite like that outlined in *Epipsychidion*, rapidly degenerated into a "Brown Demon.... She is an artful, superficial, ugly, hermaphroditical beast of a woman, and my astonishment at my fatuity, inconsistency, and bad taste was never so great, as after living four months with her as an inmate. What would Hell be, were such a woman in Heaven?"[17] Likewise, the "story of Shelley's Italian platonics" ends with the "Noble and Unfortunate" Emilia married to Biondi and leading him "*a devil of a life.*"[18] The "Juno" *Epipsychidion* had celebrated turns out to be "a cloud," a girl extraordinary only in her talent for sponging money.

The critic who tries to understand *Epipsychidion* in terms of the uneasiness he feels as he reads it has not necessarily fallen into the affective fallacy. The poem is a structural anomaly, filled with false starts and crosscurrents of thought which, colliding as absurdities, shift the meanings of the metaphors like sand. The astronomical mechanism of lines 277–383 is clumsy because it is apologetic. Shelley tries to hide under a complicated figure two embarrassing matters-of-fact: that he has never juggled his emotions with any greater agility than he does the solar system here, and that he has been through all this before with other women, other "somethings-or-other." Because he lacks the narrative distance which would enable him to treat such contretemps with the humor they deserve, a genuine tragedy like Harriet's suicide plunges him into bathos.

The position of the Actaeon-simile is most significant. Appearing between what I read as the rejection of Harriet, "whose voice was venomed melody" (256 ff.) and the meeting with Mary, it glosses over the fact of desertion leading to death. Collation with parallel passages in *The Cenci* and *Adonais* has shown that this image always signals the presence of a fratricide's remorse. Here that guilt is ineffectual because it is covert; Shelley will not call it by its name.[19] The initial evasion enervates the long astronomical conceit it introduces, and culminates in the following supreme vulgarism, masquerading as periphrasis. "These words conceal," Shelley says,

> how my soul was as a lampless sea,
> And who was then its Tempest; and when She,
> The Planet of that hour, was quenched, what frost
> Crept o'er those waters, till from coast to coast
> The moving billows of my being fell
> Into a death of ice, immovable.
>
> (319, 311–316)

The corpse of Harriet—once "my purer mind ... the inspiration of my song"—had been fished out of the Serpentine, bloated from a month's immersion and far advanced in pregnancy, perhaps by her husband; the cadaver still wore his wedding-ring.

Unless the reader is very sentimental indeed, the inadequacy of that "quenched Planet" to the circumstance it prettifies may tempt him to laugh. Metaphor has again failed Shelley, but in a way more frightening than before, because poetic integrity has collapsed with it. Shelley is now more concerned to excuse his actions than to do them actual or "poetic" justice. The symbolist deprecates the world of experience he has undertaken to illuminate and lapses into that fake eloquence, known as phrasemaking, which always attends the divorce of words from things. Perhaps he should not have tried in the first place to close the gap between noumena and phenomena, between the ageless idea and those compounds of matter and form which, being created, are imperfect and must pass away.

"The error," Shelley confessed to Gisborne, "consists in seeking in a mortal image the likeness of what is perhaps eternal." This is a venial sin. But Actaeon does heinous injury when, instead of seeking the tenor *in* the mortal vehicle, he imposes the everlasting likeness *upon* a girl too frail to bear it. She suffers, and he is guilty of professional negligence, at the very least. Ovid's question becomes meaningless, for there ceases to be any practical moral difference between *scelus* and *error* when the poet forgets that, unfortunately for poetry, a distinction must be drawn between metaphor and human life. Shelley begins to suspect that he had better give up both. "Die," he urges at the end of *Adonais*, "If thou wouldst be with that which thou dost seek!" (464–465). The only metaphor strong enough for the wedding of souls or of antithetical planes of existence is now a mockery of the aphorism which closes the marriage service: "No more let Life divide what Death can join together" (477). Nature and art are too degenerate, or too fleeting, to convey the excellence that remains, as it did for the Gnostics, imperishably transcendent:

> Rome's azure sky,
> Flowers, ruins, statues, music, words, are weak
> The glory they transfuse with fitting truth to speak.
> (466–468)

The "error," Shelley told Gisborne, cannot easily be avoided by "spirits cased in flesh and blood." On the same day—two days after Mary's miscarriage—he also wrote to Trelawny: "should you meet with any scientific person capable of preparing the *Prussic Acid*, or *essential oil of bitter almonds* I should regard it as a great kindness if you could procure me a small quantity. It requires the greatest caution in preparation & ought to be highly concentrated; I would give any price for this medicine."[20]

VIII
Motes of a Sick Eye

Naïve, Sentimental, Gnostic and Polysemous Poetry

The Triumph of Life progresses to an unanswered question, not dialectically, but through a series of irreconcilable contraries which suggest both the answer and its hollowness. The antinomies of Shelley's last work are subtler than those of "Mont Blanc," *The Revolt of Islam* and *Prometheus Unbound*—matter and mind, oppression and freedom, hatred and imagination—and quieter in their effects on the poet, for they do not yield workable or believable syntheses. The terms of each dichotomy stand, like those of 1816–1819, a world's width apart, but now they are more protean and far more insidious than the Eagle and the Snake. Once again, devils come disguised as angels, as devils always do when they mean to tempt rather than to frighten us.

Love is the most terrible of these ambivalent categories, for it descends from Ormuzd or Ahriman, to save or to damn, and blurs the distinctions between the warring or mutually indifferent elements it seeks to bind. The untranslatable semitone which determines that Faust's Gretchen is *gerettet* rather than *gerichtet* by her love (and we shall see that Shelley called at last for death in the words of Goethe's poem) is shaded no more finely than is the question that destroys Plato because in his senility he neglects to ask it: is desire born of and projected by the heart upon its mundane object, or is it the world's own weapon, an ambush directed *at* the heart?

"And Life, where long that flower of Heaven grew not,
  Conquered that heart by love which gold or pain
Or age or sloth or slavery could subdue not."[1]

(257–259)

Opposed to the heart, the principle of self and the repository of the eternal Forms, is Life, who comprehends carnality and all worldly ambition in the poem's primary polarity. Socrates proposed self-understanding as the beginning of philosophy, but his axiom has saved neither the recorder of his dialogues nor Rousseau, each vanquished by his "own heart alone." On the other side stand

"The Wise,

"The great, the unforgotten: they who wore
  Mitres & helms & crowns, or wreathes of light,
Signs of thought's empire over thought."

(208–211)

By ignoring the Delphic injunction *gnothi seauton* (within which maxim, Shelley had long felt, "all real knowledge may be comprised")[2] these heart-deniers have enslaved themselves to Life. Regenerate, Promethean man, "the King/ Over himself," would not have crowned abstraction over slippery truth, geometry over nature's vitality, grammatical paradigms over the fluidity of language, thought over itself (*P.U.*, III, iv, 196–197). The unruly heart surrenders prisoner to Life anyone who imposes a false orderliness upon it:

"their lore

"Taught them not this—to know themselves; their might
Could not repress the mutiny within,
  And for the morn of truth they feigned, deep night

"Caught them ere evening."

(211–215)

The contention of Life and the heart for mastery in every soul suggests the poem's second dilemma, the divorce which frustrates and saddens any writer who pauses to analyze his artifact into its components:

> Mind from its object differs most in this:
> Evil from good; misery from happiness;
> The baser from the nobler; the impure
> And frail, from what is clear and must endure.
>
> *(Epipsychidion,* 174–177)

Metaphor is born at the point where mind collides with its experience of the world. Despising, fearing, or otherwise alienated from nature, "romantic" art cannot strike a balance between tenor and vehicle except by abdicating into a false innocence. In the age of Homer the imaginative subject not only infused but wholly vanished into the concrete image and produced what Schiller calls *naïve* poetry: the object possessed the artist; he was the work, and the work was himself.[8] Because the naïve author effaced his personality, the reader still discovers his own emotions in the catholicity of a "classic" and purges them through its perfect order. Shelley's Rousseau points to

> "the great bards of old who inly quelled
>
> "The passions which they sung, as by their strain
>   May well be known: their living melody
> Tempers its own contagion to the vein
>
> "Of those who are infected with it."
>
> (274–278)

When Goethe told Eckermann (2 April 1829) that the classic was healthy and the romantic sickly, he had in mind the generation of Chateaubriand. Shelley makes their father Rousseau anatomize himself in much the same terms:

> "I
> Have suffered what I wrote, or viler pain!—
>   "And so my words were seeds of misery."
>
> (278–280)

Form is the only healer. Personal expression is morbid because it cools the poet's fever by projecting in an aggravated form his sickness upon others. The romantic writer spews his *Confessions* or his *Leiden* publicly, infects the neighborhood, and feels better at once. The vileness and pain behind his words have not dissolved into his art, which remains poisonous, not cathartic. Rousseau is *sentimental* too, by Schiller's definition. Estranged from the degraded, chaotic earth which must, for lack of a better, serve as vehicle, and exiled from his half-remembered, prenatal home, he still feels towards the latter Shelley's "devotion to something afar/ From the sphere of our sorrow" ("To———," 1821). Refusing to traduce eternity by compounding with time, Rousseau achieves a pyrrhic victory:

"I was overcome
By my own heart alone, which neither age

"Nor tears nor infamy nor now the tomb
Could temper to its object."

(240–243)

As Love, the pimp, entices Plato's heart to join the entourage of Life, so the midwife Nature aborts Rousseau through the tunnel of a second birth into a world one step further removed from the imperial palace whence he came. Rousseau awakes one April morning under a Purgatorial mountain after "the oblivious spell" of gestation's sleep, which has erased nearly every intimation of prior existence elsewhere:

"Whether my life had been before that sleep
The Heaven which I imagine, or a Hell

"Like this harsh world in which I wake to weep,
I know not."

(332–335)

He rises and follows a sun-flecked stream through a roofless cavern to the middle of the mountain. There, on the floor of a blazing well or fountain, stands

> "A shape all light, which with one hand did fling
> Dew on the earth, as if she were the Dawn."
>
> (352–353)

She is the false Matilda who announces not Beatrice and Revelation, drawn in the Car of the Church by the gryphon Christ, but the veiled phantom Life, whose charioteer is quadruply blind.[4] Dante saw Matilda across the chiaroscuro Lethe; the Nepenthe Rousseau's Shape bids him drink blots out not the memory of sin but the last " 'gentle trace/ Of light diviner than the common Sun' " (337–338). This Circe is the second of the poem's masked devils, a parody of Earth in the sixth stanza of Wordsworth's *Ode: Intimations of Immortality*:

> Earth fills her lap with pleasures of her own;
> Yearnings she hath in her own natural kind,
> And, even with something of a mother's mind,
>   And no unworthy aim,
>   The homely nurse doth all she can
> To make her foster-child, her inmate Man,
>   Forget the glories he hath known,
> And that imperial palace whence he came.

Optical imagery bears the same symbolic import in *The Triumph of Life* that it does in the *Ode*. The grown Wordsworth can see only refracted or reflected light: a rainbow, a rose, the moon, "Waters on a starry night." The sunshine is "a glorious birth," but not *the* glory that has passed away. A source of light apparently *sui generis*, the sun actually shadows, to borrow Keats's phrase, a magnitude brighter than a thousand suns. The last gleam of visionary excellence fades "into the light of common day," thanks to the practical zeal of one's parents. The child lies amid his own handiwork with "light upon him from his father's eyes" and "Fretted by sallies of his mother's kisses"—fretted in the double sense that the maternal attack vexes him and checkers his mind with the shade of prison bars.

The dew scattered by Rousseau's "'shape all light'" creates a rainbow: "'on the dusky grass/ Iris her many coloured scarf had drawn'" (356–357). We know what she heralds. The rainbow's beauty is as meretricious as Life itself, *Adonais*' staining "dome of many-coloured glass." An emblem of the fragmented manifold over against the One, the light broken in Jupiter's prism cannot be reconstituted into the primal blank radiance until Prometheus' agony and Asia's love have canceled history. The awful symbol of God's covenant with Noah has, Keats says, been unwoven by discursive reasoners and entered into "the dull catalogue of common things." No longer a testament of hope, the rainbow signifies to Blake the defeat of imagination in modern times by single vision. It stands for the sleep of Newton, who with the mocker Rousseau saw "particles of light" where to exiled and dreaming Israel a promise was manifested through and stretched beyond the sands of their "Red sea shore."

Life's chariot is as cold and bright as the Moon's love, which "warms not but illumines" the speaker of *Epipsychidion*, or as the city of death and beaming ice piled up on Mont Blanc by "Frost and the Sun," or as the midnight sun of intellect pursued by Frankenstein to the Pole:

And a cold glare, intenser than the noon
    But icy cold, obscured with   light
The Sun as he the stars. Like the young moon . . .

So came a chariot on the silent storm
Of its own rushing splendour.

(77–79, 86–87)

The hierarchy of light established here unlocks the moral of Shelley's allegory. The moon of Life blinds Rousseau, who vainly seeks to hide the "holes" that "Were or had been eyes" (187–188). Just as the "cold white light of morning" and the "blue moon" put the "hues of heaven" to flight in *Alastor*, Life dims the rainbow and the "'shape all light,'" who first appeared

Motes of a Sick Eye

"Amid the sun, as he amid the blaze
  Of his own glory, on the vibrating
Floor of the fountain, paved with flashing rays."

(349–351)

Nature in turn extinguishes the gleam of a happier, earlier world, " 'the spark with which Heaven lit my spirit,' " as the sun puts out the stars:

"All that was seemed as if it had been not,
  As if the gazer's mind was strewn beneath
Her feet like embers, & she, thought by thought,

"Trampled its fires into the dust of death,
As Day upon the threshold of the east
  Treads out the lamps of night, until the breath

"Of darkness reillumines even the least
  Of heaven's living eyes."

(201, 385–392)

The stars represent not only imagination and its divine source, but also a third class of poets distinct from the naïve classics and from the sentimentalists. They include Lucan, Sidney, Chatterton and Keats, those "kings of thought" whose spirits early flowed back to the "burning fountain" mocked by the *Triumph*'s flashing Lethe; they inherit thrones "Far in the Unapparent," whence they shower sidereal influence upon the world and beacon the sailor-poet (*Adonais*, 430, 399). Rousseau calls them

"the sacred few who could not tame
Their spirits to the Conqueror, but as soon
  As they had touched the world with living flame

"Fled back like eagles to their native noon."

(128–131)

We may call them *gnostic* poets, in the sense that they either detested or denied the reality of the material world. Two of the four mentioned in *Adonais* killed themselves; all "waged contention with their time's decay," and all are said by Shelley to have suffered flesh and the sun as the obscure night of the soul. They resemble Arnold's saving "remnant" and Thom Gunn's "sad captains":

> winnowed from failures,
> they withdraw to an orbit
> and turn with disinterested
> hard energy, like the stars.

As *Adonais* puts it,

> The splendours of the firmament of time
> May be eclipsed, but are extinguished not;
> Like stars to their appointed height they climb,
> And death is a low mist which cannot blot
> The brightness it may veil.
>
> (388–392)

The escaped gnostics would not grant the conqueror Life the sport of their intransigence, the continuing spectacle of their refusal, though tortured, to tame their spirits to her. Rousseau's heroism is futile. Life cannot temper his heart to its worldly "object," but she can and does blind him. If instead he had killed himself young, he might have joined the gnostics as a *living* eye of Heaven. They survive in our nether world as what Auden called Yeats and all dead poets, "a way of happening, a mouth." They survive in and as their poems, the one relic of the past that cannot pass away and the one purging flame which Nature cannot trample to ashes. Otherwise her triumph and that of her supercessor Life are absolute.

Nature, the mock Urania, fades like the dawn-star Lucifer as the dreadful car rumbles through the forest with "savage music, stunning music" (435). Life arrives like "*Night* Primeval" and "*Chaos* old" at the end of the second *Dunciad*, and like Pope's Dulness—the Muse as Antichrist—her purpose is to sear the eyes of the poet and to confound the work of the Logos, the Imagination, the demiurgic *Lux fiat*.

A fourth kind of poet is implied in *The Triumph of Life* by his absence from it. *A Defence of Poetry* quotes Tasso as saying that God and the poet alone deserve the title of Creator. But if the divine or human maker is not consubstantial with his artifact, if he is different or distant enough from it that he comments upon or manifests any emotion, including love, *towards* the work from *within* the work, he lapses into Schlegelian irony. Insofar as he does so unwittingly—not, for example, by the manipulation of a persona—he becomes what one may call a *polysemist*.[5] His work will have "many meanings," not all of them intended and not all of them relevant.

Ordinarily, when the imagination confronts the sensorium's photograph of a natural object or the memory's painting of a past experience, the operation of one upon the other generates metaphor. Sentimental metaphor is imperfect because the poet, having made his private feelings public, does not satisfactorily resolve them into the image which is their vehicle. The sentimentalist may know what he is doing; the polysemist never does, for he has moved one step beyond simple creation into reflexive criticism of his own composition. His moral and aesthetic censors work mischief upon the tentative metaphor even then taking shape and bring forth as the final metaphor a feebler synthesis—a mongrel which subsumes no true irony, because the process that yielded it was unconscious. The polysemist does not reside in his work as the sentimentalist does. His unique weakness is that in him which, as he writes, already reads the reviews.

Polysemism subverts imagination and its artifact most notably in *Epipsychidion*. "Actaeon's" unconfessed guilt over the death of Harriet debilitates the astronomical figure of his subsequent erotic history. And the poem's opening section demonstrates that doubts of the adequacy of a trope, even as it is being coined, guarantee its banality. Polysemism, or subliminal romantic irony, is presumptive evidence of a clash between the man as a man and the man as an artist and moralist. It wrecks only those metaphors which it is not seen to threaten in the moment of their conception. In the end, we need biography and must even try, with trepidation, to recover "intention" when we read Shelley, who admitted with reference to *Adonais*, his "least imperfect" production, that "The poet & the man are two different natures: though they exist together they may be unconscious of each other, & incapable of deciding upon each other's powers & effects by any reflex act."[6]

Adonais avoids the polysemism that menaces most elegists who in the fate of others weep their own by separating Shelley-Actaeon-Dionysus-Cain-Christ, the frail mourner, from the mourned Shelley-Keats. *The Triumph of Life* further sophisticates this device; it abstracts Shelley, the poet now narrating his vision in the past tense, from an outdated persona named "I" and projects the poet's present feelings (and the story of his desertion by a Shape who looked like the One, the morning star) onto the true persona, the cicerone Rousseau. The demarcation of two lines on either side of "I" and his passionate reactions to the moment, hemming him in from the analytic retrospect of the author and from his doubleganger Rousseau, saves the poem *from* sentimentalism and polysemism *for* conscious irony.

Shelley borrowed this stratagem from Dante, whom *A Defence of Poetry* describes in much the same imagery used for the gnostic poets of *Adonais* and *The Triumph of Life*: "the Lucifer of that starry flock which in the thirteenth century shone forth from republican Italy, as from a heaven, into the darkness of the benighted world. His very words are instinct with spirit; each is as a spark, a burning atom of inextinguishable thought."[7] The "I" of the poem asks Rousseau questions to which the answers are already evident, just as Dante, Chaucer and Keats annoy Vergil, the Eagle and Moneta with stupidities in aid of narrative irony. The *Commedia* also suggested Shelley's epic catalogue of dead fools and martyrs and the mistaking of a dead soul for a lower form of life. Hell's whirlwind sweeps the lustful towards Dante like starlings or singing cranes; Shelley at first overlooks Rousseau, whom he thinks an old root covered with white grass instead of hair. Finally, Shelley has begun to practice a "sweet new style" which contrasts as refreshingly with that of *Adonais* as

Motes of a Sick Eye

Dante's lucidity does to the "quibbles" of Shakespeare and the heavy ironies of Milton's synthetic vernacular.

The most surprising feature of *The Triumph of Life* is its urbanity. The thematic symbolism of *Epipsychidion*'s couplet and the numerology of the "Ode" stanza have yielded to a terza rima evocative only of its classic antecedent. One by one, Shelley bids farewell to his heresies. Historical Gnosticism takes a curtain call as Shelley trots out Pope Gregory, someone named John, and other orthodox puppets,

> men divine
>
> Who rose like shadows between Man & god
>   Till that eclipse, still hanging under Heaven,
> Was worshipped by the world o'er which they strode
>
>   For the true Sun it quenched.
>
> (288–292)

The non-Christian occult appears one last time as Rousseau points out "'Zoroaster, Solomon,'" the author of the Dendera Zodiac and, possibly, Hermes Trismegistus: "'those/ Great forms to whom Egypt & India/ Owed what they were & are.'"[8] This episode was, significantly, canceled in draft.

Shelley's third heresy, his obscurantism, has evaporated. Although the poem is difficult, its sources—Dante, the *Trionfi* of Petrarch, Lucifera's procession in *The Faerie Queene*, *Comus*, Pope and Wordsworth—are not unfamiliar to educated readers. Shelley puns but once: the "flower of heaven" and the "star that ruled" Plato's doom translate Aster, the boy who "conquered the heart by love" (256–258). The letters of 1822 do not brag of the "abstruse" nature and "esoteric" audience of poems like *Epipsychidion*;[9] there is no more perverse glorying in such "dim words" as those which "obscure" Emilia (33).

Shelley resolves his second heterodoxy—the question whether the vehicle of a given metaphor is worthy of its tenor—in a way which suggests that he is saying goodbye to more than his heresies. *The Triumph of Life* holds out a richer alternative to its merely technical solution of the problems of polysemism: the poet can always rid himself of the man who undermines him by returning his body to nature, that superannuated jilt so stale to his imagination. The polysemist may, in other words, join the gnostics. "What Adonais is, why fear we to become?" (459).

All aesthetic questions raised by the poem serve the larger one of how, or whether, to live. Crushed between the irreconcilable antinomies of Life and the heart, intellect and the mutiny within, mind and its object—having lost, like Wordsworth after the Terror, "All feeling of conviction, and, in fine,/ Sick, wearied out with contrarieties"—Shelley did not yield up moral questions in despair. Despair is the emotional paralysis struck through the dreamer or meliorist by his *first* glimpses of the intransigence of things as they nastily are. Shelley passed beyond it to a stoicism that permitted him to endure the world so long as it pleased him to do so—so long, perhaps, as the summer lasted—and held him ready at any moment to quit it quietly.

The Triumph of Life has been called a palinode by those disposed to regard the younger Shelley as a Jeremiah against "society" for "nature's" sake. The earlier chapters of this study have shown that after 1817 Shelley drew no absolute distinctions between nature and art, landscape and human institution. The *Paterfamilias*, the evil Spirit who has dominion in this imperfect world, might be induced equally from the designs of His first- and second-hand artifacts. Because only the invisible remained hopeful, the poet could no longer praise all things palpably bright and beautiful. He could only exploit their dubiously adequate emblematic content. *The Triumph of Life*'s rejection of the "natural religions" of Rousseau and Wordsworth is hardly a late development. The massive indifference which momentarily seemed to inhabit the Mont Blanc glacier awoke to sadism in *The Cenci*. The earth depicted in "Ode to the West Wind" and *Adonais* was "still life"—that genre which the French call *nature morte*—except as the "plastic stress" of the one Spirit swept through the "dross." We recall too Ahasuerus' exposure of "this Whole/ Of suns, and worlds" as an ephemeron,

> motes of a sick eye, bubbles and dreams;
> Thought is its cradle and its grave.

And Shelley had, of course, composed a prose *Refutation* of Paine's and "Palley's" deism simultaneously with *Queen Mab*.

The Triumph of Life recants nothing but the poet's heresies and his long-waning political optimism. A Fury had unintentionally aroused pity in Prometheus by crowing that goodness never coexists with power, nor wisdom with love, in fallen men.

> The good want power, but to weep barren tears.
> The powerful goodness want: worse need for them.
> The wise want love; and those who love want wisdom.
>
> (I, 625–627)

The abyss between action and motive had grown unbridgeable by 1822, when Shelley, looking at Napoleon's phantom, grieved

> to think how power & will
> In opposition rule our mortal day—
>
> And why God made irreconcilable
> Good & the means of good.
>
> (228–231)

The Triumph of Life renounces, without regret, the poet's heritage from the Enlightenment and Godwin. The "spoilers spoiled" (235) pass by in chains: Kant, Voltaire, and the princes the latter educated. Shelley has at last expelled them from his pantheon:

> "the world & its mysterious doom
>
> "Is not so much more glorious than it was
> That I desire to worship those who drew
> New figures on its false & fragile glass
>
> "As the old faded."
>
> (244–248)

Demogorgon had dampened the celebration of the apocalypse by warning that the momentum which forces a cycle to millennial crisis may in time, if we are not watchful, unbar the pit to which Destruction has been hurled. The chiliastic *Hellas* ends with a far more "bitter prophecy," stated as a question: shall the wheel inevitably lurch downward to war, "hate and death"? Shelley's and the world's weariness of the past mirrors an impatience with poetry—a sequential art whose products will, like those of all arts, perish. A historical pattern of timeless moments is no longer good enough. The fleeting tangency of time and eternity at high noon on the great circle does not reclaim the preceding and following nights of vice, ignorance, and rancor. Shelley can only "cling to moral and political hope, like a drowner to a plank."[10] So too with the "moment" of a good poem, however close it may come to drawing angels down. "I wish," Shelley wrote Peacock in the last January of his life, "I had something better to do than furnish this jingling food for the hunger of oblivion, called *verse*."[11]

The ease and grace of *The Triumph of Life* are born of effort which stops short of strain. There is no more shrillness at the verge of the ineffable because after *Adonais* Shelley has not cared to fly that high: "My mind is at peace respecting nothing so much as the constitution & mysteries of the great system of things—my curiosity on this point never amounts to solicitude."[12] The metaphysical and moral insouciance of the last poems contributes, paradoxically, to their metaphysical and moral strength; whether in this success Shelley resembles Yeats's Zen crane, who may "take a trout/ If but I do not seem to care," or the phlegmatic who, desiring little, is capable of much, remains a futile but fascinating question. The engagingly muted tone of the Casa Magni album-pieces to Jane Williams reflects both Shelley's growing urbanity and an uncharacteristic lightness of affection. Unlike the "young and foolish" Yeats, Shelley was taking love "easy, as the leaves grow on the tree" and taking his verse, which he composed while sailing, that way too; "if Poetry comes not as naturally as the Leaves to a tree," Keats had said, "it had better not come at all." The last poems were designed to clarify contraries which Shelley no longer hoped to resolve. And like the poems, the letters and the visions of June express neither content nor despair, but simply an approach to silence.

". . . the sea is flooding the house & it is all coming down"

What in fact became of Shelley after the *Don Juan* vanished into fog and smother that July afternoon? The traditional verdict of accidental death rests on the testimony of two interested witnesses. One of them was less than expert; the other, it now appears, deliberately falsified the record.

In 1964 the British Museum acquired the originals of two letters published and heavily rewritten by Trelawny in his *Recollections of the Last Days of Shelley and Byron* (1858). The first of these, addressed by Captain Daniel Roberts to Mary Shelley on 14 September 1822, deals with the salvage of the *Don Juan*. "Everything is complete in her," Roberts announced, "and clearly proves that she was not upset, but I think must have been filled by a heavy sea."[13] Trelawny represented himself as the recipient of this note and printed the sentence as follows: "Every thing is in her, and clearly proves, that she was not capsized. I think she must have been swamped by a heavy sea."[14] The emendations from "upset" to "capsized" and from "filled" to "swamped" are not as innocent as they look.

The British Museum papers include a deck plan, presumably drawn by Roberts, which shows that Shelley's yacht was not open (as is generally supposed), but fitted with a cabin enclosed to protect sofas and bookshelves. All Roberts told Mrs. Shelley, then, was that the *Don Juan* did not turn keel over; if she had, the pig-iron ballast would have torn through the topsides, and the cargo would have followed. In strict nautical usage, a boat is said to capsize either when an overwhelming sea "swamps" her or when she heels so far to leeward that a heavy sea washes inboard and "fills" her. The latter mishap occurs when too much sail is handled recklessly. As Trelawny saw when he shaded the letter's diction, Roberts suspected that the *Don Juan*'s skipper was responsible for her loss.

Trelawny tampered even more grossly with a letter Roberts wrote to him on 18 September. The printed version ends with a forged postscript: "On a close examination of Shelley's boat, we find many of the timbers on the starboard quarter broken, which makes me think for certain, that she must have been run down by some of the feluccas in the squall."[15] There is indeed a postscript in the MS., but it concerns two horses, one of whom, "Poor Alf," had "kicked his feet all to pieces against the stone stabling. . . . The hoofs stink horribly, but there is no appearance of green." Roberts offered no opinion on the cause of the wreck. Trelawny not only fabricated the addition; he also suppressed advice unflattering to himself and to an unknown lady: "to a man of your quick comprehension I need but say '*report spreads fast*.' do not let a few paltry seconds of lust (for it is nothing else) get the better man of you."

Shelley scholars have never settled what sort of a boat the *Don Juan* was. Frederick L. Jones, for instance, has claimed that Edward Williams' *Journal* sketch of a catboat with spinnaker depicts Shelley's yacht.[16] Trelawny's description of her as "Torbay rigged" has also bred confusion.[17] He probably alluded to the famous "Brixham trawler" design (Brixham is on the south side of Torbay). In Shelley's day these fishing boats were cutters, but during the century they were gradually refitted as ketches. If in 1858 Trelawny was thinking of the latter rig, he was at least accurate in remembering that the *Don Juan* had two masts. A woodcut in his *Records of Shelley, Byron, and the Author* (1878) represents the yacht as a gaff-rigged, topmasted yawl, approximately forty feet overall (exclusive of the bowsprit). The *Don Juan* was, of course, only twenty-four feet long, and in Roberts' deck plan the mainmast is shown stepped so far aft that she can only have been a schooner. Williams likewise describes a schooner in his *Journal*, and his drawing of Byron's *Bolivar* and the *Don Juan* shows the latter carrying mainsail, foresail, main and fore gaff-topsails, flying jib, jib, and forestaysail.[18] Finally, the Governor of Viareggio reported on 12 September 1822 that two boats belonging to Stefano Baroni had "while fishing discovered, at the bottom of the sea . . . a small vessel, schooner rigged."[19]

Despite his naval rank, Roberts was not the seaman his friends thought him. His testimony is suspect on that account and because, if the *Don Juan* did capsize with all sail set, he was morally guilty of manslaughter. Few novices, however imprudent, would fit out a twenty-four foot shallop as a topsail schooner, much less put to the open sea in her. But who would resist "expert" advice, especially when it promised greater fun? On Sunday, 16 June, "Roberts unrigged the Don Juan and got the masts on deck—his men employed putting tressel-trees to the masts as he intends to fit 2 topmasts to her."[20] The following Friday Roberts' gang "Fitted the topmasts ataunt, with these up," Williams crowed, "she looks like a vessel of 50 tons."[21]

To Captain Roberts' ignorance must be added Shelley's and Williams' lack of common sense. Both flattered themselves that they were " 'seasoned salts,' " despite Trelawny's protest to Williams that, "You will do no good with Shelley . . . until you heave his books and papers overboard; shear the wisps of hair that hang over his eyes; and plunge his arms up to the elbows in a tar-bucket. And you, captain, will have no authority, until you dowse your frock coat and cavalry boots."[22]

At Leghorn in mid-July Roberts assured Mary Shelley that through a telescope he had seen the schooner's crew "taking in their topsails" as the *temporale* struck.[23] He salvaged the wreck in September and, according to Trelawny, "found her topsails down and her other sails fast. Trelawny tells me that in his, Roberts' & every other sailor's opinion that she was *run down*."[24] Roberts himself maintained much later that he had found "the topsails furled—topmasts lowered."[25] What, then, are we to make of his report to Trelawny on 18 September that, "The two masts carried away just above the board—bowsprit off close to the bows"? The Captain did not necessarily lie to Mrs. Shelley. If the leeward stays had held, the snapped spars would have been recovered, tethered to the hull; a full set of seven sails was in fact sold at the auction of the wreck. Still, dismasting normally results from a violent jibe or from broaching to with excess canvas. Trelawny curiously failed to mention Roberts' telescope observations or the question of topsails in his *Recollections*. But he did include another eyewitness report: "the captain of one of the feluccas . . . asserted that he . . . had seen Shelley's boat go down off Via Reggio, with all sail set."[26]

If Dan Roberts was willfully inconsistent in his testimony, he was understandably self-regarding. But Trelawny had no such motive. He garbled Roberts' letters to save Shelley—and perhaps Roberts—from posterity's imputation of criminal negligence. One question remains: did Trelawny in fact know of such negligence, or did he assume that history has a dirty mind?

A few years after Shelley drowned, "Count" John Taaffe anticipated Trelawny's relation of the supposed eyewitness account of the anonymous felucca captain. The tale has often been dismissed as puerile. But when we begin to suspect that Shelley, Williams and Charles Vivian did not die by accident—that, moreover, Trelawny sacrificed his few scruples in an attempt to throw historians off the right track—Taaffe's report becomes worth a fresh look:

> The crew of a vessel going into Leghorn had seen them soon after they put to sea, and foreseeing that they could not long contend with such tremendous waves, bore down upon them and offered to take them on board. "A shrill voice," which is supposed to have been Shelley's, was distinctly heard to say "No." The Captain, amazed at their infatuation, continued to watch them with his telescope. The waves were running mountains high—a tremendous surf dashed over the boat which to his astonishment was still crowded with sail. "If you will not come on board for God's sake reef your sails or you are lost," cried a sailor thro' the speaking trumpet. One of the gentlemen (Williams, it is believed), was seen to make an

effort to lower the sails—his companion seized him by the arm as if in anger.[27]

Did Shelley deliberately capsize his over-rigged plaything? It is not solely the responsibility of biographers to tackle this question. The critic as well must ask to what extent Shelley's death and the hallucinatory events leading up to it clarify the metaphoric habits of his entire career. *Ad hominem* arguments are at best impolite. But the verdict of murder and suicide in Shelley's case seems to have been dodged most athletically by those biographers who have tried hardest to tone down his blasphemy or even to find "Christian elements" in his poems. Once more it is worth pointing out that the versions of Christian myth which captivated Shelley were those that supported an ethic of *passive* suicide. Self-starvation, for example, was applauded by many Gnostics as a victory snatched from the sadistic pseudo-Demiurge. To be clinical about it, psychiatry has taught us what it means to be "accident-prone." The sequel will, I believe, support the unprovable speculation that Shelley gave in to and thereby cheated what he conceived of as Wrath.

"You know," Shelley had told Peacock in 1818, "I always seek in what I see the manifestation of something beyond the present & tangible object."[28] The aftermath of *Epipsychidion* disabused him; the stamp of eternal correspondence borne by mortal images is always counterfeit. In 1822 he confessed "the error" in his last letter to John Gisborne and in "The Zucca," addressed to all the women he had pursued:

I loved—oh, no, I mean not one of ye,
  Or any earthly one, though ye are dear
As human heart to human heart may be;—
  I loved, I know not what—but this low sphere
And all that it contains, contains not thee,
  Thou, whom, seen nowhere, I feel everywhere.
From Heaven and Earth, and all that in them are,
Veiled art thou, like a   star.

Saint Augustine's quandary—*quaerebam quid amarem*—had been Shelley's only in his lack of a name for the unearthly Lady he had sought through the two Harriets, Mary and Emilia, each of whom had for some moments soothed the nympholepsy she could not cure. "Some of us," he had written in 1821, "have in a prior existence been in love with an Antigone, & that makes us find no full content in any mortal tie."[29] And now, at the beginning of the last half-summer, the nymph herself was transformed into a lamia.

Insofar as the Fancy is, in Coleridge's words, "a mode of Memory emancipated from the order of time and space," the lyricist is at odds with the lover. One works mnemonically; the other *exists*, an ontologist would say, only when he confronts the woman herself rather than the brain's picture of her. But Shelley's eye in 1822 looked wider of the "tangible object" than the terms of art demand of any literary lover. The recollected image of Jane Williams pleased him at least as highly as her actual presence had done:

> She left me, and I staid alone
> Thinking over every tone,
> Which though now silent to the ear
> The enchanted heart could hear . . .
> And feeling ever—o too much
> The soft vibrations of her touch
> As if her gentle hand even now
> Lightly trembled on my brow
> And thus although she absent were
> Memory gave me all of her
> That even fancy dares to claim.[30]

These "Lines Written in the Bay of Lerici" identify the stargoddess unnamed in "The Zucca." As Urania, she had enticed the sailor to steer by the translated soul of Adonais, through which she shone, into the teeth of the gale. Emilia had earlier manifested the One, then so called, and "lured me towards sweet Death" (73). But at San Terenzo the lodestar marks a trap, and the deity who kindles it kills for profit:

And the fisher with his lamp
And spear, about the low rocks damp
Crept, and struck the fish who came
To worship the delusive flame.

The callous idol of thought does not cheat desire, for the swimmer towards the flame longs to be consumed. Does it matter that the Power behind the light repays the adoration of fish, moths, and men with no loftier sentiment than hunger or avarice? The Blakean symbiosis of Prolific and Devourer is so horrible that felicity now consists for Shelley, as it had for Swift, in "the Possession of being well deceived":

Too happy, they whose pleasure sought
Extinguishes all sense & thought
Of the regret that pleasure [leaves,[31]]
[Destroying[32]] Seeking Life alone not peace.

"Lines Written in the Bay of Lerici" is the single poem concerning Jane Williams which attempts even a vague description of her and the only one that never addresses her in the second person. Holding her remembered image in his mind's eye, Shelley projects the cynicism her presence would evoke onto the fisherman actually before him. Because he likes the girl, he looks, in effect, the other way. He suggests indirectly, even politely, his new awareness of female sexuality as the Devourer. Women of flesh and blood do not, unfortunately, consume their lovers in the moment of climax; they wither men—or so it seems to Shelley—by the "regret" which is the afterbirth of "pleasure," by an attritive melancholy like that found by Keats in the temple of Delight. Orgasm leaves the heart high-sorrowful and cloyed because women, whatever their conscious feelings for men, participate in the fraudulence of that *Ewig-Weibliche* which triumphs in Shelley's last major fragment. Nature, who looks like Matilda, Urania, and the Witch of Atlas, betrays Rousseau to Life, the mock-Beatrice who drains men dry.

The religious imagination has always linked the ideas of orgasm and pentecost by that of bodily dissolution. Crashaw's Saint

Teresa poems express this mystery by punning on the verb "to die" in both the Christian sense of purgation into eternal life and the cant sense of ejaculation. Shelley's symbolism baptizes the theosophical *eros* both in the fire flashed as a signal from the ground of being and in the watery medium through which the fire is seen. The suicidal moth is attracted by starlight tarnished in its passage through the misty veil of the air; the lamp lures fish to the surface. A "burning fountain" draws Adonais to his eternal home, and a Shape who shines on the waters of the well like the sun "amid the blaze/ Of his own glory" seduces Rousseau. Consummation coincides with extinction in the "fire for which all thirst."

Hart Crane's ghost proclaims itself through Robert Lowell's mouth "the Shelley of my age." Crane himself derived sexual hope from the "infinite consanguinity" subsisting between his lover and the ocean, from that kinship to which the sea-water in our veins bears witness. Shelley states only that the "shapes too bright to see" who people his dreams "walk upon the sea, and chant melodiously" (*P.U.*, II, v, 108, 110). Whether they reflect God's nature or merely his own vanity, he cannot meet them face to face until he plunges into the mirror. Shelley revives for our times the metaphoric habit whose Wagnerian name, *Liebestod*, has become jargon, and whose motto might well be Crane's: "Permit me voyage, love, into your hands."

Political pessimism and personal bitterness made Shelley their victim in the last year of his life. "My firm persuasion," he told Hunt, "is that the mass of mankind as things are arranged at present, are cruel deceitful & selfish, & always on the watch to surprize those few who are not—& therefore I have taken suspicion to me as a cloak, & scorn as an impenetrable shield."[33] When the Hoppner scandal broke over their heads, he sent Mary cold comfort: "A certain degree & a certain kind of infamy is to be borne, & in fact is the best compliment which an exalted nature can receive from the filthy world of which it is it's Hell to be a part."[34] One week later he proposed to her two plans of retreat: "I would retire with you & our child to a solitary island in the sea, would build a boat, & shut upon my retreat the flood-

Motes of a Sick Eye

gates of the world. . . . The other side of the alternative . . . is to form for ourselves a society of our own class, as much as possible, in intellect or in feelings."[35] Otherwise, because "good far more than evil impulses—love far more than hatred—has been to me, except as you have been it's object, the source of all sort[s] of mischief," he would withdraw alone "from the contagion" of what he had just called in *Adonais* "the world's slow stain." He does not mention the possibility of opening the floodgates which are not of the world.

On 25 June 1816 a squall had threatened to capsize the boat in which Shelley was sailing with Byron on Lake Geneva. Moore reported in his *Life of Byron* (1844) that, "as Shelley was no swimmer," Byron "insisted upon endeavouring, by some means, to save him. This offer, however, Shelley positively refused; and seating himself quietly upon a locker, and grasping the rings at each end firmly in his hands, declared his determination to go down in that position, without a struggle."[36] "I felt in this near prospect of death," Shelley wrote Peacock, "a mixture of sensations, among which terror entered, though but subordinately."[37] The next day he added a circumstance which gains interest in the light of Donald Reiman's speculation that the "Rousseau" of *The Triumph of Life* is the hero of *La Nouvelle Héloïse* rather than the author of the *Confessions*: "our danger from the storm took place precisely in the spot where Julie and her lover were nearly overset, and where St. Preux was tempted to plunge with her into the lake."[38]

Writing "in dejection, near Naples" two years later, Shelley had longed to "hear the sea/ Breathe o'er my dying brain its last monotony." And now, very near the end, he held curious conversations with Trelawny. There is no trusting Trelawny, but the fiction—if such it be—is uncomfortably close to what we know:

> "If we had been in a squall to-day [Trelawny said] with the main-sheet jammed, and the tiller put starboard instead of port, we should have had to swim for it."
>
> "Not I: I should have gone down with the rest of the pigs

in the bottom of the boat," said Shelley, meaning the iron pig-ballast.[39]

Shelley's joke meant more than that he could not swim, if we accept the record of the one lesson he may have taken:

> I was bathing one day in a deep pool in the Arno, and astonished the Poet by performing a series of aquatic gymnastics, which I had learnt from the natives of the South Seas. On my coming out, whilst dressing, Shelley said, mournfully:
> "Why can't I swim, it seems so very easy?"

Trelawny claims to have encouraged and briefly instructed his friend, who at once

> doffed his jacket and trowsers, kicked off his shoes and socks, and plunged in, and there he lay stretched out on the bottom like a conger eel, not making the least effort or struggle to save himself. He would have been drowned if I had not instantly fished him out. When he recovered his breath, he said:
> "I always find the bottom of the well, and they say Truth lies there. In another minute I should have found it, and you would have found an empty shell. It is an easy way of getting rid of the body."[40]

This version of the love-death metaphor had been with Shelley since *Alastor*, whose hero gazes into a well that

> Images all the woven boughs above,
> And each depending leaf, and every speck
> Of azure sky, darting between their chasms;
> Nor aught else in the liquid mirror laves
> Its portraiture, but some inconstant star.
>
> (459–463)

Looking up, the Poet meets "Two starry eyes, hung in the gloom of thought" (490). These belong to his Lady, the goal of the quest which began as a voyage:

> A restless impulse urged him to embark
> And meet lone Death on the drear ocean's waste;
> For well he knew that mighty Shadow loves
> The slimy caverns of the populous deep.
>
> (304-307)

In 1822 the play of light on the sea raised ghosts as well as metaphors. "After tea," Williams noted in his *Journal* for the sixth of May,

> while walking with S[helley] on the terrace and observing the effect of moonshine on the waters, he complained of being unusually nervous, and stopping short he grasped me violently by the arm and stared steadfastly on the white surf that broke upon the beach under our feet. Observing him sensibly affected I demanded of him if he was in pain—but he only answered, saying "There it is again!—there!"—He recovered after some time, and declared that he saw, as plainly as then he saw me a naked child rise from the sea, clap its hands as if in joy and smiling at him.[41]

Shelley had always been the prey of waking visions. So clearly had he seen his demonic assailant at Tan-yr-allt that he was able to draw its picture.[42] He fled the room one evening at Villa Diodati, nauseated by the fantasy that Mary's nipples were eyes. But the worst horror was reserved for Casa Magni:

> He dreamt that lying as he did in bed Edward & Jane came in to him, they were in the most horrible condition, their bodies lacerated—their bones starting through their skin, the faces pale yet stained with blood, they could hardly walk, but Edward was the weakest & Jane was supporting him—Edward said—Get up, Shelley, the sea is flooding the house & it is all coming down. S[helley] got up, he thought, & went to the [*sic*] his window that looked on the terrace & the sea & thought he saw the sea rushing in. Suddenly his vision changed & he saw the figure of himself strangling me, that had made him rush into my room, yet fearful of frightening me he dared

not approch [*sic*] the bed, when my jumping out awoke him, or as he phrased it caused his vision to vanish.⁴³

The waters of death not only invaded at last the margin that lay, for Shelley, between full consciousness and sleep; they vitiated his waking perceptions too. Allegra walked on moonlight and the sea; the sea flooded the house. The world "underneath the grave" reasserted its ancient prerogative over "that which thou beholdest" by manifesting its phantasmagoria to the bodily eye. There, in the world of putrefaction and potentiality,

> do inhabit
> The shadows of all forms that think and live
> Till death unite them and they part no more.
> (*P.U.*, I, 196–199)

Like the Magus Zoroaster, who "Met his own image walking in the garden," Shelley encountered on 23 June his doubleganger, his daemonic self or evil genius, who showed him the corruption of his heart by acting out the uxoricide hidden at its core. Marvell's comparison of the mind to an "ocean where each kind/ Does straight its own resemblance find" reflects a popular superstition which Shelley now had to stare down. "For know," the Earth had told Prometheus, "there are two worlds of life and death." Now there was only one. The *kakodaimon* bade the poet follow and merge with him there: "he told me," Mary recalled, "that he had had many visions lately—he had seen the figure of himself which met him as he walked on the terrace & said to him—'how long do you mean to be content.' "⁴⁴

Shelley pondered this invitation precisely as Faust had. Goethe's angels are empowered to save the man *wer immer strebend sich bemüht*, even though his strength is demonic; the striver's might enslaves the devils, who cannot harm him so long as he does not rest. "I always go on," Shelley told Trelawny, "until I am stopped, and I never am stopped."⁴⁵ But the demons can seize whoever finds the contentment against which his doubleganger warned the poet. It is easy to misinterpret the mood of

Motes of a Sick Eye

Shelley's last days. Outwardly at peace, he was racked with mental pain greater than he had ever known. "I am not well," he told Claire Clairmont. "My side torments me; my mind agitates the frame which it inhabits, and things go ill with me—that is within—for all external circumstances are auspicious."[46] Seven weeks later he clarified this paradox: "I read and enjoy for the first time these ten years something like health.—I find however that I must neither think or feel, or the pain returns to its old nest."[47]

Why, then, did he express to Horace Smith, a week before his death, such satisfaction with the passing moment? "I still inhabit this divine bay, reading Spanish dramas & sailing & listening to the most enchanting music. We have some friends on a visit to us, & my only regret is that the summer must ever pass."[48] The answer is again Goethean. If ever I lie on a bed of sloth, Faust bets Mephistopheles, if ever you flatter me that I find pleasure in myself, let that be my last day. The devil accepts the wager. Faust continues:

> Werd ich zum Augenblicke sagen:
> Verweile doch! Du bist so schön!
> Dann magst du mich in Fesseln schlagen,
> Dann will ich gern zugrunde gehn!
>
> (1699–1702)

The day Faust enjoins time to stop, the demons can clap him into chains, for that day he wishes to die. Shelley uttered the suicidal formula on 18 June (the same day he asked Trelawny to procure him prussic acid), when he wrote to John Gisborne, as follows, of the *Don Juan*: "Williams is captain, and we drive along this delightful bay in the evening wind, under the summer moon, until earth appears another world. Jane brings her guitar, and if the past and the future could be obliterated, the present would content me so well that I could say with Faust to the passing moment, 'Remain, thou, thou art so beautiful.' "[49]

This was the long-delayed signal. The devils could come and take him. "I stand, as it were," Shelley continued to Gisborne, "upon a precipice, which I have ascended with great, and cannot descend without *greater*, peril, and I am content if the heaven above me is calm for the passing moment." The sorcerer's pose of contentment with Faust's *Augenblick* and his invocation of celestial calmness were ironic, for they were spells. His words charmed his summer to end, like *Adonais*, with the riving of the "massy earth and spherèd skies." As he had warned Gisborne two months earlier, Goethe's drama is "an unfit study for any person who is a prey to the reproaches of memory, & the delusions of an imagination not to be restrained."[50]

The doubleganger had at this point been walking up and down outside Casa Magni for three days:

> Now Jane though a woman of sensibility has not much imagination & is not in the slightest degree nervous—neither in dreams or otherwise. She was standing one day, the day before I was taken ill, at a window that looked on the Terrace with Trelawny—it was day—she saw as she thought Shelley pass by the window, as he often was then, without a coat or jacket—he passed again—now as he passed both times the same way—and as from the side towards which he went each time there was no way to get back except past the window again (except over a wall twenty feet from the ground) she was struck at seeing him pass twice thus & looked out & seeing him no more she cried—"Good God can Shelley have leapt from the wall? Where can he be gone?" Shelley, said Trelawny—"no Shelley has past—What do you mean?" Trelawny says that she trembled exceedingly when she heard this & it proved indeed that Shelley had never been on the terrace & was far off at the time she saw him. Well we thought [no] more of these things & I slowly got better.[51]

Shelley's letter to Gisborne invited the devil to cross the threshold. In the early morning hours of 23 June, it invaded Mary's bedroom. Eternity had inaugurated the last phase of its assault upon time.

Very near the end Ned Williams cracked an anti-ecclesiastical joke whose weird aptness forbids a smile. Here is the final entry in his *Journal*:

> *Thursday, July 4.* Fine. Processions of Priests & religiosi have for several days past been active in their prayers for rain—but the Gods are either angry or Nature is too powerful.[52]

The same day Shelley sent Jane an odd little note, to which she replied, half humorously, on 6 July: "Why do you talk of never enjoying moments like the past, are you going to join your friend Plato or do you expect I shall do so soon?"[53] Two days later her husband and Shelley were at sea; the weather broke, and Williams tried to uncleat the halyards. Had the metaphor come right at last? How unlikely is it that Shelley seized his friend by the arm, "as if in anger"?

Blake was the amanuensis of authors in eternity, and "daimons" descended to give Yeats "metaphors for poetry." Through the window of Shelley's art we envision or hallucinate a midnight thronged with dreadful faces, "shapes too bright to see"; in our poverty of doctrine, we cannot tell if they are angels or devils. The doublegangers who dwell in the dark mirror-realm "underneath the grave" may or may not be our true selves; we should in any case beware of them. "Remember," a "communicator" told Yeats, "we will deceive you if we can."

Shelley asks whether we are in fact the dreams and light imaginings of something else, and if so, to what end. Is incarnation the process of becoming by which the comatose Godhead awakens and names Himself? Coleridge compared the new-born child's imaginative construction of his own identity to "the eternal act of creation," the poetic Word by which infinity defines itself: I AM THAT I AM. This could be the intended use of pain, disease, and the body's eventual betrayal of every noble sentiment. Perhaps we have willed ourselves into three-dimensional existence seeking to achieve a higher degree of consciousness by splintering our fingernails against the dead wall of limitation.

A reading of Shelley compels these reflections and their parody. His images, for all their precision, seem to bleed away into white light about the edges. Material existence was for him, as for all gnostics, the eclipse of eternity's fiery sphere; a crown of incandescent vapors played and flickered beyond the rim of the round, black blot. But was the sun really there? Perhaps Shelley saw no more than the aura that transfigures the epileptic's world as he wails upon the slippery, steep, and narrow verge of seizure. The vulgar cry of "vagueness" against his imagery is justified, and I hope to have shown that it is entirely beside the point.

God may in the end be a fever of ourselves. Shelley never denied the possibility. His only certainty was the skepticism implied in the name Sophia Prunicos. When the Holy Spirit took flesh from the sea, she fell into blindness and vindictiveness. We are her temple, Saint Paul says, and our wisdom, insofar as it is of the body only, will be left-handed, adulterous, and for sale.

Appendix

Dr. Polidori and the Genesis of *Frankenstein*[1]

The received history of the contest in writing ghost-stories at Villa Diodati during the "wet, ungenial" June of 1816 is well known to every student of the Byron-Shelley circle.[2] It is, as we shall see, an almost total fabrication.

I

On 20 October 1820, Hester Thrale Piozzi wrote from Bath to Frances Burney D'Arblay, "How changed is the taste of verse, prose, and painting! since *le bon vieux temps*, dear Madam! Nothing attracts us but what terrifies, and is within—*if* within—a hair's-breadth of positive disgust. . . . some of the strange things they *write* remind me of Squoire Richard's visit to the Tower Menagerie, when he says 'They are *pure* grim devils,'—particularly a wild and hideous tale called Frankenstein."[3]

Never, it has been thought, since Donne, Jonson, and every other wit in London composed commendatory verses to *Coryats Crudities*, has so much talent joined in a common project to so little purpose. Yet Mrs. Piozzi, who had become rather *derrière-garde* since her Streatham days, need not have worried. The heyday of the *Schauerroman* was done, as the contestants themselves seem to have realized. Shelley's and "Claire" Clairmont's stories have vanished without a trace, and Byron abandoned his after a few pages. *Frankenstein* (1818) contains no supernature, and in the one other Diodati story published with the author's full will, Polidori's *Ernestus Berchtold* (1819), a ghost and a djinn make only brief, embarrassed, peripheral appearances.

Byron's vampire-story was published as "A Fragment" with *Mazeppa* in 1819, but only in self-defense.[4] "Poor Polidori" had been foolish enough to leave the manuscript of his *The Vampyre* with the Countess of Breuss, who, by previously challenging his ability to complete Byron's story, had ensured his doing so. She then gave it to another person, presumably the mysterious Mme. Gatelier, who forwarded it to Henry Colburn. He in turn printed the tale under Byron's name in *The New Monthly Magazine* for April of 1819. Polidori's immediate protest that the work was his own touched off a dog-fight which, even by the standards of the Regency publishing world, was exceptionally savage. From a free-for-all involving Colburn, his editor (who promptly resigned), John Murray, Messrs. Sherwood, Neely, and Jones, and Byron himself, only Polidori emerged with his reputation very much the worse for wear. Although he was the one person who had acted both honorably and in full possession of the facts, the doctor was a born bungler and remains to this day unfairly branded a pirate, parasite, and liar.[5] The triumphant word was Byron's, in his disclaimer written to the editor of *Galignani's Magazine:* "If the book is clever, it would be base to deprive the real writer, whoever he may be, of his honours; and if stupid, I desire the responsibility of nobody's dullness but my own. . . . I have besides a personal dislike to 'Vampires,' and the little acquaintance I have with them would by no means induce me to divulge their secrets."[6]

Byron's vampire, Augustus Darvell, is another in the long file of criminal wanderers who fly, harried by the specter of sadistic love, through the proud, bad verses of the so-called Oriental Tales. In June 1816 Byron was writing the psychosexual picaresque out of his system in what is probably his masterpiece of non-humorous verse, the Third Canto of *Childe Harold's Pilgrimage*. This poem was completed ten days after he made his abortive start on "A Fragment." He was, moreover, growing weary of narrative verse and about to turn mainly to drama and satire. Gothic prose must have seemed a stale departure. "A Fragment" ends with Darvell's "undeath" in a Muslim graveyard from a strange inner corruption. He rots before our very eyes. Byron gives him up as a sorry spectacle indeed, and the reader is likewise content to leave him lying there in the moonlight, like John Randolph's mackerel, to shine and stink.

Polidori's novel on the same subject is a far from contemptible piece of work, though it is not read today. A sensationally popular stage version was produced in Paris on 13 June 1820;[7] J. R. Planché's "free translation" of this piece was written, rehearsed, and rushed onto the stage of the English Opera House by 9 August.[8] That the success of this play was not matched until the debut of Richard Brinsley Peake's *Presumption: or the Fate of Frankenstein* at the same theater in 1823, is surely one of literary history's smaller ironies. Both melodramas were at last pitchforked into oblivion by a work of near-genius—*Der Freischütz*.[9]

Lord Ruthven, Polidori's version of Augustus Darvell, is done to seeming death by the comparatively clean means of a bandit's bullet. The change is symptomatic, for the doctor orders us out of the miasmic closeness of Byron's atmosphere into the tonic air of a deliberately misleading realism. He is sometimes even witty, as when he describes Aubrey's education: "Left also to himself by guardians, who thought it their duty merely to take care of his fortune, while they relinquished the more important charge of his mind to the care of mercenary subalterns, he cultivated more his imagination than his judgment. He had, hence, that high romantic feeling of honour and candour, which daily ruins so many milliners' apprentices."[10] The sanity and gentility of Polidori's narrative pose enforce by contrast the irruptive shock of the unthinkable.

Although Lord Byron's public personality was more a product of the early Gothic romance than a direct influence upon later examples of the genre, his portrait in Lord Ruthven is unmistakable. So also is that of the vampire's naïve companion: "allowing his imagination to picture every thing that flattered its propensity to extravagant ideas, he soon formed this object into the hero of a romance, and determined to observe the offspring of his fancy, rather than the person before him."[11] Aubrey's final recognition of Ruthven as he really is does not prevent a catastrophe as dreadful as that which struck down his Byronomane creator.

His Lordship is a leech. But just as no man is a poet, much less a matinee idol, to his physician, so no master credits his valet with a soul. Polidori to Byron was "exactly the kind of person to whom, if he fell overboard, one would hold out a straw to know if the adage be true that drowning men catch at straws."[12] Polidori came from a distinguished literary family (his father had been Alfieri's secretary) and was the uncle of Dante Gabriel, William Michael, and Christina Rossetti. Young, classically handsome, and possessed of a gift for writing which surprises every modern reader who has taken the judgments of the Shelley circle at face value,[13] he was fatally conceited. His vanity and sensitivity to every imagined slight, his "eternal nonsense, and *tracasseries*,"[14] make Goldsmith look in the comparison like Patient Grissil. None the less, when he drank prussic acid at the age of twenty-five,[15] England lost a religious novelist of some promise. Like Keats, whose dates (1795–1821) he shares, he composed his own epitaph. He found it in the plea of his mythical ancestor to another wanderer and former comrade and placed it, slightly altered, on the title page of *Ximenes*: "Parce pias scelerare manus: non me tibi Troia Externum tulit. . . . Quòd Polydorus ego."[16]

2

In her 1831 Introduction Mary Shelley claimed that the story independently begun by Polidori at Villa Diodati was "some terrible idea about a skull-headed lady, who was so punished for peeping through a keyhole—what to see I forget—something very shocking and wrong of course; but when she was reduced to a worse condition than the renowned Tom of Coventry, he did not know what to do with her, and was obliged to despatch her to the tomb of the Capulets, the only place for which she was fitted" (p. 9).

When Mary Shelley admits to forgetting particulars, we may usually assume that she remembers nothing. No statement in her account of the writing party at Diodati, or even of the inception of her own idea, can be trusted, as we shall now see. For example, she recalls that, "Some volumes of ghost stories, translated from the German into French, fell into our hands. There was the History of the Inconstant Lover, who, when he thought to clasp the bride to whom he had pledged his vows, found himself in the arms of the pale ghost of her whom he had deserted" (p. 9). These two volumes were the work of Jean Baptiste Benoît Eyriès (1767–1846), who published them anonymously as *Fantasmagoriana, ou Recueil d'Histoires d'Apparitions de Spectres, Revenans, Fantômes, etc.; traduit de l'allemand, par un Amateur* (Paris, 1812). Mary Shelley's "History of the Inconstant Lover" is actually called "La Morte Fiancée," and the ghost who takes Libussa's place in Count Marino's bed on their wedding night is not that of the jilted Apollonia, but of a lady deserted some two or three centuries earlier. Mrs. Shelley continues:

> There was the tale of the sinful founder of his race, whose miserable doom it was to bestow the kiss of death on all the younger sons of his fated house, just when they reached the age of promise. His gigantic, shadowy form, clothed like the ghost in Hamlet, *in complete armour, but with the beaver up,* was seen at midnight, by the moon's fitful beams, to advance slowly along the gloomy avenue. The shape was lost beneath the shadow of the castle walls; *but soon a gate swung back, a step was heard, the door of the chamber opened,* and he advanced to the couch of the blooming youths, cradled in healthy sleep. Eternal sorrow sat upon his face as he bent down and kissed the forehead of the boys, who from that hour withered like flowers snapt upon the stalk. *I have not seen these stories since then; but their incidents are as fresh in my mind as if I had read them yesterday.*[17]
>
> (p. 9)

"Les Portraits de Famille" is the story here recalled in an altered form. Eyriès's ghost wears "un manteau gris," but no armor; his journey from the garden to the children's bedside is silent and invisible. None of this would be of the slightest importance, were it not that Mary Shelley insists so positively upon the accuracy of her memory. If Italian noblemen have sexual intercourse with the wrong ghosts, and Hamlet's father does not stamp along corridors "with the beaver up," what credit can there be for the skull-headed lady? Polidori's own word, introductory to *Ernestus Berchtold*, is preferable: "The tale here presented to the public is the one I began at Coligny [*sic*], when Frankenstein was planned, and when a noble author having determined to descend from his lofty range, gave up a few hours to a tale of terror, and wrote the fragment published at the end of Mazeppa."[18]

The failure of every commentator (to the best of my knowledge) to cast serious doubt upon the accuracy of Mary Shelley's Introduction is probably owing to the extreme rarity of the *Fantasmagoriana*,[19] described by the only scholar who claims to have read it as "a poor sort of book."[20] The discovery of the faultiness of Mrs. Shelley's recollections in this regard prompts a further examination of her account of the original conception of *Frankenstein*. The entire story quickly falls to the ground.

Mrs. Shelley records the sequence of events as follows: (1) the party read the *Fantasmagoriana* during some wet weather; (2) "'We will each write a ghost story,' said Lord Byron; and his proposition was acceded to. There were four of us"; (3) "I busied myself *to think of a story*—a story to rival those which had excited us to this task. . . . *Have you thought of a story?* I was asked each morning, and each morning I was forced to reply with a mortifying negative"; and finally,

> Many and long were the conversations between Lord Byron and Shelley, to which I was a devout but nearly silent listener. During one of these, various philosophical doctrines were discussed, and among others the nature of the principle of life, and whether there was any probability of its ever being

discovered and communicated. . . . Night waned upon this talk, and even the witching hour had gone by, before we retired to rest. When I placed my head upon my pillow, I did not sleep, nor could I be said to think. My imagination, unbidden, possessed and guided me, gifting the successive images that arose in my mind with a vividness far beyond the usual bounds of reverie. I saw—with shut eyes, but acute mental vision—I saw the pale student of unhallowed arts kneeling beside the thing he had put together.

(pp. 10–11)

Polidori's *Diary* records for 17 June 1816, "The ghost-stories are begun by all but me."[21] 16 June is the probable date of Byron's suggestion,[22] for several reasons. First, enthusiasm for the project waned quickly, so we may assume that it was formed no more than a week earlier. 14 June was the first time since the tenth that the entire party (there were, of course, *five* of them) had been together at Diodati. But the weather was dry, for Polidori "rode almost all day," and Mary Shelley says that the *Fantasmagoriana* was read to pass the time while "incessant rain . . . confined us for days to the house" (p. 9). It showered on 15 June, and Polidori sprained his ankle on the wet grass after leaping over a wall; after-dinner conversation, however, involved a play Polidori had written and then a scientific discussion with Shelley. On the sixteenth the rain must have begun in earnest, for Polidori records that Shelley "slept here, with Mrs. S. and Miss Claire Clairmont." They would not have done so except for really nasty weather, as their own house, the Maison Chappuis, was but an eight-minute walk from Villa Diodati.

The discussion between Shelley and Polidori on the fifteenth was noted down by the latter as "a conversation about principles, —whether man was to be thought merely an instrument." This is almost certainly the conversation alluded to by Mary Shelley and quoted above, regarding "the nature of the principle of life."[23] Mrs. Shelley remembered Byron as her husband's partner in this discussion, but will that bear even superficial examination? Shelley was an accomplished amateur chemist, and Polidori not only a physician, but a first-rate one and fresh out of Edinburgh.[24] He is far more likely than his noble employer to have involved himself, not to say held up his own end, in the following conversation:

> They talked of the experiments of Dr. Darwin ... who preserved a piece of vermicelli in a glass case, till by some extraordinary means it began to move with voluntary motion. Not thus, after all, would life be given. Perhaps a corpse would be re-animated; galvanism had given token of such things: perhaps the component parts of a creature might be manufactured, brought together, and endued with vital warmth.
>
> (pp. 10–11)

The conclusive piece of evidence is that Polidori had the year before published a dissertation on somnambulism misleadingly entitled *De Oneirodynia*.[25] Sleep-walking was then a topic embraced with what we now call hypnotism under the general heading of "animal magnetism." As a pseudoscience it is forever associated with the name of Friedrich (or Franz) Anton Mesmer, who died in the year that Polidori received his degree. On the respectable side this enquiry into the nature of a subtle, universal fluid became the researches into galvanism and electricity of Sir Humphry Davy, whose *Elements of Chemical Philosophy* (1812)[26] Mary Shelley got around to reading in October, while composing what is probably now Chapter 2 of *Frankenstein*. It is also closely related to Erasmus Darwin's experiments in medicine, botany, and electro-chemical tropism. Finally, of course, animal magnetism is linked with the name of Benjamin Franklin, who headed the French royal commission which in 1784 exploded Mesmer's theories. His experiment with the kite and key is reproduced by Victor Frankenstein's father in Chapter 1 of the 1818 edition of that novel.

Polidori was perforce an expert. When on the evening of 15 June "all agreed" that his play (either *Cajetan* or *Boadicea*) "was worth nothing,"[27] he made a typically desperate attempt to soothe his injured vanity by dragging the conversation around to his most recent undoubted success.[28]

If we can accept Mary Shelley's word that this was the same night in which she had her waking dream of the scientist's filthy creation standing "at his bedside, opening his curtains, and looking on him with yellow, watery, but speculative eyes" (p. 11), then the entire chronology of conception is altered.[29] The nucleus of the story was already fully developed in her mind when on the following evening the party read two of the eight stories in the *Fantasmagoriana* and Byron made his suggestion. The next morning she was at her desk with the others.

Most scholars have heretofore assumed either that Mary Shelley started a different story, later dropped, on 17 June,[30] or that she invented her "modern Prometheus" and his profane Adam after "the abortive tales [of] the others in the house party had already [been] begun and abandoned."[31] The difficulty has always been that Mary Shelley's journal is missing for the all-important period from 14 May 1815, to 20 July 1816. In fairness to the lady, we may assume that she lost it before 1831.

3

The importance of all this is that it shifts critical emphasis with regard to *Frankenstein*, enabling us to see the novel unembarrassed by the Gothic tradition, some of whose ancillary characteristics it none the less preserves. The *Fantasmagoriana* could not in any case have been much of a source, for, excepting Calzolaro's unfulfilled promise (in "La Tête de Mort") to afford his audience "quelques moments agréables avec des expériences d'électricité et de magnétisme" (I, 242), not one concession is made to contemporary psychology and physical science, or to the aesthetic truth of any age. *Frankenstein* may be vulgarly termed science fiction, but more properly Mary Shelley wished to write an anti-humanist morality quite exempt, as Shelley put it in the 1818 Preface, "from the disadvantages of a mere tale of spectres or enchantment." Factitious science, "however impossible as a physical fact," was to afford "a point of view to the imagination for the delineating of human passions more comprehensive and commanding than any which the ordinary relations of existing events can yield" (p. 5).[32]

This embarrassment with the outdated "shudder-novel" was shared by Polidori and, probably, was the major cause of the other contestants' rapid loss of interest in their own tales. The doctor candidly admitted in his Introduction to *Ernestus Berchtold* that, "A tale that rests upon improbabilities, must generally disgust a rational mind; I am therefore afraid that, though I have thrown the superior agency into the back ground as much as was in my power, still, that many readers will think the same moral, and the same colouring, might have been given to characters acting under the ordinary agencies of life; I believe it, but had agreed to write a supernatural tale, and that does not allow of a completely every-day narrative" (pp. vii–viii).

Polidori makes amends for the condition unhappily agreed to by an understatement of narrative and a clinical accuracy of natural description seldom encountered (to say the least) in the contemporary novel. He numbers the streaks of the tulip with the eye of a trained botanist. His landscapes are those of a naturalist's pencil sketch, not of a Salvator Rosa canvas. By contrast, Mary Shelley's "sublime" diction in, say, the key Mont Blanc passage, protests too much and spoils the effect by forcing it. You can lead a reader to the Arve glacier, but you can't make him look. The only stylistic faults of *Ernestus Berchtold* (which certainly deserves a modern edition) are technical. Polidori's sentences often either lack a main verb or else pile up one coordinate clause on another and run on and on for pages.

Polidori thought of himself primarily as a religious poet, though his best work is a novel whose subtitle, "the Modern Oedipus," imitates "the Modern Prometheus." Mary Shelley too tried to give the novel mythic dimensions. "Supremely frightful," she said of her Promethean scientist, "would be the effect of any human endeavour to mock the stupendous mechanism of the

Creator of the world. His success would terrify the artist; he would rush away from his odious handiwork, horror-stricken" (p. 11). Four years later she attempted two verse plays, *Prosperine* and *Midas*. When in 1819 Leigh Hunt told her that, "Polyphemus.... always appears to me a pathetic rather than a monstrous person, though his disappointed sympathies at last made him cruel," she answered, "I have written a book in defense of Polypheme have I not?"[33]

Mary Shelley had at this time a sneaking fondness for Polidori, whom the others so despised. Both of them felt out of place in the company of two geniuses and an overgrown nymphet: "since incapacity and timidity always prevented my mingling in the nightly conversations of Diodati, they were, as it were, entirely tête-à-tête between my Shelley and Albé."[34]

Whereas the doctor reacted to the inequality of the situation with bumptious violence, Mary Shelley wrote a story for which, she insisted, "I certainly did not owe the suggestion of one incident, nor scarcely of one train of feeling, to my husband" (p. 12). On the eighteenth of June she called Polidori "her brother (younger),"[35] which is surely the kindest word anyone had thrown his way for days. Mrs. Shelley was pleased with the queer man who had given her the vital spark for her story.[36] But it is not for this reason that she would have resented the later, metaphorically ironic remark that "*Frankenstein* was written when her brain, magnetized by [Shelley's] companionship, was capable of an effort never to be repeated."[37]

Notes

Introduction

1. *Theology Today*, V (January, 1949), p. 591.

2. Letter to John Gisborne, 26 January 1822; letter to Charles Ollier, 16 February 1821. *The Letters of Percy Bysshe Shelley*, ed. Frederick L. Jones (Oxford, 1964), II, 388, 263.

3. This vexed term here denotes an impulse in the poet, not a quality of his finished work. The latter is of course the prevailing academic acceptation. See I. A. Richards, *Practical Criticism* (New York, 1929), pp. 280–287.

4. William Butler Yeats, *Essays and Introductions* (London, 1961), I. *Ideas of Good and Evil*, "The Philosophy of Shelley's Poetry" (1900), p. 65.

5. *The English Romantic Poets: A Review of Research*, ed. Thomas M. Raysor, 2nd ed. (New York, 1956), "Shelley," p. 204.

6. I. A. Richards, *Principles of Literary Criticism*, 3rd ed. (London, 1928), p. 218.

7. T. S. Eliot, "The Metaphysical Poets" (1921), *Selected Essays*, 2nd ed. (New York, 1950), p. 247.

8. T. S. Eliot, "Shelley and Keats," *The Use of Poetry and the Use of Criticism* (London, 1933), p. 88.

9. *Ibid.*, pp. 99–100.

10. Letter to John Trusler, 23 August 1799. *The Complete Writings of William Blake*, ed. Geoffrey Keynes (London, 1957), p. 793.

I Disinheritance

1. This development is outlined by Kenneth Neill Cameron in *The Young Shelley: Genesis of a Radical*, 2nd ed. (New York, 1962), ch. 2, "From Fox to Godwin," pp. 52–100.

2. Letter to John Murray, 25 December 1822. *The Works of Lord Byron. . . . Letters and Journals*, ed. Rowland E. Prothero (1898–1901), VI, 157.

3. For a handy summary of recent work in the field, see Sir Ivor Jennings, *Party Politics*, II. *The Growth of Parties* (Cambridge, 1961), pp. 26–82.

4. *Ibid.*, p. 79.

5. Cameron, pp. 60–61.

6. Letter to Elizabeth Hitchener, 26 January 1812. *Letters*, I, 239.

7. Letter of 23 April 1810. *Letters*, I, 10.

8. Letter to Lady Jane Shelley, December (?) 1856. Quoted by Thomas Jefferson Hogg, *The Life of Percy Bysshe Shelley* (1858), I, 7–8.

9. Hogg, I, 9.

10. *St. Irvyne; or, The Rosicrucian: A Romance* (1811). *The Complete Works of Percy Bysshe Shelley*, Julian Edition, ed. Roger Ingpen and Walter E. Peck (London, 1926–1930), V, 180.

11. Harry Levin, *The Overreacher. A Study of Christopher Marlowe*, 2nd ed. (Boston, 1964), pp. 26–27.

12. Hogg, I, 40.

13. Cameron, pp. 55–56.

14. Letter from Mary Shelley to Maria Gisborne, ca. 27 August 1822. *The Letters of Mary W. Shelley*, ed. Frederick L. Jones (Norman, 1944), I, 189.

15. Letter to Hogg, ? 14 May 1811. *Letters*, I, 85.

16. *Ibid.*

17. Letter of 17 May 1811. *Letters*, I, 90.

18. Letter to Hogg, 11 January 1811. *Letters*, I, 42.

19. *Ibid.*

20. Frederick L. Jones long ago proved that *The Necessity of*

Atheism was mainly Hogg's work. See "Hogg and *The Necessity of Atheism*," *PMLA*, LII (1937), 423–426; also Cameron, pp. 93–95.

21. Letter of 10 January 1812. *Letters*, I, 228.

22. Letter from P.B.S. to Timothy Shelley, ? 13 April 1811. *Letters*, I, 60.

23. Hogg, I, 97.

24. Eliot, "Shelley and Keats," p. 89.

25. Hogg, I, 104.

26. *Ibid.*, I, 99.

27. *Ibid.*, I, 141.

28. *The Complete Works of William Hazlitt*, ed. P. P. Howe (London, 1932), XI, *The Spirit of the Age*, "William Godwin," p. 24.

29. *The Collected Writings of Thomas De Quincey*, ed. David Masson (London, 1897), XI, *Notes on Gilfillan's Literary Portraits*, "William Godwin," p. 328.

30. *The Spirit of the Age*, p. 27.

31. *Ibid.*, p. 26.

32. The third of these, *Imogen: a Pastoral Romance from the Ancient British* (1784), has been recovered and reprinted in *Bulletin of the New York Public Library*, LXVII (1963), 17-32, 119-134, 191-202, 261-270, 328-340, 395-410.

33. *Sketches of History in Six Sermons* (1784), I. "The Resignation of Aaron," p. 20.

34. *Ibid.*, III. "The Arraignment of Jesus," p. 88.

35. Preface to the 1832 reprint of *Fleetwood: or, The New Man of Feeling* (1805) in Bentley's "Standard Novels" series. Reprinted in *The Adventures of Caleb Williams: or, Things As They Are*, ed. with an Introduction by George Sherburn (New York, 1960), p. xxix. All quotations from *Caleb Williams* are taken from this edition. Sherburn's basic text is that of the third edition (1797) collated with Bentley's "Standard Novels" edition (1831).

36. Sherburn, p. 321.

37. *Ibid.*, p. 354.

38. *Ibid.*, p. 146.

39. *Ibid.*, p. 212.

40. *Ibid.*, p. 169.

41. *Ibid.*, p. 313.

42. *Ibid.*, pp. 166–167.

43. *Ibid.*, p. 372.

44. *Ibid.*, p. 279.

45. *Ibid.*, p. 343.

46. See the opening paragraphs of *A Defence of Poetry, Works,* VII, 109.

47. Sherburn, p. 370.

48. The manuscript collection of James Richard Scarlett, eighth baron Abinger, of Clees Hall, Bures, Suffolk. Sixteen-reel microfilm copies of these papers exist at the Bodleian Library and Duke University. The Abinger MSS. have not yet been catalogued, but the Godwin materials are contained in Bodleian Reels 72–76. For a detailed description, see Lewis Patton, "The Shelley-Godwin Collection of Lord Abinger," *Library Notes* (Duke University Library), no. 27 (April, 1953), pp. 11–17. Italics within quotations throughout the remainder of this chapter are mine.

49. Abinger MSS., "Memoirs," pp. 34–35. This document is sometimes wrongly referred to as the "Autobiographical Fragment." On a half-sheet of paper preceding the MS. itself a hand other than Godwin's has inscribed "Autobiographical Fragment/Complete 1756–1769," but at the top of Godwin's own first page he has written "Memoirs," followed by two letters which (at least in the Bodleian microfilm copy) are illegible. These reminiscences are continued in an additional fragment bearing the superscription, "Autobiographical Notes/1773–1796."

50. *Ibid.*, pp. 42–43.

51. *Ibid.*, p. 35.

52. Sherburn, p. 364.

53. Abinger MSS., undated letter to the Rev. Samuel Newton. It is probably the provoker of or the reply to Newton's letter of 4 December 1793.

54. *The Spirit of the Age,* p. 25.

55. *Collected Writings,* III, *London Reminiscences,* ch. 1, "Sir Humphry Davy: Mr. Godwin: Mrs. Grant of Laggan," p. 25.

56. 1832 preface to *Fleetwood.* Sherburn, p. xxvii.

57. Suppressed Preface to the first edition of *Caleb Williams* (12 May 1794). Sherburn, p. xxiii.

58. Sherburn, p. 364.

59. *Ibid.*, p. 344.

60. *Memoirs of the Author of a Vindication of the Rights of Woman* (1798), pp. 196–197, 199.

61. *A Defence of Poetry, Works,* VII, 118.

II The Rosy Cross and the Wandering Jew

1. "Kipling Good," *The Spectator,* no. 6993 (6 July 1962), p. 13.

2. Hogg, I, 69–70.

3. Cameron, p. 98.

4. The text, authorship, dating and publication history of this poem are excessively problematic. See Cameron, pp. 335–342.

5. Other minor uses of the legend of Ahasuerus include "Ghasta; or, The Avenging Demon" in *Original Poetry by Victor and Cazire* (1810), "The Wandering Jew's Soliloquy" (1810?), and *Alastor* (1815), ll. 675–681. "The Assassins" (1814), in which this figure begins to metamorphose into Prometheus, will be discussed in Chapter Five.

6. For my discussion of the pre-Romantic Ahasuerus and of Schubart's poem, I am greatly indebted to Edgar Rosenberg, *From Shylock to Svengali: Jewish Stereotypes in English Fiction* (Stanford, 1960), pp. 190–199. The best extended study of Ahasuerus is Werner Zirus, *Der ewige Jude in der Dichtung, vornehmlich in der englischen und deutschen* (Leipzig, 1928). See also Eino Railo, *The Haunted Castle: A Study of the Elements of English Romanticism* (London, 1927).

7. *Works,* I, 152.

8. *Works,* IV, 347–396.

9. Published by 11 December 1810, but dated 1811. *Works,* V, 105–199.

10. This phrase is transferred verbatim to Wolfstein in the "Conclusion" of *St. Irvyne* (198). All references are to the first, four-volume edition of *St. Leon.*

11. *Frankenstein; or, The Modern Prometheus* (1818; 1831). Page references throughout the book are to the Doubleday "Dolphin" edition of *Frankenstein* (Garden City, N. Y., ca. 1960). The text is that of the revised, improved, Bentley's Standard Novels edition of

1831, and includes both Mary Shelley's Introduction to that and Shelley's unsigned Preface to the first edition.

12. Hogg, I, 54. Cf. Shelley's letter to Godwin, 29 July 1812: "But *words* are the very things that so eminently contribute to the growth and establishment of prejudice. . . . words are merely signs of ideas. . . . The science of things is superior to the science of words." *Letters*, I, 317–318. The italics are Shelley's.

13. *Ibid.*, I, 58.

14. *Ibid.*, I, 59.

15. *Ibid.*, I, 60.

16. *Ibid.*, I, 60, 62.

17. *Ibid.*, I, 63.

18. *Ibid.*, I, 64.

19. See Walter Edwin Peck, "Shelley and the Abbé Barruel," *PMLA*, XXXVI (1921), 347–353. All my page references will be to the first American edition of the *Memoirs*, 4 vols. (Hartford-New York-Elizabethtown, 1799); this is taken directly from the second London edition.

20. Letter of 27 February 1812. *Letters*, I, 264.

21. See Bernard Fay, *Revolution and Freemasonry, 1680–1800* (Boston, 1935); Gaston Martin, *La Franc-Maçonnerie Française et la Préparation de la Révolution*, 2nd ed. (Paris, 1926); Crane Brinton, *The Jacobins*, 2nd ed. (New York, 1961). Martin (p. 280) explodes Barruel and his English counterpart, John Robison, author of *Proofs of a Conspiracy against all the Religions and Governments of Europe, carried on in the Secret Meetings of Free Masons, Illuminati and Reading Societies* (1797). Brinton refutes (pp. 14–15) the charge that the Jacobin Clubs grew out of the Lodges.

22. See Arthur Edward Waite, *The Brotherhood of the Rosy Cross* (London, 1926), p. 430; F. de P. Castells, *Our Ancient Brethren the Originators of Freemasonry* (London, 1932), p. 230.

23. Lewis Spence, *An Encyclopaedia of Occultism*, 2nd ed. (New Hyde Park, New York, 1960), s.v. "Rosicrucians."

24. Letter of 20 December 1810. *Letters*, I, 27, 29. The italics are Shelley's.

25. Letter of 3 January 1811. *Letters*, I, 35–36. The italics are Shelley's.

26. Note to VII, 135–136. *The Complete Poetical Works of Percy Bysshe Shelley*, ed. Thomas Hutchinson (Oxford, 1905), p. 820.

27. See also the series "Four Poems to Mary" in *The Esdaile Poems*, ed. Neville Rogers (Oxford, 1966).

28. Letter to Hogg, 3 January 1811. *Letters*, I, 35.

29. Letter to Elizabeth Hitchener, 11 June 1811. *Letters*, I, 100-101. The italics are Shelley's.

30. Note to VII, 13. Hutchinson, p. 812.

31. Letter of 15 August 1821. *Letters*, II, 339.

32. *Der Fall Wagner* (1888), 3. The translation is mine. The italics are Nietzsche's.

III Mont Blanc and the Magus Zoroaster

1. *Mary Shelley's Journal*, ed. Frederick L. Jones (Norman, 1947), p. 53.

2. *The Spirit of the Age*, p. 23.

3. Hazlitt made his one direct reference to Frankenstein's monster in a discussion of the novels of Charles Brockden Brown four years later. "American Literature—Dr. Channing" (*Edinburgh Review*, October, 1829), *Works*, XVI, 319.

4. *Frankenstein*, ed. cit., pp. 13-14.

5. *Child of Light, a Reassessment of Mary Wollstonecraft Shelley* (Hadleigh, Essex, 1951), pp. 135-136.

6. *Journal* (22 July 1816), p. 51.

7. Shelley wrote, probably of this scene, that "The encounter and argument between Frankenstein and the Being on the sea of ice, almost approaches, in effect, to the expostulation of Caleb Williams with Falkland. It reminds us, indeed, somewhat of the style and character of that admirable writer, to whom the author has dedicated his work, and whose productions he seems to have studied." "On *Frankenstein*," *Works*, VI, 264. "Sea of ice" most likely translates *Mer de Glace*, as the Arctic is referred to later in the same review as "the Frozen Ocean."

8. *The Spirit of the Age*, p. 23.

9. *Pierre; or, the Ambiguities*, ed. Henry A. Murray (New York, 1949), p. 194. Melville purchased a copy of *Frankenstein* from Richard Bentley in London some time between the eighteenth and the twenty-fourth of December, 1849. *Pierre*, of course, was published in 1852.

10. *The Subtler Language* (Baltimore, 1959), Chapter 6. My departures from Wasserman's interpretation express my discomfort with his method. It seems to me dangerous to apply Shelley's philosophical essays at all rigorously to his poems. His political prose and his attacks on religious establishment are consistent and, the few times they are relevant, safe enough; the richly figurative *Defence of Poetry* is as much a poem as a discourse. But such ontological exercises as the "Essay on Life" (1818) were devised by an intellect which, in its anxiety to define its own limits, asserted answers to questions which the poems—and especially "Mont Blanc"—always reopened. The tangled metaphysics of the letters to Hogg and Miss Hitchener should warn us that Shelley's mind, for all its love of system, was not systematic. The "Intellectual Philosophy" which Wasserman derives from the prose does not, I think, exist anywhere else. To adapt Pascal's reflection, the imagination has reasons which the reason knows nothing of.

11. Letter of 25 July 1816. *Letters*, I, 500.

12. These connotations were first detected by Harold Bloom, *Shelley's Mythmaking* (New Haven, 1959), p. 27.

13. Letter to Peacock, 6 November 1818. *Letters*, II, 47.

14. Letter to Peacock, 25 February 1819. *Letters*, II, 80.

15. *Ibid.*, p. 79.

16. Letter to Peacock, 23–24 January 1819. *Letters*, II, 73.

17. Letter to Peacock, 23 March 1819. *Letters*, II, 86.

18. Letter to Peacock, 23–24 January 1819. *Letters*, II, 73.

19. Letter to Peacock, 17 or 18 December 1818. *Letters*, II, 62–63.

20. See C. E. Pulos, *The Deep Truth. A Study of Shelley's Scepticism*, 2nd ed. (Lincoln, 1962), p. 62.

21. Letter to Thomas Butts, 22 November 1802. *The Complete Writings of William Blake*, ed. Geoffrey Keynes (London, 1957), p. 817.

22. *Ibid.*, p. 818.

23. *Works*, VII, 109.

24. *Works*, VI, 141.

25. This summary derives mainly from Edwin Hatch, *The Influence of Greek Ideas on Christianity*, 2nd ed., ed. Frederick C. Grant (New York, 1957), pp. 174–188.

26. Letters to Elizabeth Hitchener, 11 June 1811, and to Hogg, 6 January 1811. *Letters*, I, 101, 39. The italics are Shelley's.

27. Letter of 23 July 1816. *Letters*, I, 499.

28. "At a later period in Persia, it [the power of evil] was the *Serpent;* who, under the name of Ahrimanes, formed the basis of the system of Zoroaster." *Ruins of Empires*, p. 208, quoted by Kenneth N. Cameron, "A Major Source of *The Revolt of Islam*," *PMLA*, LVI (1941), 201. The italics are the translator's.

29. The "Magus Zoroaster" passage had been gestating since 1812, when Shelley asked,

> Who painteth the shadows that are beneath
>   The wide-winding realms of the peopled tomb?
> Or uniteth the hopes of what shall be
>   With the fears and the love for that which we see?

"Reality," *The Esdaile Poems*, ed. Neville Rogers (Oxford, 1966), pp. 39–40.

30. *A Blake Dictionary* (Providence, 1965), s.v. "Shelley." Harold Bloom finds this "passionate identification . . . delightfully arbitrary on Damon's part" and, for reasons not at all clear to me, "alas, chronologically impossible." "Foster Damon and William Blake," *The New Republic* (5 June 1965), p. 25.

31. Keynes, p. 677.

32. *Letters*, I, 89. The italics are Shelley's.

IV The Paterin Beatrice

1. Note to *Prometheus Unbound*. Hutchinson, p. 271.

2. *Essay on Christianity. Works*, VI, 235.

3. *Essay on Christianity*, pp. 239–240.

4. First printed by Mrs. Shelley in her second edition, *The Poetical Works of Percy Bysshe Shelley* (1839). *Works*, II, 159–166.

5. *On the Devil, and Devils. Works*, VII, 95.

6. *Ibid.*

7. See Elizabeth Nitchie, *Mary Shelley, Author of "Frankenstein"* (New Brunswick, N. J., 1953), p. 148.

8. Letter of 8 November 1820. *Letters*, II, 245.

9. J. C. L. Simonde de Sismondi, *Histoire des Républiques Italiennes du Moyen Âge*, II (Paris, 1809), 352–354. The translation is mine; the italics are Sismondi's. The uncommon spelling, "Paterini," indicates this work as Mary Shelley's major source. See *Journal*, pp. 115–116

(3 January–25 February 1819). The entry for 20 January includes the following sentence: "Shelley and I read Sismondi." Since Mary made but one other entry between 13 and 30 January, there is no way of telling whether her husband read Sismondi more than once during those two weeks. The clear kinship of the two Beatrices has led me to assume without more direct evidence that the passages quoted here were among those known to Shelley.

10. Most of my information on the Paterini has been taken from Steven Runciman, *The Medieval Manichee: A Study of the Christian Dualist Heresy* (Cambridge, 1947). I have also used the *Encyclopedia of Religion and Ethics*, the *Dictionary of Sects, Heresies, Ecclesiastical Parties, and Schools of Religious Thought*, and *The Catholic Encyclopedia*.

V The Ophite Demogorgon

1. See Erwin Panofsky, *Studies in Iconology: Humanistic Themes in the Art of the Renaissance*, 2nd ed. (New York, 1962), pp. 216–217 and n. 149.

2. *Shelley* (New York, 1940), I, 682.

3. *Works*, VI, 165–166.

4. *Ibid.*, p. 164.

5. *Ibid.*, p. 168.

6. *Ibid.*, pp. 170–171.

7. *Ibid.*, p. 157.

8. *Ibid.*, p. 155.

9. *Journal*, p. 43.

10. Ophite influence upon Shelley's serpent-symbolism was first claimed by Ernst Sieper, "Spuren ophitisch-gnostischer Einflüsse in den Dichtungen Shelleys," *Herrigs Archiv*, CXX (1908), 315–331. Later scholars, such as A. M. D. Hughes and Carl Grabo (see n. 33 below), have referred in passing to possible Ophite influence on Shelley. A. A. Prins re-examines the question in some detail in "The Religious Background of Shelley's *Prometheus Unbound*," *English Studies Presented to R. W. Zandvoort on the Occasion of His Seventieth Birthday: a Supplement to* English Studies, XLV (1964), 223-234.

11. See James A. Notopoulos, "Shelley and Thomas Taylor," *PMLA*, LI (1936), 502–517. The direct biographical evidence, though compelling, is too scanty to be conclusive. Professor Notopoulos also

points out that Peacock fictionalized or imagined a Shelley-Taylor friendship in *Melincourt* (1817). For an opposed view, see Frank B. Evans, "Thomas Taylor, Platonist of the Romantic Period," *PMLA*, LV (1940), 1060–1079.

12. Here is a typical passage: "For it was one of the natural consequences of his [Kerinthus' gnostic] theory, that the human spirit in spite of the thick rind of cold and opake matter, in which it has been clad ever since its detrusion from the empyreal abodes, has never been so totally obscured, that some sparks and rays of the all-circumfluent ocean of fire and light, eternally flowing from the abyss of the deity, have not penetrated into it, as it were, through the chinks and crevices of this incrustation. . . ." C. M. Wieland, *Private History of Peregrinus Proteus the Philosopher*, trans. anon. (London, J. Johnson, 1796), II, 136–137.

13. *The Decline and Fall of the Roman Empire* (1783–1790), ch. xlvii, n. 11.

14. See Notopoulos, p. 515.

15. See Hans Jonas, *The Gnostic Religion* (Boston, 1958), p. 34. Most of my information on Gnosticism is taken from this learned, clearly written, and witty study, which comes closer than any other I have seen to making consistent sense out of these heresies. They were factious to begin with, and the study of them has since been darkened by the poverty of manuscript tradition and the rancor of their patristic and later orthodox confounders. The most literate early study of the general subject is Plotinus' *Against the Gnostics* (*Enneads*, II, 9). Hippolytus' *Philosophumena* contains the only detailed contemporary account of the Naassenes other than that of Saint Irenaeus. Hippolytus' text was not recovered, however, until the middle of the nineteenth century.

16. *Five Books of S. Irenaeus, Bishop of Lyons, Against Heresies*, trans. John Keble (London, 1872), p. 83. Saint Irenaeus wrote his great work in Greek between 182 and 188, but his text has come down to us in an anonymous Latin translation. Modern scholarship has recovered many passages of the original as quoted by Epiphanius; these unfortunately do not include the chapter on the Ophites. The Latin is, as Gibbon generously remarked, "barbarous," and I have therefore chosen to quote from Keble's comparatively lucid English version in the text of this study. I shall reproduce the apposite Latin passages in this and succeeding footnotes. For these I have preferred the emended and heavily annotated text given by Ubaldo Mannucci (Rome, 1907) to that of J.-P. Migne's *Patrologiae Graecae Cursus*

Completus, VII (1857): "quoddam primum lumen in virtute Bythi, beatum, et incorruptibile, et interminatum: esse autem et hoc Patrem omnium, et vocari primum hominem. Ennoeam autem eius progredientem, filium dicunt emittentis, et esse hunc Filium hominis, secundum hominem. Sub his autem Spiritum sanctum esse. . . ." (*Irenaei Lugdunensis Episcopi Adversus Haereses Libri Quinque*, I, xxx, 1).

17. See Paul Shorey, *Platonism, Ancient and Modern* (Berkeley, 1938), p. 106.

18. ". . . propter quae contristatum Ialdabaoth, et desperantem, conspexisse in subiacentem faecem materiae, et consolidasse concupiscentiam suam in eam, unde natum filium dicunt. Hunc autem ipsum esse Nun in figura serpentis contortum, dehinc et spiritum, et animam, et omnia mundialia: inde generatam omnem oblivionem, et malitiam, et zelum, et invidiam, et mortem. Hunc autem serpentiformem et contortum Nun eorum adhuc magis evertisse Patrem dicunt tortuositate. . . . Unde exsultantem Ialdabaoth in omnibus his quae sub eo essent gloriatum, et dixisse: 'Ego Pater et Deus, et super me nemo.' Audientem autem matrem clamasse adversus eum: 'Noli mentiri, Ialdabaoth: est enim super te pater omnium primus Anthropus, et Anthropus filius Anthropi.' Conturbatis autem omnibus ad novam vocem, et inopinabili nuncupatione, et quaerentibus unde clamor, ad avocandos eos, et ad se seducendum, dixisse Ialdabaoth dicunt: 'Venite, faciamus hominem ad imaginem nostram.' " (*Adv. Haer.*, I, xxx, 5–6; Keble, p. 85.) Italics in the second paragraph are Keble's.

19. See Jonas, ch. 2, *passim*.

20. ". . . supergredi praeceptum Ialdabaoth; Eva autem quasi a Filio Dei hoc audiens, facile credidit, et Adam suasit manducare de arbore, de qua dixerat Deus, non manducare. Manducantes autem eos cognovisse eam quae est super omnia virtutem dicunt, et abscessisse ab his qui fecerant eos. Prunicum autem videntem, quoniam et per suum plasma victi sunt, valde gratulatam, et rursum exclamasse, quoniam, quum esset Pater incorruptibilis, olim hic semetipsum vocan Patrem mentitus est." (*Adv. Haer.*, I, xxx, 7; Keble, p. 86.)

21. ". . . et magnanimes exstiterunt, cognoscentes quoniam ad tempus corpus circumdatum est eis." (*Adv. Haer.*, I, xxx, 9; Keble, p. 87.)

22. "Quidam enim ipsam Sophiam serpentem factam dicunt: quapropter et contrariam exstitisse factori Adae, et agnitionem hominibus immisisse, et propter hoc dictum serpentem omnium sapientiorem." (*Adv. Haer.*, I, xxx, 15; Keble, p. 90.)

23. Jonas, p. 93. Italics Jonas'.

24. *Ibid.*, p. 198.

25. *Collection des Anciens Alchimistes Grecs*, ed. M. Berthelot (Paris, 1888), II, part 3, "Les Oeuvres de Zosime," xlix, *Gnesia hypomnimata peri tou Omega stoicheiou*, par. 3, p. 229. The translation is mine.

26. Jonas, pp. 176–177.

27. See Henry G. Lotspeich, "Shelley's 'Eternity' and Demogorgon," *PQ*, XIII (1934), 309–311.

28. An excellent discussion of Boccaccio's Demogorgon may be found in Edward B. Hungerford, *Shores of Darkness* (New York, 1941), pp. 179–180.

29. *The Works of Thomas Love Peacock*, Halliford Edition, ed. H. F. B. Brett-Smith and C. E. Jones (London, 1931), VII, 94.

30. *Timaeus*, trans. R. G. Bury (Cambridge, Mass., 1929), pp. 51, 53.

31. William K. Wimsatt, Jr., points out that "The Kantian 'Reason' which Coleridge, following Fichte and Schelling, improved from a hypothetically constructive to a gnostic faculty does not appear in Shelley's system. The honor conferred upon poetic imagination, though nebulous, is the highest possible." William K. Wimsatt, Jr., and Cleanth Brooks, *Literary Criticism: A Short History* (New York, 1957), p. 423.

32. *Works*, VII, 109.

33. See especially Grabo, *Prometheus Unbound: An Interpretation* (Chapel Hill, 1935), p. 73; this is perhaps the classic modern presentation of the Demogorgon-Necessity equation. On pp. 78–79 of the same study Professor Grabo suggests in a footnote that "Jupiter's denial of knowledge, the birthright of their being, is an idea reminiscent of Gnosticism." He goes on to mention probable parallels to "Ophist" mythology in the snake-symbolism of "The Assassins," *The Revolt of Islam*, and *Prometheus Unbound*. That Professor Grabo should have overlooked the imaginative aspect of the Gnostic snake— and thereby of Demogorgon—is due, I think, to his having translated *nun* or *nous* simply as "reason." A similar brief discussion in *The Magic Plant: The Growth of Shelley's Thought* (Chapel Hill, 1936) contains the following argument: "Sophia, minister of the Ultimate, tempts man to knowledge by means of her familiar, the snake. Through knowledge and reason man frees himself from the evil domination of the God of his creation. The snake, therefore, is the symbol of reason which frees man from superstition and tyranny" (p. 136). Frank Lea, in *Shelley and the Romantic Revolution* (London, 1945), argues that the victory of Prometheus is that of imagination. No reference is

made to any religious system. "The understanding—what Shelley called the 'calculating faculty'—when it strives to comprehend the intuition of the eternal, ceases to be a tyrant; and when it is united with intuition, becomes imagination itself—the true imagination or Reason, Demogorgan [sic]" (p. 122).

34. *A Defence of Poetry, Works,* VII, 118.

35. *Works,* VI, 188.

36. See *Epipsychidion,* 267–274; *Adonais,* 274–279.

37. See Edwin Hatch, *The Influence of Greek Ideas on Christianity,* 2nd ed., ed. Frederick C. Grant (New York, 1957), pp. 182–188. See also Adolph Harnack, *History of Dogma,* 3rd ed., trans. Neil Buchanan (reprinted New York, 1961), II, 206–212.

38. *De Civitate Dei,* XI, 24–28.

39. G. Wilson Knight equates Prometheus with Christ, Jupiter with "the satanic attributes of God the Father," and Demogorgon "with the human imagination or Holy Spirit during the era of conflict." Asia supersedes Demogorgon in the era of peace. *The Starlit Dome,* 2nd ed. (London, 1959), p. 204.

40. *The Four Zoas,* Night iv, 26–27. *The Complete Writings of William Blake,* ed. Geoffrey Keynes (London, 1957), p. 298.

41. *Jerusalem,* Plate xcvi, 22. Keynes, p. 743.

42. See Carlos Baker, *Shelley's Major Poetry: The Fabric of a Vision* (Princeton, 1948), p. 116; Arthur Wormhoudt, *The Demon Lover* (New York, 1949), p. 99.

43. Origen, *Contra Celsum,* trans. ed. Henry Chadwick (Cambridge, 1953), VI, 25, p. 340. The editorial italics indicate that Origen is quoting from Celsus.

44. Quoted *ibid.,* n. 2.

45. Jonas, pp. 116–117.

46. See James A. Notopoulos, *The Platonism of Shelley: A Study of Platonism and the Poetic Mind* (Durham, 1949), p. 187.

47. *Works,* VII, 103.

48. *Shelley's Prose in the Bodleian Manuscripts,* ed. André H. Koszul (London, 1910), p. 122.

49. *The Four Zoas,* Night vii, 147–148. Keynes, pp. 323–324.

50. *Ibid.,* 155. Keynes, p. 324.

51. *The Collected Works of C. G. Jung,* Vol. IX, Part II, *Aion:*

Researches into the Phenomenology of the Self, trans. R. F. C. Hull (London, 1959), p. 188. The italics are the translator's.

52. *Five Questions Concerning the Mind*, trans. Josephine L. Burroughs, in *The Renaissance Philosophy of Man*, ed. E. Cassirer, P. O. Kristeller, J. H. Randall, Jr. (Chicago, 1948), p. 208. For amplification of the ideas summarized in the paragraph preceding the quotation, see Panofsky, pp. 136–137.

53. Professor Notopoulos' *Platonism* is of course the standard work on the subject. See especially part I, chs. 2, 4.

54. *Maria Gisborne and Edward E. Williams, Shelley's Friends, Their Journals and Letters*, ed. F. L. Jones (Norman, 1951), p. 45.

55. Godwin's "Journal," XXIII, in the Abinger MSS. Lewis Patton is presently preparing an edition of this manuscript.

56. Quoted by Jonas, p. 55.

57. Panofsky, p. 135.

58. William Godwin, *Thoughts on Man, His Nature, Productions, and Discoveries* (London, 1831), "Of the Rebelliousness of Man," pp. 99–100.

59. *The Complete Works of Samuel Taylor Coleridge*, ed. W. G. T. Shedd (New York, 1854), I. *The Statesman's Manual*, Appendix B, p. 458.

VI Orpheus and the West Wind

1. Hogg, I, 56.

2. Letter to John Gisborne, 22 October 1821. *Letters*, II, 363.

3. *Revaluation: Tradition and Development in English Poetry* (London, 1936), pp. 216–220. See Frederick A. Pottle's reply, "The Case of Shelley," *PMLA*, LXVII (1952), 589–608. Both critiques have been reprinted in *English Romantic Poets: Modern Essays in Criticism*, ed. M. H. Abrams (New York, 1960), pp. 268–306.

4. *Mythology and the Romantic Tradition in English Poetry* (Cambridge, Mass., 1937), pp. 158–159.

5. So far as I know, the "Ode" stanza has only been imitated once. Frost employed it for far quieter purposes in "Acquainted with the Night."

6. This image is frequently misunderstood. The palaces and towers are actually submerged, not merely reflected by the water. See the letter to Peacock of 17 or 18 December 1818: "The colours of the

water & the air breathe over all things here the radiance of their own beauty. After passing the Bay of Baiae & observing the ruins of its antique grandeur standing like rocks in the transparent sea under our boat, we landed to visit Lake Avernus." *Letters*, II, 61.

7. On 17 December 1812 Shelley ordered Edward Moor's *The Hindu Pantheon* (1810) from Thomas Hookham. *Letters*, I, 342.

8. Désirée Hirst, *Hidden Riches: Traditional Symbolism from the Renaissance to Blake* (London, 1964).

9. Letter to Hogg, 26 November 1813. *Letters*, I, 380.

10. Arthur Koestler, *The Sleepwalkers* (London, 1959), p. 28. Quoted by Hirst, p. 29.

11. See also *A Defence of Poetry* on the poetic principle: "Man is an instrument over which a series of external and internal impressions are driven, like the alternations of an ever-changing wind over an Aeolian lyre, which move it by their motion to ever-changing melody. But there is a principle within the human being, and perhaps within all sentient beings, which acts otherwise than in the lyre and produces not melody, alone, but harmony, by an internal adjustment of the sounds or motions thus excited to the impressions which excite them. It is as if the lyre could accommodate its chords to the motions of that which strikes them, in a determined proportion of sound; even as the musician can accommodate his voice to the sound of the lyre" (*Works*, VII, 109–110). Shelley had earlier employed this metaphor to convey a panpsychistic answer to orthodox Christianity: "There is a Power by which we are surrounded, like the atmosphere in which some motionless lyre is suspended, which visits with its breath our silent chords, at will" (*Essay on Christianity, Works*, VI, 231).

12. *Works*, VII, 135.

13. *Notes on Sculptures, Works*, VI, 320.

14. *Ibid.*, p. 323.

15. Ordered from Ollier in Thomas Taylor's translation (*The Description of Greece*, 1784), 24 July 1817. *Letters*, I, 548.

16. *Note Books of Percy Bysshe Shelley*, ed. H. Buxton Forman (Boston, 1911), I, 174.

17. *Ibid.*, I, 171–172; also Neville Rogers, *Shelley at Work: A Critical Inquiry* (Oxford, 1956), p. 224.

18. Shelley of course knew the *Metamorphoses* thoroughly. He is last reported to have read the entire work in 1817. *Journal*, p. 90.

19. Quoted and presumably translated by Robert Graves, *The Greek Myths* (New York, 1959), I, 114.

20. Walter W. Skeat, *An Etymological Dictionary of the English Language*, 2nd ed. (Oxford, 1910).

VII Actaeon, the Phrasemaker

1. As quoted by Earl R. Wasserman, who has consulted the MSS. of Shelley's prose, in *Shelley's* Prometheus Unbound: *A Critical Reading* (Baltimore, 1965), p. 51.

2. Carlos Baker, *Shelley's Major Poetry: The Fabric of a Vision* (Princeton, 1948), p. 53.

3. Charles Dealtry Locock, ed. *The Poems of Percy Bysshe Shelley* (London, 1911), II, 453.

4. Neville Rogers, *Shelley at Work: A Critical Inquiry* (Oxford, 1956), p. 245.

5. The eighteen-line stanza of *Prothalamion* uses only five rhymes; neither poem follows Dante's scheme exactly. The form was never fixed, not even in the *Convivio*, whose first and third canzoni employ thirteen- and twenty-line stanzas respectively. Shelley was reading the *Vita Nuova* early in 1821, while composing *Epipsychidion*.

6. A new gas formed by the combination of equal volumes of different gases will occupy a space equal to the original volume of either.

7. Bod. MS. Shelley adds. e. 8, p. 167 rev. See Rogers, pp. 235–236, 340–341.

8. Hogg, I, 117–118.

9. "Fragments Connected with *Epipsychidion*," Hutchinson, p. 427.

10. Shelley ordered the *Historical Library* of Diodorus Siculus from "Clio" Rickman on 24 December 1812. *Letters*, I, 344.

11. Letter to Lord Byron, 4 May 1821. *Letters*, II, 289.

12. Cf. ll. 19–20 of the 1821 poem ("Swifter far than summer's flight") variously entitled "Song," "A Lament," and "Remembrance": "Violets for a maiden dead—/Pansies let *my* flowers be."

13. Note to V, 189: "Even love is sold." *Works*, I, 141–142.

14. Shaw dismissed *Epipsychidion* in his Preface to "The Black Girl in Search of God" (1934) as "literary gas and gaiters"; in *Everybody's Political What's What* (1944) he added that the poem was at best "a wonderful effort by a supreme master of language to utter the unspeakable; but the result is a rhapsody of nonsense that has no contact with natural history." Quoted by Roland A. Duerksen, "Shelley and Shaw," *PMLA*, LXXVIII (1963), 118b.

15. The italics are Shelley's. Carlos Baker argues (pp. 231-238) that the Planet (which he identifies with the Comet), the Moon and the Sun stand not for actual women but for "unruly Emotion," Reason and Imagination, or the appetitive, higher mortal and immortal souls of Plato. I find this interpretation most attractive, especially in view of Shelley's prefatory lines from Dante: "My Song, I fear that thou wilt find but few/Who fitly shall conceive thy reasoning,/Of such hard matter dost thou entertain." But the supreme clumsiness with which Shelley stages his astronomical conceit, together with Dante's own insistence upon the personal basis of any allegory ("Philosophy," in the canzone quoted, is also a flesh-and-blood "lady of the window"), points clearly to the simultaneous presence of autobiography.

16. *Works*, VII, 128.

17. Letter to Hogg, 3 December 1812. *Letters*, I, 336.

18. Mary Shelley to Maria Gisborne, 7 March 1822. *Letters of M.W.S.*, I, 160-161. The italics are Mrs. Shelley's.

19. Shelley's announcement to Lord Byron (17 January 1817) of the discovery of Harriet's body shows precisely this reluctance to contemplate the gruesome image and its moral meaning, together with his eagerness to shift the blame: "My late wife is dead. The circumstances which attended this event are of a nature of such awful and appalling horror, that I dare hardly avert to them in thought. The sister of whom you have heard me speak may be truly said (though not in law, yet in fact) to have murdered her for the sake of her father's money" (*Letters*, I, 529-530). On 17 August 1820 Shelley replied as follows to Southey's accusations: "You select a single passage out of a life otherwise not only spotless but spent in an impassioned pursuit of virtue, which looks like a blot, merely because I regulated my domestic arrangements without deferring to the notions of the vulgar, although I might have done so quite as conveniently had I descended to their base thoughts—this you call *guilt*. . . . you accuse me wrongfully. I am innocent of ill, either done or intended; the consequences you allude to flowed in no respect from me" (*Letters*, II, 231). The italics are Shelley's.

20. *Letters*, II, 432-433. The italics are Shelley's.

VIII Motes of a Sick Eye

1. Text from Donald H. Reiman, *Shelley's "The Triumph of Life": A Critical Study* (Urbana, 1965).

2. Letter to Mary Godwin, 28 October 1814. *Letters*, I, 414.

3. "Das Objekt besitzt ihn gänzlich. . . . *er* ist das Werk, und das Werk ist *er*." *Über naive und sentimentalische Dichtung* (1795), *Schillers Werke*, ed. Erwin Ackerknecht (Munich, 1957), II, 657.

4. Shelley translated *Purgatorio*, XXVIII, 1–51 in the winter of 1820 at Pisa. The significance of Rousseau's "Shape all light" was missed by every modern critic before Harold Bloom. I wish, therefore, to record my indebtedness to the brilliant final chapter of *Shelley's Mythmaking* (New Haven, 1959).

5. M. H. Abrams, to whom I am indebted for this term, defines it somewhat differently: a work is polysemous insofar as it has "bidirectional reference—both outward and inward, 'objective' and 'subjective.'" Mr. Abrams, who is at this point discussing Friedrich Schlegel, notes his own debt to Aquinas and Dante ("Letter to Can Grande della Scala"), who "maintained that secular works of literature may, like the Scriptures, be made 'polysemous,' or significant both of literal and various kinds of allegorical truths." *The Mirror and the Lamp: Romantic Theory and the Critical Tradition*, 2nd ed. (Oxford, 1960), p. 240.

6. Letter to John and Maria Gisborne, 19 July 1821. *Letters*, II, 310. Shelley is speaking specifically of his inability to assess the worth of *Adonais*, which the Gisbornes have praised highly.

7. *Works*, VII, 131.

8. See Reiman, Appendix C, p. 242.

9. Letter to Charles Ollier, 16 February 1821. *Letters*, II, 263.

10. Letter to Lord Byron, 4 May 1821. *Letters*, II, 291.

11. *Letters*, II, 374.

12. Letter to Thomas Medwin, 22 August 1821. *Letters*, II, 341-342.

13. British Museum Add. MSS. 52361. Besides the two letters and the deck plan discussed here, the collection contains two letters from Roberts to Byron, dated 21 April and 5 June 1823.

14. Edward Trelawny, *Recollections*, reprinted as *The Last Days of Shelley and Byron*, ed. J. E. Morpurgo (Garden City, N. Y., 1960), p. 116.

15. *Ibid.*, p. 117.

16. Reproduced following p. 126 of *Maria Gisborne and Edward E. Williams, Shelley's Friends, Their Journals and Letters*, ed. F. L. Jones (Norman, 1951).

17. Trelawny, p. 78.

18. This sketch is now in the British Museum. Newman White reproduces it in *Shelley*, II, following p. 368.

19. This report, preserved in the archives of the Duchy of Lucca, is quoted by Ivan Roe, *Shelley: The Last Phase* (New York, 1953), p. 236.

20. *Gisborne and Williams*, p. 154.

21. *Ibid.*, p. 155.

22. Trelawny, p. 82.

23. Mary Shelley to Maria Gisborne, 15 August 1822. *Letters of M.W.S.*, I, 183.

24. Mary Shelley to Jane Williams, 15 October 1822. *Letters of M.W.S.*, I, 197. The italics are Mary Shelley's.

25. Mary Shelley to Maria Gisborne, 2 May 1823. *Letters of M.W.S.*, I, 223. Here is the complete passage: "Roberts had bought the hulk of that miserable boat—new rigged her—even with higher masts than before—he has sailed with her at the rate of 8 knots an hour, and on such occasions tried various experiments, hazardous ones, to discover how the catastrophe that closed the scene for us two poor creatures happened. It is plain to every eye. She was run down from behind. On bringing her up from 15 fathom all was in her—books, telescope, ballast, lying on each side of the boat without any appearance of shifting or confusion—the topsails furled—topmasts lowered—the false stern (Jane can explain) broken to pieces and a great hole knocked in the stern timbers. When she was brought to Leghorn, every one went to see her—and the same exclamation was uttered by all—She was run down by that wretched fishing boat which owned that it had seen them." It must be remembered that Mrs. Shelley had this story from Roberts eight months after he had salvaged the *Don Juan* and had written two letters which imply the contrary of the position set forth here. Roberts may have been dealing honestly with the widow. But it is also possible that by May he and Trelawny had agreed on the comfortable verdict enshrined in the *Recollections* forgeries. Finally, of course, the stern may have been damaged in the course of salvage.

26. Trelawny, p. 102.

27. Reported in the *Journal of Clarissa Trant, 1800–1832* (London, 1925), pp. 198–199. Quoted by Walter E. Peck, *Shelley: His Life and Work* (Boston, 1927), II, 287 n.

28. Letter of 6 November 1818. *Letters*, II, 47.

29. Letter to John Gisborne, 22 October 1821. *Letters*, II, 364.
30. Text from G. M. Matthews, "Shelley and Jane Williams," *RES*, N.S., XII (February, 1961), 40–48.
31. Added by Richard Garnett, *Relics of Shelley* (1862).
32. Canceled in the MS., but preferred by Garnett to "Seeking."
33. Letter of 25 January 1822. *Letters*, II, 382. For specific political grievances, see the letter to Horace Smith of 29 July 1822, *Letters*, II, 442.
34. Letter of 8 August 1821. *Letters*, II, 320.
35. Letter of 15 August 1821. *Letters*, II, 339.
36. Quoted in *Letters*, I, 483–484 n.
37. Letter to Peacock, 12 July 1816. *Letters*, I, 483.
38. *Ibid.*, p. 486. See Reiman, p. 60.
39. Trelawny, p. 82.
40. *Ibid.*, p. 49.
41. *Gisborne and Williams*, p. 147.
42. The Tan-yr-allt assault *may*, despite Hogg's and Peacock's insistence to the contrary, have taken place elsewhere than in Shelley's fancy. H. M. Dowling argues ("The Attack at Tanyrallt," Keats-Shelley Memorial Association *Bulletin*, XII [1961], 28–36) that a practical joke was played on Shelley in order to drive him and his radical opinions out of the district.
43. Mary Shelley to Maria Gisborne, 15 August 1822. *Letters of M.W.S.*, I, 180.
44. *Ibid.*
45. Trelawny, p. 54.
46. Letter of 10 April 1822. *Letters*, II, 404.
47. Letter to Claire Clairmont, 28 May 1822. *Letters*, II, 427.
48. Letter of 29 June 1822. *Letters*, II, 442–443.
49. *Letters*, II, 435–436.
50. Letter of 10 April 1822. *Letters*, II, 406.
51. Mary Shelley to Maria Gisborne, 15 August 1822. *Letters of M.W.S.*, I, 180–181.
52. *Gisborne and Williams*, p. 156.
53. *Ibid.*, p. 161.

Appendix

1. In the course of this study I have so frequently questioned Mary Shelley's biographical accuracy and critical intelligence that I have decided to reprint here my particular reasons for doubting her word generally. The essay that follows first appeared, in a slightly different form, in *Studies in English Literature*, III (1963), 461–472.

2. Mary Shelley, Introduction to the 1831 edition of *Frankenstein, or the Modern Prometheus* in Colburn and Bentley's Standard Novels series; John William Polidori, *The Vampyre; a Tale* (London, Sherwood, Neely, and Jones, 1819), "Extract of a Letter from Geneva." This letter is certainly not by Polidori himself. W. M. Rossetti may be correct in ascribing it to Mme. Gatelier (*The Diary of Dr. John William Polidori*, ed. W. M. Rossetti [London, 1911], Introduction, p. 13).

3. *Diary and Letters of Madame D'Arblay*, ed. Austin Dobson (London, 1905), VI, 388–389.

4. "A Fragment" is now most readily accessible in *The Works of Lord Byron, Letters and Journals*, ed. Rowland E. Prothero, III (London, 1899), Appendix IX, 446.

5. The full story is contained in Rossetti's Introduction and incidental notes to the *Diary*.

6. *Letters and Journals*, IV, 288.

7. [Pierre François Adolphe Carmouche, Charles Nodier, Achille Jouffroy] *Le Vampire; mélodrame en trois actes, avec un prologue, par* MM*** (Paris, 1820).

8. *The Vampire; or, the Bride of the Isles: a romantic melo-drama in two acts* (London, 1820).

9. See Elizabeth Nitchie, *Mary Shelley* (New Brunswick, N. J., 1953), Appendix IV, "The Stage History of *Frankenstein*," pp. 218–231. Reprinted from the *South Atlantic Quarterly*, XLI (October, 1942), 384–398.

10. *The Vampyre*, pp. 29–30.

11. *Ibid.*, pp. 31–32.

12. Thomas Moore, *Letters and Journals of Lord Byron: with Notices of His Life* (London, 1830), II, 29. Quoted by Leslie Marchand, *Byron: a Biography* (New York, 1957), II, 626.

13. We must except his thoroughly incompetent verse: *Ximenes, the Wreath, and Other Poems* (London, 1819); *The Fall of the Angels, a Sacred Poem* (London, 1821). The latter employs a peculiar ten-line stanza (ababccdede), but is otherwise pseudo-Miltonic throughout.

14. *Letters and Journals*, IV, 140. Quoted by Marchand.

15. According to Rossetti (p. 4), it was "perfectly well known in his family" that Polidori had committed suicide and that "the easy-going and good-naturedly disposed coroner's jury" had connived in hushing up the fact. This question has recently been re-opened by Henry R. Viets, M.D., Curator of the Boston Medical Library and author of a forthcoming biography of Polidori, in his article, " 'By the Visitation of God': the Death of John William Polidori, M.D., in 1821," *British Medical Journal*, II (30 December 1961), 1773-1775. Dr. Viets here attempts to discredit the Polidori-Rossetti family tradition, but I find his argument unconvincing. It stands or falls with Dr. Viets's assumption that it took "a half-hour, perhaps longer," for the Polidoris' maid to fetch and return with, "on the run," a physician who lived "only two streets away."

16. *Aen.* III, 42-43, 45. The final hemistich should read "Nam Polydorus ego."

17. Italics mine.

18. *Ernestus Berchtold; or, the Modern Oedipus. A Tale* (London, 1819), Introduction, p. v.

19. The Union Catalogue of the Harvard University Library lists only one American copy, in the Library of Congress.

20. Rossetti, p. 126.

21. This entry is confirmed by Byron's placement of the date, 17 June 1816, at the top of "A Fragment." Some doubt might be cast upon the accuracy of the printed *Diary* from Rossetti's having used a transcript made by his aged aunt, Miss Charlotte Polidori—evidently an English lady of the Cassandra Austen stamp—who had excised all reference to "improper" sexual conduct and then destroyed the MS. Rossetti had, however, worked with the MS. while preparing his *Memoir of Shelley* in 1869, and he vouches for the transcript's authority being "only a shade less safe than that of the original" (p. 11).

22. Professor Marchand (II, 628) assigns the suggestion to the fourteenth or fifteenth. But White (*Shelley*, I, 443-444) assumes—likewise without stated evidence—that it came on the sixteenth.

23. The identification was first made, tentatively, by Rossetti (p. 124), but no one has since followed up his suggestion.

24. Polidori received his medical degree at the "singularly early age . . . of nineteen." So young a man must have shown extraordinary talent and promise to have been recommended by Sir Henry Halford to an international celebrity like Byron the following year (Rossetti, p. 2).

25. *Disputatio Medica Inauguralis, Quaedam de Morbo, Oneirodynia Dicto, Complectens* (Edinburgh, 1815). The copy in the Houghton Library at Harvard is inscribed, "Our dearest Mother's own copy./ Christina to William M. Rossetti/September 1887." Polidori's concluding sentence affords us an interesting glimpse of the frontiers of psychotherapy in the year of Waterloo: "Verbera, electricitas, balnea frigida, si ita posita sint ut aeger in ea incidat cum e lecto somnambulans migrat, forsitan paroxysmorum reditum impedient." In modern medicine, of course, the term *oneirodynia* refers not to somnambulism but nightmare.

26. This is Frederick L. Jones's suggestion for the "Introduction to Davy's Chemistry" cited by Mary Shelley at the end of her journal for 1816. *Journal*, p. 73.

27. *Diary*, p. 123.

28. On 5 June Polidori had also conversed with Dr. Odier on somnambulism and had been given an MS. by him on the subject.

29. The common experience of insomnia when sleeping for the first time in a strange house suggests the alternative possibility—admittedly speculative—that the nightmare occurred in the early morning hours of 17 June.

30. Even Rossetti makes this entirely unwarranted assumption, p. 126.

31. Elizabeth Nitchie, *Mary Shelley* (New Brunswick, N. J., 1953), p. 27.

32. For some reason Shelley mentions only "two other friends" (himself and Byron?) as taking part in the writing contest.

33. *Shelley and Mary* (privately printed, 1882), II, 370; *Letters of M.W.S.*, I, 65. This exchange is quoted in Nitchie, p. 17 n.

34. *Journal* (19 October 1822), p. 184.

35. *Diary*, p. 127.

36. The greatest single influence upon Mary Shelley's first novel was, of course, the anti-humanist *Tendenzroman* as practiced by her father.

37. Richard Garnett, ed., *Tales and Stories by Mary Wollstonecraft Shelley* (London, 1891), Introduction, p. v.

Index

Abinger, James Richard Scarlett, eighth Baron, 252n
Abrams, Meyer H., 267n
Acts of Kyriakos and Julitta, 154
Acts of the Apostle Thomas, 154
Adamson, H., *The Muses' Threnodie*, 66–67
Aeschylus:
    Choephoroe, 130, 146
    Prometheus Bound, 129
Agrippa, Cornelius, 172
Albigensians, 64, 69, 112, 121, 123–125, 128, 160
alchemy, 35, 66, 67, 154
Alfieri, Vittorio, 240
Alighieri, Dante, 166:
    Convivio, 168, 185, 187, 190, 191, 194, 217, 265n, 266n
    Inferno, 88, 190, 216
    "Letter to Can Grande della Scala," 267n
    Paradiso, 192
    Purgatorio, 192, 211, 267n
Allingham, William, 27
Amis, Kingsley, 50
Anaxagoras, 142
Andrea, Johann Valentin, *Fama Fraternitatis*, 66
Apologists, 149
Aquinas, Saint Thomas, 267n
Ariosto, Lodovico, 143
Aristotle, 33, 110; *De Anima*, 142
Arnold, Matthew, 27, 35, 47, 164, 165, 214
Auden, W. H., 167, 214
Augustine, Saint:
    Confessions, 101, 202
    De Civitate Dei, 149, 152
Avogadro's Law, 188, 265n

Baker, Carlos, 184, 262n, 266n
Barruel, Augustin, 63, 68;
    Memoirs, 63–67, 70, 100
Beckford, William, 27
Bell's Court and Fashionable Magazine, 52
Bentley, Richard, 255n
Berkeley, Bishop George, 73, 108
Blake, William, 15, 18, 21, 39, 56, 96–98, 99, 104, 147, 155, 173, 212, 227, 235:
    Four Zoas, The, 152, 155–156
    Jerusalem, 107, 152

Marriage of Heaven and Hell, The, 104
Bloom, Harold, 256n, 257n, 267n
Boccaccio, Giovanni, *Genealogia Deorum Gentilium*, 142, 143, 154
Boehme, Jacob, 172
Bogomils, 123–124
Bonaparte; *see* Napoleon
Breuss, Countess of, 238
Brinton, Crane, 254n
Brontë, Emily, *Wuthering Heights*, 27
Brown, Charles Brockden, 255n
Browning, Robert, 163
Burdett, Sir Francis, 24
Burke, Edmund, 34, 85
Bush, Douglas, 165
Byron, Allegra, 232
Byron, George Gordon, Lord, 24, 25, 34, 167, 222, 229, 237, 239–240, 242–245, 247, 266n, 267n, 271n, 272n:
Cain, 198
Childe Harold's Pilgrimage, 75, 163, 238
Don Juan, 168
"Fragment, A," 238–239, 270n, 271n
Manfred, 75, 198
Mazeppa, 238, 242

Cabalism, 64
Cainites, 135
Calvinism, 34, 35, 37, 38, 40, 41–42, 113, 114; *see also* Sandemanianism

Cambridge Platonists, 172
Cameron, Kenneth Neill, 250n, 251n, 253n, 257n
Carlyle, Thomas, 113
Castells, F. de P., 254n
Categorical Imperative, 160; *see also* Kant
Cathari; *see* Albigensians
Catholic Emancipation, 25, 30
Chateaubriand, François-René, Vicomte de, 209
Chatterton, Thomas, 213
Chaucer, Geoffrey, 18, 27, 216
Church of England, 33, 34
Cicero, 138
Clairmont, Claire, 133, 201, 233, 237, 243
Clement V, Pope, 64
Clement VIII, Pope, 114
Colburn, Henry, 238
Coleridge, Samuel Taylor, 15, 20, 34, 40, 61, 72, 74, 76, 82, 98, 158, 162, 226, 235, 261n
Condorcet, Jean Antoine, 63, 64
Correggio, 165
Coryats Crudities, 237
Cowper, William, 194
Crane, Hart, 130, 189, 228
Crashaw, Richard, 74, 227–228
Curran, Amelia, 164

D'Alembert, Jean le Rond, 63
Dalton, John, 188
Damon, S. Foster, 107
Danton, Georges Jacques, 63
D'Arblay, Frances Burney, 237
Darwin, Erasmus, 244

Davy, Sir Humphry, 244
deism, 23, 58, 66, 71, 109, 220
Dendera Zodiac, 100, 217
De Quincey, Thomas, 37, 44
Descartes, René, 72
Desmoulins, Camille, 63
Diodorus Siculus, *Historical Library*, 195, 265n
Dissent, 18, 34, 37; see also Calvinism
Docetists, 124
Donne, John, 74, 75, 191, 237
Dowling, H. M., 269n
Drummond, Sir William, *Academical Questions*, 158
Dryden, John, 19
Duerksen, Roland A., 265n

Edwards, Jonathan, 94
Eliot, T. S., 19, 34, 87
Epiphanius, 259n
Eugenius III, Pope, 64
Evans, Frank B., 259n
Eyriès, J.-B. B., *Fantasmagoriana*, 241–242, 243, 245, 271n

Fay, Bernard, 254n
Fibonacci series, 170
Fichte, Johann, 158, 261n
Ficino, Marsilio, 164:
  Corpus Hermeticum, 172
  Quaestiones quinque de mente, 157–158
Fludd, Robert, 172; *Utriusque Cosmi . . . Historia*, 173
Forster, E. M., 27:
  Howards End, 18
  Longest Journey, The, 200
Fox, Charles James, 24, 25

Franklin, Benjamin, 244
Freemasonry, 14, 18, 63–67, 68
Freischütz, Der, 239
Freud, Anna, 44
Freud, Sigmund, 117
Frost, Robert, 48, 80, 263n

Galignani's Magazine, 238
Garnett, Richard, 269n, 272n
Gatelier, Mme., 238, 270n
Genesis, 156
Gibbon, Edward, *Decline and Fall*, 133–134, 259n
Giorgio, Francesco, *De Harmonia Mundi*, 172
Gisborne, John, 189, 202, 204–205, 225, 233–234, 267n
Gisborne, Maria, 159, 267n
Gladstone, William Ewart, 24
Gnosticism, 14, 15, 68–69, 102–103, 106, 124–128, 132–134, 138–141, 154–155, 157–162 *passim*, 204, 217, 225; see also Cainites, Docetists, Mandaeans, Marcionites, Ophites, Peratae, Sethians, Sodomites, Valentinians; *for late forms, see* Manicheism
Godwin, William, 30, 35*ff*, 59, 60, 86, 87, 94, 108, 155, 159–161, 219, 272n:
  Caleb Williams, 29, 34–48, 55, 83, 84, 157, 161–162, 255n
  Fleetwood (Preface), 38, 45
  Imogen, 251n
  Life of Chatham, 37
  "Memoirs," 41–44

Memoirs of the Author of a Vindication of the Rights of Woman, 47
Political Justice, 35–37, 39, 41, 44, 45, 46, 81
St. Leon, 29, 46, 55–57, 62
Sketches of History, 38
Thoughts on Man, 162
Goethe, J. W. von, 209: *Faust,* 29, 197, 207, 232–234
Wilhelm Meisters Lehrjahre, 113, 199
Golden Rectangle, 170
Goldsmith, Oliver, 240
Grabo, Carl, 258n, 261n
Graham, Edward Fergus, 27
Grattan, Henry, 30
Graves, Robert, 264n
Gregory VII (?), Pope, 217
Grove, Harriet, 70, 226
Guillotin, Dr., 63
Gunn, Thom, 214

Hammer, Joseph von, *Geschichte der Assassinen,* 133
Harnack, Adolph, 262n
Hartley, David, 47, 95
Hatch, Edwin, 256n, 262n
Hawthorne, Nathaniel, *The Marble Faun,* 122
Hazlitt, William, 36, 37, 44, 81, 87
Heine, Heinrich, *Memoirs of Herr von Schnabelwopski,* 74, 75
Heraclitus, 138
Hermes Trismegistus, 64, 138, 172; *see also* Ficino

Herrick, Robert, 27
Hesiod, *Works and Days,* 139
Hippolytus, *Philosophumena,* 259n
Hirst, Désirée, 172
Hitchener, Elizabeth, 66, 71, 202, 256n
Hobbes, Thomas, 89
Hogg, Thomas Jefferson, 28, 31, 32, *49–51,* 63, 70, 71, 201, 256n, 269n; *Life of Shelley,* 30, 35, 49–50, 57–60, 163, 190
Holbach, Baron d', 67, 95
Homer, *Iliad,* 130
Hookham, Thomas, 75, 264n
Hoppner scandal, 228
Horapollo, *Hieroglyphica,* 154–155
Hughes, A. M. D., 258n
Hulme, T. E., 19
Hume, David, 32, 41, 61, 67, 95
Hungerford, Edward B., 261n
Hunt, Leigh, 195, 228, 247

Illuminists, 63, 67
Innocent III, Pope, 69, 160
Irenaeus, Saint, 15, 259n; *Adversus Haereses,* 133–138, 142, 153, 154
Isaiah, 102
Ismaili Muslims, 132

"Jacobinism," 18, 34–37, 63–67, 123
James, William, 23, 33, 34
Jennings, Sir Ivor, 250n
Job, 96, 99

John, Saint, Gospel according to, 148–149
Johnson, Joseph, 155
Johnson, Samuel, 24
Jonas, Hans, 138, 154, 259*n*, 260*n*, 261*n*, 262*n*
Jones, Frederick L., 222, 250*n*, 272*n*
Jonson, Ben, 237
Journal of Clarissa Trant, 268*n*
Jung, Carl G., *Aion*, 157

Kant, Immanuel, 143, 219, 261*n*
Keats, John, 13, 167, 168, 195, 211, 212, 213, 216, 220, 227, 240
Keble, John, 259*n*
Knight, G. Wilson, 262*n*
Knights Templar, 64, 65
Koestler, Arthur, 173
Kotzebue, August von, 118

Lafayette, Marquis de, 63
Lamb, Charles, 38
Langton, Bennet, 24
La Rochefoucauld, François, Duc de, 19
Law, William, 172
Lawrence, D. H., 19, 129
Lea, Frank, 261*n*–262*n*
Leavis, F. R., 164
Levin, Harry, 29
Lewis, Matthew Gregory, 118; *The Monk*, 54, 60, 62
Lives of the Pirates, 38
Locke, John, 32, 61, 110
Locock, C. D., 184

Logos, 73, 86, 98–99, 110, 127–128, 135, *148–152*, 157
Lotspeich, Henry G., 261*n*
Lowell, Robert, 20, 79, 99, 228
Lucan, 213
Luther, Martin, 66

Macaulay, Thomas Babington, 24
Mandaeans, 135, 154
Manicheism, 14, 63, 64, 112, 122–124, 134; *see also* Albigensians, Bogomils, Paterini, Paulicians
Mannucci, Ubaldo, 259*n*
Marchand, Leslie, 271*n*
Marcionites, 128, 135, 161
Marlowe, Christopher, 29, 39, 143, 162
Martin, Gaston, 254*n*
Martinism, 64
Marvell, Andrew, 107, 161, 232
Matthews, G. M., 269*n*
Maturin, Charles Robert, 118; *Melmoth the Wanderer*, 55
Maurois, André, *Ariel*, 164
Melville, Herman:
  Moby-Dick, 79
  Pierre, 89, 122
Mesmer, F. A., 244
Michelangelo, 130
Migne, J.-P., *Patrologiae Graecae*, 259*n*–260*n*
Mill, John Stuart, 163
Milton, John, 19, 33, 143, 162, 172, 178, 196:
  Comus, 217

Lycidas, 181
Paradise Lost, 71, 81, 84, 98, 113, 125–126, 149–150, 152, 189
Mirabeau, Comte de, 64
Mithraism, 154
Molay, Jacques de, 64, 65
Monboddo, James Burnett, Lord, 154, 155
Montesquieu, Charles de Secondat, Baron de, 63
Moor, Edward, *The Hindu Pantheon*, 264n
Moore, Thomas, 25; *Life of Byron*, 229
More, Henry, 172
Mosheim, J. L., *Commentaries*, 133–134
Murray, John, 238

Naassenes, 133, 259n; *see also* Ophites
Napoleon, 24, 219
Newgate Calendar, 38
New Monthly Magazine, 238
Newton, Sir Isaac, 47, 212
Newton, John Frank, 100–101, 112
Newton, Samuel, 41–44, 46, 160
Nietzsche, Friedrich, *Der Fall Wagner*, 77
Nitchie, Elizabeth, 257n, 270n
Nonconformism; *see* Dissent
Norfolk, Charles Howard, eleventh Duke of, 25, 26, 27, 30
Notopoulos, James, 154, 262n, 263n

Odier, Dr., 272n
Ollier, Charles, 264n
Ophites, 133, *134–141*, 154–155, 162, 259n, 261n
Origen, 15; *Contra Celsum*, 153–154, 156
Orpheus, 14, 72, 107, 166, 172, 173, 175, *178–182*, 195
Ovid, *Metamorphoses*, 178–180, 183, 196, 204, 264n

Paganis, Hugo de, 64
Paine, Thomas, 219
Paley, William, 31, 32, 160, 219
Panofsky, Erwin, 258n, 259n, 263n
Pantisocracy, 34
Paracelsus, 172
Paris, Matthew, *Chronica Maiora*, 52
Paterini, 46, 64, 121, *122–125*, 128
Patton, Lewis, 252n
Paul, Saint, 101, 236:
Romans, 18
1 Corinthians, 172
Paulicians, 122–124, 128, 135
Pausanias, *Periegesis*, 178
Peacock, Thomas Love, 90, 92, 98, 100, 112, 122, 134, 220, 225, 229, 269n:
Ahrimanes, 100
Melincourt, 259n
Nightmare Abbey, 100
Rhododaphne, 134, 142, 143
Peake, Richard Brinsley, *Presumption*, 239
Peck, Walter Edwin, 254n

Peratae, 138
Petrarch (Francesco Petrarca), 160, 190; *Trionfi*, 217
Petrarchan sonnet, 167–169
Philip the Fair, King, 64, 65
Philipps, Janetta, 109
Philo Judaeus, 149
Piozzi, Hester Thrale, 237
Pistis Sophia, 154
Pitt, William, the elder, first Earl of Chatham, 25
Pitt, William, the younger, 25, 35
Planché, J. R., 239
Plato, 134, 141, 160, 235; as literary character, 207, 210, 217:
Critias, 145
Phaedo, 161
Phaedrus, 184
Republic, 89
Symposium, 164, 168–169, 184, 188
Timaeus, 124, 127, 135, 137, 142–143, 145
Plotinus, 158, 164, 259n
Polidori, Charlotte, 271n
Polidori, John William, 238–240, 242–247, 270n, 271n, 272n:
Boadicea, 244
Cajetan, 244
De Oneirodynia, 244, 272n
Diary, 243, 271n
Ernestus Berchtold, 238, 242, 246
Fall of the Angels, The, 271n
Vampyre, The, 238–240

Ximenes, 240, 271n
Pope, Alexander, 34; *The Dunciad*, 150, 214, 217
Pottle, Frederick A., 263n
Pound, Ezra, 17, 19
Price, Dr. Richard, 34
Price, Uvedale, 85
Priestley, Joseph, 34
Prins, A. A., 258n
Proclus, 134, 180
Pulos, C. E., 256n
Pythagoras, 149, 171, 172, 173; *Les Vers dorés* (trans. Fabre d'Olivet), 173

Quarterly Review, 30

Railo, Eino, 253n
Reiman, Donald, 229, 266n, 267n, 269n
Revelation of St. John the Divine, 95, 102, 156, 181
Richards, I. A., 17, 20, 249n
Richardson, Samuel, *Clarissa Harlowe*, 154, 155
Rickman, "Clio," 265n
Rimbaud, Arthur, 163
Roberts, Capt. Daniel, 221–224, 267n, 268n
Robison, John, 254n
Roe, Ivan, 268n
Rogers, Neville, 185, 264n, 265n
Rogers, Samuel, 25
Roman Catholic Church, 114–115
"Rosa Matilda" (Charlotte Dacre), 60
Rosa, Salvator, 246

Rosenberg, Edgar, 253*n*
Rosicrucianism, 17, 62–67, 73
Rossetti, Christina, 240, 272*n*
Rossetti, Dante Gabriel, 27, 240
Rossetti, William Michael, 240, 270*n*, 271*n*, 272*n*
Rousseau, Jean-Jacques, 218, 229; as literary character, 209–214, 216
Rubens, Peter Paul, 130
Runciman, Steven, 258*n*

Sandemanianism, 41–43, 46, 159–160
Santayana, George, *Winds of Doctrine*, 23, 24, 33
Schelling, Friedrich, 72, 158, 261*n*
Schiller, Friedrich, 209, 210, 267*n*
Schlegel, Friedrich, 215, 267*n*
Schubart, Christian F. D., *Ahasver*, 52–53, 60, 68, 70, 73
Sethians, 135
Shakespeare, William, 52, 197
Shakespearean sonnet, 168–169
Shaw, George Bernard:
  "Black Girl in Search of God, The," 265*n*
  Everybody's Political What's What, 265*n*
  Man and Superman, 199–200
Shelley, Sir Bysshe, grandfather of S, 25, 26
Shelley, Elizabeth, mother of S, 27, 31
Shelley, Elizabeth, sister of S, 27, 31, 50
Shelley, Harriet Westbrook, first wife of S, 74, 201–203, 215, 226, 266*n*
Shelley, Hellen, sister of S, 28, 29
Shelley, Mary Wollstonecraft Godwin, second wife of S, 77, 80, 129, 133, 155, 159, 161–162, 171, 200–203, 205, 221, 223, 226, 228, 231–232, 234, 268*n*, 270*n*:
  Frankenstein, 29, 44–45, 46, 56, *81–89*, 95, 161, 212, 237–238; composition of, 240–247.
  History of a Six Weeks' Tour, 98, 109.
  Midas, 247.
  "Mortal Immortal, The," 53.
  Proserpine, 247.
  Valperga, 121–125, 127–128.

Shelley, Percy Bysshe, works:

Poetry
  Adonais, 74, 75, 80, 107, 11–112, 165, 167, 175, 180, 181, 185, 186, *194–197*, 203, 204, 212, 213, 214, 216, 218, 220, 226, 228, 229, 234, 262*n*, 267*n*.
  Alastor, 74, 130, 202, 212, 230–231, 253*n*.
  Cenci, The, 71, 108, 110, *111–121*, 122, *125–128*, 144, 156, 159, 184, 198, 203, 218.

Index

"Cloud, The," 171.
Daemon of the World, The, 154, 155, 173–174.
"England in 1819," 167.
Epipsychidion, 15, 60, 74, 75, 76, 97, 165, 168, 181, *183–194*, *196–205*, 212, 215, 217, 226, 262*n*, 265*n*, 266*n*.
"Four Poems to Mary," 255*n*.
Hellas, 51, 73–74, 114, 218–219, 220.
"Hymn to Intellectual Beauty," 28, 101, 165.
"Indian Serenade, The," 164.
"Lift not the painted veil," 167.
"Lines: 'When the lamp is shattered,'" 164.
"Lines Written in the Bay of Lerici," 226–227, 228.
"Mont Blanc," 56, 73, 80, *89–101*, *107–110*, 148, 184, 207, 212, 218.
"Ode to Liberty," 177.
"Ode to the West Wind," 14, 165, *166–182*, 184, 185, 194, 217, 218, 263–264*n*.
Original Poetry by Victor and Cazire, 60, 253*n*.
"Orpheus," 174–175, 180.
"Ozymandias," 167.
"Passage of the Apennines," 96–97.
Posthumous Poems (1824), 109.
Prince Athanase, 191.

Prometheus Unbound, 14, 15, 16, 17, 47–48, 58, 79–80, 93, 99–100, 101, *104–107*, 110, 111, 112, 121, 122, 125–126, 128, 129–132, *139–148*, *149–152 passim*, 175, 177, 197–198, 201, 207, 219, 220, 228, 232, 261*n*.
Queen Mab, 51, 52, 61, 62, 67, *68–72*, 74, 75, 133, 155, 199–200, 219.
"Reality," 257*n*.
Revolt of Islam, The, 76, *101–103*, 104, 106, 130, 148, 154, 189, 190, 207. 261*n*.
Rosalind and Helen, 190.
Sensitive Plant, The, 190.
"Sonnet to Byron," 167.
"Stanzas Written in Dejection," 111, 229.
"Swifter far than summer's flight," 265*n*.
"To——" (1821), 210.
"To the Nile," 167.
Triumph of Life, The, 13, 60, 97, 108, 150, 166, 185, *207–221*, 228.
Wandering Jew, The, 24, 51, *53–54*, 55, 60, 62.
"Wandering Jew's Soliloquy," 253*n*.
Witch of Atlas, The, 192, 227.
"Zucca, The," 225–226.

Prose

"Assassins, The," 68, 74, *131–133*, 155, 253*n*, 261*n*.

Defence of Poetry, A, 97, 143, 144, 154, 175, 193, 201, 215, 216, 256*n*, 264*n*.
Essay on Christianity, 112, 140, 264*n*.
Essay on the Devil, and Devils, 102, 113, 114, 117, 154.
Essay on Life, 256*n*.
Essay on Love, 184.
Essay on the Punishment of Death, 146.
Necessity of Atheism, The, 32, 61.
Notebooks (Bixby-Huntington), 178.
Notes on Sculptures, 176–178.
"On *Frankenstein*," 255*n*.
Refutation of Deism, A, 219.
St. Irvyne, 27, 29, 51, 55, 57, 60, 62.
Zastrozzi, 60.
Shelley, Sir Timothy, father of S, 25, 26, 30–33, 115, 160
Shelley, William, son of S, 171
Sherburn, George, 251*n*
Shorey, Paul, 260*n*
Sidney, Sir Philip, 164, 168–169, 213
Sieper, Ernst, 258*n*
Simon Magus, 140
Sismondi, J. C. L. Simonde de, *Histoire des Républiques Italiennes*, 122–123, 257*n*
Skeat, Walter W., 265*n*

Smith, Horace, 233
Socrates, 13
Sodomites, 135
Solomon, King, 65, 217
Southey, Robert, 34, 266*n*
Spark, Muriel, 83
Spence, Lewis, 254*n*
Spenser, Edmund:
Epithalamion, 185
Faerie Queene, The, 101, 102, 130, 143, 154, 166, 172, 217
Prothalamion, 265*n*
State Trails (1794), 36, 37
Stevens, Wallace, 96
Stockdale, J. J., 61, 62
Stoicism, 98–99, 108, 110, 138, 149
Strindberg, August, *Creditors*, 107
Swedenborg, Emanuel, 172
Swedenborgianism, 18
Swift, Jonathan, 227
Swinburne, Algernon Charles, 67

Taaffe, "Count" John, 224
Tasso, Torquato, 72, 150, 215
Taylor, Thomas, 134, 258–259*n*, 264*n*
Tennyson, Alfred, Lord, "Tithonus," 52
Teresa, Saint, 165
Tertullian, 159
Toltecs, 130
Trelawny, Edward J., 205, 234, 268*n*:
Recollections, 221–224, 229–230, 232–233

Records, 222
Trevelyan, G. M., 24

Valentinians, 124, 128, 134, 138
Vampire, Le, 270n
Vergil, *Aeneid*, 185, 186, 240, 271n
Viets, Henry R., 271n
Villiers de l'Isle-Adam, Auguste, Comte de, *Axel*, 62
Vivian, Charles, 223
Viviani, Emilia, 185, 190, 200–202, 217, 226; *see also* Epipsychidion *under* Shelley
Volksbuch, 52–53
Volney, Constantin François, Comte de, 64, 101, 112, 154, 155
Voltaire, François M. A. de, 51, 63, 67, 70, 219

Wagner, Richard:
Fliegende Holländer, Der, 75, 77
Parsifal, 75–76
Tannhäuser, 76
Tristan und Isolde, 76, 77, 228
Waite, A. E., 254n
Wasserman, Earl, 90, 256n, 265n
Weaver, Bennett, 16
Webster, John, *The White Devil*, 118–119
Weishaupt, Adam ("Spartacus"), 63
Wendover, Roger of, *Flores Historiarum*, 52
Whig Party, 23–27, 30, 51
White, Newman Ivey, 131, 268n
Wieland, Christoph Martin, *Peregrinus Proteus*, 134, 259n
Wilder, Amos Niven, 14
Williams, Edward E., 222–224, 231, 233–235
Williams, Jane, 50, 220, 226–227, 231, 233–235, 268n
Wimsatt, William K., Jr., 261n
Wollstonecraft, Mary, 44, 47, 189
Wordsworth, William, 19, 27, 34, 167–168:
"Mutability," 168
Ode: Intimations of Immortality, 161, 211, 217
Prelude, The, 97, 218
"Tintern Abbey," 184
Wormhoudt, Arthur, 262n
Wyatt, Sir Thomas, 169

Yeats, William Butler, 15–18 *passim*, 24, 27, 87–88, 97, 188–189, 214, 220, 235

Zirus, Werner, 253n
Zoroastrianism, 14, *100–103*, 106, 112, 124, 130–131, 134, 138, 159, 217
Zosimos, 138–139